DIVIDED PARENTS, SHARED CHILDREN

EUROPEAN FAMILY LAW SERIES

Published by the Organising Committee of the
Commission on European Family Law

DIVIDED PARENTS, SHARED CHILDREN

Legal Aspects of (Residential) Co-Parenting in England, the Netherlands and Belgium

Natalie NIKOLINA

intersentia

Cambridge – Antwerp – Portland

Intersentia Ltd
Sheraton House | Castle Park
Cambridge | CB3 0AX | United Kingdom
Tel.: +44 1223 370 170 | Email: mail@intersentia.co.uk

Distribution for the UK:
NBN International
Airport Business Centre, 10 Thornbury Road
Plymouth, PL6 7 PP
United Kingdom
Tel.: +44 1752 202 301 | Fax: +44 1752 202 331
Email: orders@nbninternational.com

Distribution for the USA and Canada:
International Specialized Book Services
920 NE 58th Ave. Suite 300
Portland, OR 97213
USA
Tel.: +1 800 944 6190 (toll free)
Email: info@isbs.com

Distribution for Germany and Switzerland:
Stämpfli Verlag AG
Wölflistrasse 1
Postfach 5662
3001 Bern
Switzerland
Tel.: +41 31 300 66 77
Email: verlag@staempfli.com

Distribution for other countries:
Intersentia Publishing nv
Groenstraat 31
2640 Mortsel
Belgium
Tel.: +32 3 680 15 50
Email: mail@intersentia.be

Divided Parents, Shared Children. Legal Aspects of (Residential) Co-Parenting in England, the Netherlands and Belgium
Natalie Nikolina

ISBN 978-1-78068-341-6
D/2015/7849/131
NUR 822

British Library Cataloguing in Publication Data. A catalogue record for this book is available from the British Library.

ACKNOWLEDGEMENTS

Writing this book sometimes felt like raising a child: it takes up all your time, focus and energy, you are always thinking about it, worrying you're not good enough to be doing this, and at the end you must send it out into the world on its own. They say it takes a village to raise a child. It definitely took a (proverbial) village to raise this particular baby. So many wonderful people have made this book possible. Too many to mention here, but I shall try nonetheless.

First and foremost my deep gratitude goes to my supervisor Katharina, for taking a chance on me in the first place, for being an inspiration, for your patience, your support, your time, and your enormous positivity. You always kept faith in me and my abilities, even when I would lose it myself (which happened on a regular basis).

The Molengraaff Institute has been a home to me for over four years and the people there remain dear to me. It was a warm and inspirational environment to work in and I leave it with some wistfulness. A special thank you goes out to Merel, for making me feel welcome and patiently explaining everything when I was very intimidated to make the transition from student to co-worker, to Evelien for being the best roomie one could wish for, and to Jaki for always willing to listen to me vent.

I have always said that law cannot operate in a vacuum and therefore it was very important to me to include demographic and sociological data in this book. I could never have done this without the help of Tanja, Anne-Rigt and Sarah. Sarah deserves a special mention as she has been a sister-in-arms throughout my PhD and became a dear friend.

Thank you to everyone who has made my research and stay abroad possible and provided much needed insights into the English and Belgian legal systems: Frederik Swennen, Dimitri Mortelmans, Heather Draper, Sonia Harris-Short, Rebecca Probert and all the supporting staff.

Titia, Peter and Klaartje, who helped me with the editing and the lay-out of this book, have been particularly accomodating, going above and beyond to help me finish on time and with the least amount of stress. You were an incredible help at the difficult last stage.

Last, but not least: my loved ones. Withouth the constant support, love and care from my family and friends this book would not have existed. Mam, Dick, oma, dank jullie wel voor al jullie steun! Rodger and Carola, you know how important you are to me and how much I love you. My dear friends, I am blessed with so many of you. You have filled these five years with happiness.

To everyone else who have helped me on this journey, but I did not have the space to mention here: thank you!

Natalie Nikolina
Nieuwegein, 27 July 2015

CONTENTS

CHAPTER 1
INTRODUCTION

1.1. STUDY BACKGROUND

Never before have there been as many changes in the position and the structure of the family in Dutch society as in the last 50 years. Both our concept of what it means to be a parent and what consists of a family unit have evolved and are still evolving drastically. As the law is in place to protect and reflect society, modern family law is also rapidly reforming to accommodate the many societal changes.

In the area of post-separation parenting, the demand for the genders to be treated equally, the growing awareness of not just the need to protect children, but also their intrinsic rights, and the growing number of separations and the establishment of new families have required the law to find new solutions as to how to deal with post-separation issues.

'[T]he norms associated with fatherhood have shifted in recent decades toward a new concept that embraces both economic support and childcare responsibilities'.[1] The growing awareness of the importance of contact with fathers for the children's well-being after parental separation, and the growing involvement of fathers in childcare during marriage, have caused fathers to be more involved in their children's lives after parental separation.[2] Subsequently, fathers have started to demand more favourable contact, care and residence arrangements in the courts, and they want to see greater legal equality between parents.[3]

As the position of fathers changed, so did the position of children. This change had come about even earlier and on a more international scale. More and more international and European instruments emphasize children's rights while the best interests of the child have become the main consideration in national family law. How to safeguard these interests when more and more children experience the often traumatic situation of their parents' separation is a question that is at the forefront of a great deal of discussion among policy makers, legislators and legal professionals. In

1 S. WESTPHAL, *Are the kids alright?*, 2015, p. 43.
2 S. WESTPHAL, 2015, pp. 57-58.
3 See for information on the rise of father's rights movements the country-specific Chapters 3, 4 and 5.

the Netherlands alone, approximately 57,000 children a year experience parental separation. That is more than one in four children.[4]

As parental separation can have many negative effects on the children, such as behavioural problems, stress and depression, and in many cases causes the loss of parental resources,[5] it is important to know what can be done to diminish these negative effects and what kinds of post-separation arrangements have the best outcomes in terms of children's well-being.

This combination of a high number of parental separations, the need to find the best way to ensure children's well-being, and the call for more equality between parents has resulted the relatively new post-separation arrangement, residential co-parenting, an arrangement in which the child shares the time he or she resides with either parent more or less equally, being much discussed. An arrangement in which the parents actively share the care for their child after separation is generally seen by the Dutch legislator as beneficial for the child and as a 'safety net' to prevent the negative effects of parental separation. However, a great deal is still unknown about both the legal and practical reality of co-parenting and academics have expressed fears that residential co-parenting might expose children to instability, increase anxiety in children and expose them to ongoing parental conflict.[6]

While it was originally proposed to make residential co-parenting a preferential model, this was eventually deemed to be a step too far, and the new Promotion of Continued Parenting and Proper Divorce Act (*Wet bevordering voortgezet ouderschap en zorgvuldige scheiding*), which came into force in 2009, did not contain such a preference, but granted the child the right to equal care by both parents. This right to equal care caused some confusion among parents and legal practitioners alike due to its vagueness and discussions about residential co-parenting continued.[7]

Internationally and multidisciplinarily, co-parenting is a hot topic, as can be seen from various initiatives by research groups and discussion platforms. Last year, the first International Conference on Shared Parenting was held in Bonn, Germany, which attracted many academics, policy makers, social workers and legal professionals from all over the world.[8]

One thing that is clear from all the discussions on co-parenting is that there is a lack of knowledge: it is unclear how co-parenting should be

4 Numbers from the Dutch Central Bureau for Statistics (www.cbs.nl, last visited 29 April 2015) and the 2010 study by E. Spruijt on divorce and children presented during the Scheiden en de kinderen congress on 12 October 2010 in Driebergen, the Netherlands.
5 S. WESTPHAL, 2015, p. 63.
6 *Ibid.*
7 See sections 4.1 and 4.2 of Chapter 4 for a discussion on the Dutch law reform.
8 See the website of the International Council on Shared Parenting (ICSP): twohomes.org (last visited 29 April 2015) for more information, especially the summary of the 2014 first International Conference on Shared Parenting.

defined; if, and how often, it occurs; how the courts should deal with it; what effect it has on children's well-being; and thus also what the best course of action for the legislator would be in dealing with co-parenting. This book intends to address these issues.

As a part of a larger NWO (the Netherlands Organisation for Scientific Research) funded project entitled 'Divided parents, shared children? A combined legal and sociological perspective on children's residence arrangements after divorce and their consequences for children's well-being', the PhD research on which this book is based focuses on (residential) co-parenting arrangements from a comparative legal perspective.[9]

1.2. SELECTION OF JURISDICTIONS AND RESEARCH QUESTIONS

The choice for a comparative perspective was made due to the fact that the Netherlands is not the only country that struggles with these issues. Worldwide, many countries have dealt with co-parenting in either their legislation or case law. A comparative study can therefore offer another perspective on the issue and possibly suggest solutions to problems.

Within the scope of this book it was feasible to compare a maximum of three countries. It was decided to choose three countries within the European Union in order also to be able to examine the existence and possible influence of International, European, and EU instruments on national legislation concerning co-parenting. As this is Dutch research, prompted by Dutch legal reform and the growing interest in co-parenting in the Netherlands, the Dutch legal system had to be one of the three countries to be compared. The other two countries were chosen on the basis of their comparability and sufficient difference. This means that they had to have a similar social structure to that of the Netherlands, but had to deal with (residential) co-parenting in different ways. Eventually Belgium and England (and Wales) were chosen as they represented two opposite ways of dealing with residential co-parenting: with England lacking any legislation and the courts strongly favouring party autonomy and equality considerations in disputes concerning residence orders, while Belgium takes a more proactive approach and stimulates residential co-parenting through legislation and focuses on the practical considerations in case law. The Dutch approach lies somewhere in between these and could therefore potentially benefit from problem solving from either of these systems. Sweden, as one of the first European countries to actively promote

9 See for more information www.nwo.nl and nfn-onderzoek.nl (last visited 29 April 2015) for more information.

residential co-parenting, was also considered, but eventually disregarded due to the language barrier and the fact that a great deal has already been written on Sweden in this field.

By using the English language the three legal systems discussed, specifically the Dutch and the Belgian legal systems, have been made accessible for foreign researchers for the purpose of further research and comparison.

This book seeks to answer three main questions to further understand the phenomenon of co-parenting and to provide the legislator, the courts and parents with possible solutions for certain problems: What kind of legal framework exists in the three countries discussed with regard to (residential) co-parenting and what can these countries learn from each other's legal systems? Does residential co-parenting occur in the three countries discussed, and if so how predominant is it? Should these countries stimulate or discourage residential co-parenting through legal action?

While a large part of the answers to these questions, especially the first two questions, are descriptive in nature, some evaluation has been added in order to stimulate discussion and further research. The evaluative parts of this book are not always strictly separated from the rest. This is done in order to avoid repetition and improve readability.

1.3. TERMINOLOGY

While there has been much discussion on co-parenting every source seems to have its own definition and it is easy to lose track while seemingly talking about the same thing. Co-parenting, shared care, shared parenting, alternating residence, joint physical custody, the Dutch term *verblijfsco-ouderschap*, all these have been used to indicate similar arrangements. To avoid confusion, a choice has been made in this book in favour of a definition that makes a strict distinction between the sharing of care for a child in the legal sense and the practical arrangement of dividing the residence of the child between two homes. *Co-parenting* as understood in this book is the former: the shared care of the child, the joint exercise of parental responsibilities by both parents after parental separation. It requires both parents to be holders of (joint) parental responsibilities and to make decisions about the child's life together in co-operation with each other. *Residential co-parenting* is the term used for a semi-permanent arrangement whereby the child lives with both parents even though the parents no longer cohabit and alternates between the homes on a regular basis, spending a comparable amount of time with each parent.

Co-parenting is the umbrella term. Co-parenting exists no matter what practical residential arrangements the parents have in place as long as they are both actively involved in the child's life and make decisions about the child's life together. Residential co-parenting, on the other hand, would arguably be practically impossible without co-parenting. So, co-parents *may* have a residential co-parenting arrangement, while parents who have a residential co-parenting arrangement are *always* co-parents.

This definition warrants the following question: when does a child spend *a comparable amount of time with each parent*? A relatively broad definition of 'a comparable amount of time' has been chosen in this book in order to encompass the many empirical studies that are relied upon in the underlying PhD research. Most of these empirical studies do not give a definition of residential co-parenting, but instead rely on a self-identification of the subjects: if the parents call their arrangement residential co-parenting or indicate that they share the residence of their children (more or less) equally, their arrangements are considered to be residential co-parenting arrangements and are dealt with as such.

Therefore, when this book talks about residential co-parenting arrangements in the context of empirical research, this indicates arrangements which the parents themselves have labelled as residential co-parenting or arrangements which parents characterise as arrangements in which they (more or less) equally share the time spent with the child(ren).

If, however, the exact division of residence is known, or a theoretical/hypothetical case of residential co-parenting is meant, residential co-parenting is understood to be an arrangement in which both parents share the care for their child and the child resides between 33% and 66% of the time with each parent.[10] This time should not *only* be spent with one of the parents in the weekends and holidays, it is important that each parent is involved in most aspects of the child's everyday life.

Unless otherwise specified, the word parent refers to the legal parent of the child and the word child refers to a minor who has not reached the age of consent. In sections that deal with the acquisition of parental responsibilities, parent is intended to mean someone who is either the legal parent or can become the legal parent.

Each legal system has its own (legal) definition of parental responsibilities which is given and discussed in Chapters 3 to 5, but, generally speaking, parental responsibilities indicate a collection of rights and duties which a parent holds in order to care for and raise his or her child. In the past the terms parental authority and custody were used for this and these terms

10 These percentages are borrowed from the *Scheiding in Vlaanderen* study's definition of residential co-parenting that is extensively discussed in sections 6.2.3 and 6.3.3 of Chapter 6.

are mentioned in this book when talking about the concept of parental responsibilities from a historical perspective.

A choice has been made in this book not to define the concept of 'best interests of the child'. Countless books and papers have been devoted to this topic and academics are still to reach any kind of consensus. This book has been written from the point of view that in decisions concerning parenting, the child's best interests should be at the forefront of the discussion. This means that the (promotion of the) well-being of children should be the main consideration when legislation on parenting is made or when the courts are petitioned to make a decision. Whether something promotes or harms the well-being of children is sometimes difficult to establish. For that purpose sociological and psychological studies have been consulted and are relied upon in this book.

Finally, whenever this book mentions England or the English legal system, it is always implied that England and Wales is meant. This is for the sake of brevity and readability.

1.4. SCOPE

While interesting, it would not be feasible to look at every single aspect of co-parenting in this book. Therefore, certain topics had to be omitted.

This book focuses on legislation and case law on the division of care, the attribution and discharge of parental responsibilities, judicial involvement in the exercise of parental responsibilities, and the establishment and change of residential co-parenting arrangements. The more practical issues, mainly those concerning financial matters, as well as strictly procedural legislation, fall outside of the scope of this book.

While relocation is touched upon in this book as a part of the discussion on changes in residential co-parenting arrangements, this topic is not extensively elaborated upon due to the fact that a book specifically on relocation, based on research that is also part of the 'Divided Parents, Shared Children' project, is due to be published shortly.

While being loosely related to issues of residential co-parenthood, instruments on child abduction have also been deliberately excluded from the book. Even though child abduction can coincide with co-parenting (for example, when a co-parent abducts the child and takes him or her to another country) this connection is presumed to be rare and it is a large and complex subject matter that touches not only upon private international law, but also on elements of criminal law and public law.

1.5. METHODOLOGY

This book has been written by a legal scholar in the context of a comparative law PhD thesis and therefore the emphasis is on law. The classic approach of studying legal texts, case law and (legal) literature was employed to gain the majority of the information. However, because the issues surrounding parenting are inextricably linked to areas outside of law, it was also deemed necessary to consult sources on demographics, sociology and psychology.

When it comes to the comparison of the three legal systems, the point of departure was that these systems would be compared on an equal basis. This means that where, for example, for one legal system's case law and empirical research were used, this would also have to be done for the other two legal systems. This was occasionally complicated and the help of national experts was requested to guide this process.

In the Belgian system, the majority of the case law could only be accessed through legal journals and especially the French-language decisions only contain a minimum of facts and explanations, while the English case law is not only easy to access from online databases, but also contains extensive discussion and reasoning. Dutch case law was more readily available online than Belgian case law, but the digitalisation of decisions is not as abundant as in the English system, nor is the reasoning as extensive.

When it came to empirical research on co-parenting, which was necessary to answer the question on the prevalence of residential co-parenting in the three legal systems, Belgium had a very extensive study available, while in England a multitude of smaller studies have been conducted over the years. In the Netherlands, unfortunately very little research has been done in this area. Some empirical research therefore had to be carried out by the author of this book in order to supplement that which was available. It was decided to gather parental plans that have been approved by the Dutch courts to gain insights into what kinds of arrangements parents make upon separation, how often they choose residential co-parenting, and how the courts deal with this new obligatory instrument, the parenting plan.[11]

In order to discover whether residential co-parenting is beneficial or detrimental to the well-being of children and thus to be able to answer the third question posed in this book, whether it should be encouraged through legal action, socio-psychological research had to be consulted. Because the author of this book has no background in sociology or psychology, only existing research has been used to gather information and no new socio-psychological empirical research was conducted. Here it was not strictly necessary to limit the research conducted in the three countries

---

11 For a more in-depth methodology discussion of country-specific studies see section 6.2 of Chapter 6.

central to this book as the effects of (aspects of) residential co-parenting arrangements on children are not confined to legal systems or countries. Because it was impossible to consult all available socio-psychological research in this area due to its magnitude, most influential reviews that summarise the available studies were used instead.[12] In order to make sure that only summaries from reputable sources were used, sociologists from Utrecht University were consulted.[13]

1.6. OUTLINE

This book contains eight chapters. After this introduction, Chapter 2 sets out to develop an international and European framework within which the three legal systems function. Then the legal systems of England (and Wales), the Netherlands, and Belgium are set out in Chapters 3, 4, and 5. Each chapter on a particular legal system is divided into the following sections: history of the main legal and societal developments, background of the law currently in place, joint parental responsibilities, the child's residence, children's procedural rights and the enforcement of arrangements in case of non-compliance, and is concluded with a short summary. The successive comparison method was used to present the national systems in order to avoid the confusion of simultaneously comparing three quite different systems and to provide a clear overview of each national system for those readers unfamiliar with these systems. It was feared that some of the nuances of each system might become lost within a simultaneous comparison.

Chapter 6 deals with the socio-psychological aspects of residential co-parenting. It describes the various national empirical studies that have been used, provides facts and figures on residential co-parenting in England (and Wales), the Netherlands, and Belgium, and explains the (outside) factors which influence the well-being of children in residential co-parenting arrangements.

In Chapter 7 the English, Dutch, and Belgian legal systems are compared. This comparison follows the structure of Chapters 3 to 5 and devotes some preliminary consideration that is taken into account and is used in Chapter 8. This concluding chapter answers the three main questions of this book and provides some recommendations for the Dutch system.

---

12 For a more detailed explanation of the studies used see section 6.4 of Chapter 6.

13 T. van der Lippe, A. Poortman, and S. Westphal.

CHAPTER 2
INTERNATIONAL AND EUROPEAN FRAMEWORK[1]

2.1. INTRODUCTION

While the main focus of this book is national legislation on (residential) co-parenting, it is imperative to place such legislation within a certain context. National legislation does not operate in a vacuum; it is influenced by politics, demographic changes, behavioural changes and, within the legal sphere, supranational legislation.

In view of the growing influence of international and regional organizations, such as the European Union, and their instruments on national law, these organizations and their instruments cannot be disregarded in legal research. International and regional instruments have now become an integral part of the national systems to which they apply. Therefore, before looking at how the national systems function, which flaws they contain, or how they can be changed, it is prudent to first examine the international framework in which they have to function. This chapter is devoted to this. In order to answer the question of whether international legal instruments support (residential) co-parenting after parental separation, it analyses the international framework for co-parenthood.

This chapter includes only a discussion of those international and regional instruments that are relevant to the topic of residential co-parenting, or the broader concept of parental responsibilities. These include issues such as the allocation and exercise of parental responsibilities, the child's rights in proceedings dealing with his or her residence, the child's rights in proceedings concerning the care of or contact with the child, and the provisions concerning the child's residence after parental separation. If they add something to the main subject, other closely linked issues are also briefly considered. While related to issues of (residential) co-parenthood,

1 An earlier version of this chapter was published as an article in the Utrecht Law Review. N. NIKOLINA, 'The Influence of International Law on the Issue of Co-Parenting: Emerging Trends in International and European Instruments', *Utrecht Law Review*, Vol. 8(1), 2012, pp. 122-144.

instruments on child abduction or relocation have deliberately been excluded from this chapter and the subject-matter is only briefly and summarily included within (the rest of) this book.

Because there is no clear division between residence and contact, especially within international literature, and extensive contact can in practice mean that the child lives for a substantial amount of time with the non-resident parent, when an instrument has no provisions on residence, but does include provisions on contact that can be relevant for residential co-parenting, these provisions are included in this chapter.

Only those regional instruments are included that concern the three national systems which this book analyses. This means that at least one out of the three states has to be a member of (or otherwise affiliated with) the organisation from which the regional instrument originates.

In the following sections binding and non-binding international instruments are discussed. First, section 2.2 discusses *binding* international instruments, grouped according to the organization from which they originate. Section 2.3 presents *non-binding* instruments in the same order. Another soft law instrument by the Commission on European Family Law is added in this section. If available, each instrument's provisions on (1) the child's rights, (2) the parent-child relationship, (3) parental responsibilities, and (4) the instrument's relevance to residential co-parenting are discussed. These main features of the instruments are compared and analysed in section 2.4, highlighting the main differences between binding and non-binding instruments, other remarkable differences, and similarities in the form of recurring notions.

2.2. BINDING INSTRUMENTS

The binding international instruments discussed in this section, while having different names, such as Covenant, Convention and Charter, can all be defined as international treaties: agreements under international law entered into by actors in international law. These actors can be sovereign states or international organizations. These treaties bind the States Parties as to the rights or principles they contain. They are discussed in the order of their regional application, starting with the instruments of the United Nations, then those of the Hague Conference, the Council of Europe and, finally, the instruments of the European Union. When there are multiple instruments originating from the same organization, they are arranged by the type of legal provisions they contain: human rights first, private international law second and substantive law third. Where applicable, case law associated with the instruments is also discussed.

2.2.1. ICCPR

The International Covenant on Civil and Political Rights (ICCPR) was the first international instrument to protect the rights of the family and the child.[2] In the years following its entry into force in 1976, the ICCPR generated a large body of case law that has branched out into issues concerning parentage and contact. The two articles on which the most important case law (for this chapter) is based are Article 23 on the protection of the family and Article 24 on the protection of the child.

Article 24 lays down the rights of a child to protection (by his or her family, society and the state), to a name and to a nationality. It is for each state to determine what measures might be needed for the protection of children within its territory and jurisdiction.[3] The Human Rights Commission, in its general comment on Article 24, emphasized that children need protection in the event of the divorce of their parents: 'If the marriage is dissolved, steps should be taken, keeping in view the paramount interest of the children, to give them necessary protection and, so far as is possible, to guarantee personal relations with both parents.'[4]

Where both Article 23 and Article 24 are intended to promote and protect the development and continuity of a child's relationship with both parents after divorce, the background of this protection is different. Article 23 protects the bond between parent and child from the point of view that the *family* should be protected and kept intact as far as possible, while Article 24 is intended to ensure the protection and the best interests of the *child*. Because, generally, it is (considered to be) in the best interests of the child to have a bond with both parents, this bond should be protected. However, 'in cases where the parents and the family seriously fail in their duties, ill-treat or neglect the child, the state should intervene to restrict parental authority and the child may be separated from his family when circumstances so require.'[5]

The definition of a family is not confined to the concept of marriage and should be broadly interpreted. However, some minimum requirements for the existence of a family relationship are necessary, such as living

---

2 1966 *International Covenant on Civil and Political Rights*, 999 United Nations Treaty Series 171.

3 Human Rights Committee, *General Comment 17 (Thirty-fifth session, 1989)*, 7 April 1989, para. 3.

4 *Ibid.*, para. 6.

5 *Ibid.*

together, economic ties and a regular and intense relationship.[6] The family relationship is not automatically terminated after divorce.[7]

> 'The idea of the family must necessarily embrace the relations between parents and child. Although divorce legally ends a marriage, it cannot dissolve the bond uniting father - or mother - and child: this bond does not depend on the continuation of the parents' marriage.'[8]

Because of this bond, Paragraph 4 of Article 23 'grants, barring exceptional circumstances, a right to regular contact between children and both of their parents upon dissolution of a marriage'.[9] The States Parties also have to ensure that the right to regular contact can be successfully enforced. This was confirmed in the case of *L.P. v. Czech Republic*, in which the complainant had been prevented from (regularly) meeting his son by his ex-wife, despite the fact that he had been granted the right to see his son every other weekend by the court. Although the court repeatedly fined the ex-wife for not respecting the court's orders, these fines were not fully enforced, nor replaced by other measures. This was seen as a violation of Article 23.[10]

While the relationship between the parent(s) and child is seen as a family bond and has to be protected by the state, the protection of this relationship initially does not seem to go beyond the need to ensure that there is regular contact between the parent(s) and child. The ICCPR does not prescribe residential co-parenting, either during the relationship between the parents or after their separation. What it does prescribe is equality. Paragraph 4 of Article 23 states that States Parties should take appropriate steps to ensure the equality of rights and responsibilities of spouses as to marriage, during marriage and upon its dissolution and that in the case of dissolution, provisions should be made for the necessary protection of any children involved. The protection of the bond between the (divorced) parent(s) and child should be equally enjoyed by parents of both sexes:

> '[A]ny discriminatory treatment in regard to the grounds and procedures for separation or divorce, child custody, maintenance or alimony, visiting rights

---

6 Communication No. 417/1990, *Santacana v. Spain*, Views adopted on 15 July 1994, para. 10.2.

7 S. JOSEPH et al., *The international covenant on civil and political rights: cases, materials, and commentary*, 2004, p. 588.

8 Communication No. 201/1985, *Hendriks v. the Netherlands*, Views adopted on 27 July 1988, para. 10.3.

9 Communication No. 514/1992, *Fei v. Colombia*, Views adopted on 4 April 1995, para. 8.9.

10 Communication No. 945/2000, *L.P. v. Czech Republic*, Views adopted on 4 August 2005.

> or the loss or recovery of parental authority must be prohibited, bearing in mind the paramount interest of the children in this connection. States Parties should, in particular, include information in their reports concerning the provision made for the necessary protection of any children at the dissolution of a marriage or on the separation of the spouses.'[11]

This presupposition of equality can be applied to parenting: the equal exercise of care in the form of joint parental responsibilities and the exercise thereof, possibly by means of residential co-parenting. The case law has not (yet?) gone as far as to take this point of view.

Relevance for co-parenting
Applying both articles to the issue of co-parenting it can be said that the protection of the family and the bond between parent and child with the included presupposition of equality between the parents would strongly support a joint exercise of parental responsibilities and in no way discourage residential co-parenting. The principle of the protection of the child would also support these kinds of arrangements as part of this right's intention is to guarantee, as far as possible, personal relations with both parents, because this is seen as beneficial for the child. However, in cases where joint parental responsibilities or a residential co-parenting arrangement would have a negative effect on the child's well-being, the state should intervene.

2.2.2. CRC

While the rights set out in the major international human rights instruments apply to both adults and children, children need extra protection, because they are more vulnerable than adults. For that purpose the Convention on the Rights of the Child (CRC) restates the most crucial rights already in place through other international instruments and supplements them with rights that deal specifically with issues related to children.[12] The CRC is the most prominent international instrument protecting children's rights, not only because it specifically focuses on children's rights, but also because it is one of the very few binding international instruments which, with 194 States Parties (significantly, the United States is not among these States Parties), has almost reached universal ratification.[13]

---

11 Human Rights Committee, *General Comment 19 (Thirty-ninth session, 1990)*, 27 July 1990, para. 9.
12 *1989 Convention on the Rights of the Child*, 1577 United Nations Treaty Series 3.
13 See for signatory states and ratifications the United Nations Treaties website at: treaties.un.org (last visited 29 April 2015).

The CRC will always apply in issues concerning residential co-parenting and disputes concerning parental responsibilities, as these issues directly affect the life and welfare of children. Out of the CRC rights, the right to know and be cared for by one's parents (Article 7), the right not to be separated from one's parents against the parent(s')'s will (Article 9(1)) and the child's right to maintain personal relations and direct contact with both parents on a regular basis after separation (Article 9(3)) are the most relevant rights for this chapter.

Paragraph 1 of Article 3 lays down the general principle - to be found throughout the Convention - that in all actions concerning children the best interests of the child should be a primary consideration. Even though this notion is flexible, its interaction with the rest of the Convention is summarised quite clearly by Tobin: 'a proposed outcome for a child cannot be said to be in his or her best interests where it conflicts with the provisions of the Convention.'[14] So where one (or more) of the rights of the CRC is at stake, the notion of the best interests of the child should be applied in conjunction with this/these right(s). When no other right is applicable, the notion of the best interests of the child can be relied upon as a stand-alone principle.[15]

Another aspect to keep in mind is that the best interests of the child are *a primary* consideration; it is not prescribed by the CRC that the best interests of the child should be the *determining* consideration. This means that even if a certain decision is not in the child's best interests, it can still be taken by the relevant authority without infringing the CRC if someone else's needs (for example, one of the parents') outweighs the best interests of the child or there are practical impossibilities to act in conformity with the child's best interests.

2.2.2.1. The right to know and be cared for by one's parents

Paragraph 1 of Article 7 sets out one of the most important rights of the child (for the purpose of this chapter): the right, as far as possible, to know and be cared for by one's parents. Paragraph 2 of Article 7 obliges the States Parties to ensure the implementation of this right. The words 'as far as possible' may weaken this right, however. The danger exists that these words will give rise to an arbitrary interpretation of the right. For example, the words 'as far as possible' allow the non-disclosure of information about the biological parent(s) in the case of adoption, but what about a

---

14 J. TOBIN, 'Beyond the Supermarket Shelf: Using a Rights Based Approach to Address Children's Health Needs', *International Journal of Children's Rights*, 2006, p. 287.

15 S. DETRICK, *A commentary on the United Nations Convention on the Rights of the Child*, 1999, p. 90.

decision that one of the parents is unfit to care for the child and therefore should be completely excluded from the child's life and can a parent be thus excluded for the sole reason that the other parent does not want the child to interact with the parent in question because he or she would have a negative influence on the child?

Combined with the interpretation of Article 3 – which states that in all actions concerning children the best interests of the child should be a primary consideration – the right to know and be cared for by one's parents should be interpreted in a way that it is in the best interests of the child to know and be cared for by his or her parents.

The child does not only have the right to know and be cared for by his or her parents, but also to 'preserve his or her family relations as recognised by law without unlawful interference'.[16] In a way, this right is broader than the right to know and be cared for by one's parents as this right applies to a larger group of people and does not contain the weakening 'as far as possible' limitation; on the other hand, the right does allow *lawful* interference with family relations, which is a limitation in itself.

2.2.2.2. The right not to be separated from one's parent(s)

Article 9 deals with parental separation and focuses specifically on contact between parent(s) and the child. Paragraph 1 of Article 9 obligates States Parties to ensure that a child is not separated from his or her parents against the parents' will, unless such separation is necessary for the protection of the best interests of the child. A separation between one of the parents and the child often occurs when the parents themselves separate. The separation in such cases is physical: one of the parents leaves the family home. This would either be voluntary or as a result of a court order, thus the requirements of Paragraph 1 of Article 9 are fulfilled and the separation is in accordance with the CRC.

A decision on whether separating the child from his or her parent(s) in a specific case is in the child's best interests can only be taken by the competent authorities and should be subject to judicial review.[17] Also, all interested parties should be given an opportunity to participate in the proceedings and make their views known.[18] 'All interested parties' always include the child in question.[19]

This is supported by Article 12 which grants the child who is capable of forming his or her own views the right to express those views freely in

---

16 Paragraph 1 of Article 8 of the CRC.
17 Paragraph 1 of Article 9 of the CRC.
18 Paragraph 2 of Article 9 of the CRC.
19 S. DETRICK, 1999, p. 175.

all matters affecting him or her and it grants the child the right to be heard in any judicial and administrative proceedings affecting him or her. The views of the child should be given due weight in accordance with his or her age and maturity.[20] General Comment No. 12 on this right clarifies that

> 'all legislation on separation and divorce has to include the right of the child to be heard by decision makers and in mediation processes. Some jurisdictions, either as a matter of policy or legislation, prefer to state an age at which the child is regarded as capable of expressing her or his own views. The Convention, however, anticipates that this matter is to be determined on a case-by-case basis, since it refers to age and maturity, and for this reason requires an individual assessment of the capacity of the child'.[21]

2.2.2.3. *The right to maintain personal relations with both parents*

Once it has been determined that it is in the best interests of the child to be separated from one or both of his or her parents or one or both of the parents separates voluntarily, for example one of the parents has left the family home after divorce, Paragraph 3 of Article 9 becomes applicable to the situation. This paragraph grants the child who is separated from one or both parents the right to maintain personal relations and direct contact with both parents on a regular basis, unless - again - this is contrary to the child's best interests. This means that while the CRC prescribes a minimum of regular *contact* after separation, it does not go as far as to make *joint parental responsibilities* compulsory, nor does it prescribe any type of residential arrangements.

The rights contained in Articles 7 and 9 do not make a distinction between married, cohabiting or divorced parents, and the relationship between the parents does not seem to be of any importance at all. Instead the rights emphasize the bond between parent and child. The CRC obliges States Parties to make sure that a child develops a relationship with both his or her parents, has regular contact with them and, where possible, is cared for equally by both parents.

2.2.2.4. *The rights of parents*

The CRC does not only focus on children's rights. Multiple articles give consideration to the rights and responsibilities of parents as well.

---

[20] Paragraph 1 of Article 12 of the CRC.

[21] See CRC General Comment No. 12, p. 15, discussing the right of the child to be heard. This document can be found on the website of the Office of the United Nations High Commissioner for Human Rights at www2.ohchr.org under bodies, crc (last visited 29 April 2015).

Paragraph 2 of Article 3 lays down an obligation for States Parties to take all appropriate legislative and administrative measures to ensure that the child receives such protection and care as is necessary for his or her well-being, *taking into account the rights and duties of his or her parents*, legal guardians, or other individuals legally responsible for him or her. The difficulty in applying Paragraph 2 of Article 3 is that the States Parties on the one hand have to ensure the child's protection and care, while, on the other, they have to respect the parents' rights and duties. Upholding both can be very difficult when there are conflicting interests.

The States Parties not only have to give consideration to, but also to respect the responsibilities, rights and duties of parents (or other persons legally responsible for the child) to provide appropriate direction and guidance in the exercise by the child of the rights recognized in the CRC.[22]

It is not surprising that the CRC takes the rights and duties of the parents into account considering that it places the *primary* responsibility for the upbringing and development of the child on the child's parents (or legal guardians). Both parents have common responsibilities and the best interests of the child should be their basic concern.[23] One must keep in mind that *common responsibilities* do not necessarily mean *equal* or the *same* responsibilities. Thus the parents can have different responsibilities and it is also allowed by the CRC that one of the parents has more responsibilities than the other. Thus, it cannot be said that the parents have the right to *equally share the caring duties* as far as their children are concerned.

The CRC does not set out what responsibilities parents have or what they entail, but it does give an example in Paragraph 2 of Article 27, stating that those responsible for the child have the primary responsibility to secure, within their abilities and financial capacities, the living conditions which are necessary for the child's development. This in itself is of course quite a vague provision.

Relevance for co-parenting

The rights enshrined in the CRC can be seen as supportive of joint parental responsibilities over the child and regular contact with the child during the relationship and after separation, but nothing more. The term parental responsibilities is not used; instead the focus lies on rights and authority. And even if the term was employed, the fact that both parents have, or should have, joint parental responsibilities does not say anything about the exercise of those responsibilities, or about the child's residence.

However, one should be aware of the following. If joint parental responsibilities are to be more than just a legal label, they should be

---

22 Article 5 of the CRC.

23 Paragraph 1 of Article 18 of the CRC.

exercised. This exercise will need at least some sort of communication and the making of arrangements between the parents. Joint parental responsibilities will therefore in practice mostly lead to the joint *exercise* thereof. One can even wonder whether parental responsibilities held by both parents can be exercised effectively, or exercised at all, if they are not exercised jointly, meaning in co-operation, by the parents. Keeping this in mind, one could tentatively conclude that as the CRC explicitly encourages joint parental responsibilities (even after separation), it implicitly also encourages the joint exercise of parental responsibilities.

2.2.3. THE HAGUE CONVENTION 1996

The 1996 Convention on jurisdiction, applicable law, recognition, enforcement and co-operation in respect of parental responsibilities and measures for the protection of children (the Hague Convention), drafted by the Hague Conference of Private International Law, does not contain any substantive law; its purpose is to provide rules on the jurisdiction and applicable law in disputes concerning children, including disputes about parental responsibilities.[24] It is a private international law instrument. This Convention is remarkable because it is the first binding international instrument to talk about parental responsibilities (or more accurately responsibility) as opposed to parental authority.

The Convention states in its preamble that the best interests of the child should be a primary consideration. The hearing of the child is also seen as very important. Not providing an opportunity for the child to be heard is in fact a valid reason not to recognise a foreign measure.[25]

Paragraph 2 of Article 1 of the Convention defines the term parental responsibility so as to include parental authority, or any analogous relationship of authority determining the rights, powers and responsibilities of parents, guardians or other legal representatives in relation to the person or the property of the child.

Article 3 clarifies that the attribution, exercise, termination, restriction and delegation of parental responsibility all fall within the reach of the Convention, as do the rights of custody. This means that questions of jurisdiction and applicable law in disputes on the exercise of parental responsibilities and residential arrangements, including residential co-

---

24 *1996 Hague Convention on jurisdiction, applicable law, recognition, enforcement and co-operation in respect of parental responsibilities and measures for the protection of children*, 19 October 1996.

25 Paragraph 2 subsection b of Article 23 of the Hague Convention 1996.

parenting, also fall within the scope of this Convention. In procedures relating to those disputes, the hearing of the child is therefore important.

Relevance for co-parenting
As mentioned above, the relevance of the 1996 Hague Convention for the issue of co-parenting lies in the fact that it was the first binding international instrument to mention parental responsibility (as opposed to parental authority). Additionally, the Convention contains a provision on the right of the child to be heard.

2.2.4. ECHR

What the ICCPR is to binding international instruments, the Convention for the Protection of Human Rights and Fundamental Freedoms (ECHR), drafted by the Council of Europe, is to European instruments.[26] It is the first and the most encompassing human rights treaty which has been set up to protect the most essential rights and freedoms of the peoples of Europe. For a supranational instrument, the ECHR has one of the strongest monitoring bodies possible in the form of the European Court of Human Rights (the Court) which has generated a large body of binding case law.

Article 8 of the ECHR - and the case law based thereon - is the only article in this Convention that has direct relevance for issues linked to parenting. This article protects the right to respect for private and family life and prohibits interference by a public authority with the exercise of this right, except when the interference is in accordance with the law and is necessary in a democratic society to protect certain legitimate aims.

In a number of decisions the Court has helped to define and explain the notion of family life. First of all, family life is not confined to marriage-based relationships and may encompass other de facto family ties where the parties are cohabiting outside wedlock. A child born out of such a relationship is ipso jure part of that family unit from the moment and by the very fact of his or her birth. A bond thus exists between the child and his or her parents which amounts to family life even if at the time of his or her birth the parents are no longer cohabiting or if their relationship has ended.[27]

But even the cohabitation (prior to separation) of the parents is not a necessary requirement for the existence of family life. The existence or non-existence of family life is essentially a question of fact depending

---

26 *1950 European Convention for the Protection of Human Rights and Fundamental Freedoms*, 213 United Nations Treaty Series 221.

27 ECtHR, *Keegan v. Ireland*, Appl. No. 16969/90, 26 May 1994, para. 44.

upon the real existence, in practice, of close personal ties, in particular the demonstrable interest in and commitment by the father to the child both before and after the birth.[28]

While the mutual enjoyment by parent and child of each other's company constitutes a fundamental element of family life and domestic measures hindering such enjoyment amount to an interference with the right protected by Article 8, this does not automatically grant the parent the right to have parental responsibilities over the child, or the right of contact with the child.[29] In decisions on granting or restricting parental responsibilities, and granting, denying or restricting access to the child, as well as decisions on placing the child in care a fair balance must be struck between the interests of the child and those of the parent(s) and in striking such a balance, particular importance must be attached to the best interests of the child which, depending on their nature and seriousness, may override those of the parent(s).[30]

Article 8 is often relied upon in conjunction with Article 14: the provision on the prohibition of discrimination. Applied to cases concerning parental responsibilities and contact, these two articles are used to prevent parental responsibilities or access to the child from being denied to the parent because of discriminatory reasons. In *Salgueiro Da Silva Mouta*, for example, the Court found that awarding sole custody to the mother exclusively on the basis of the father's sexual orientation constituted discrimination and violated the ECHR.[31]

A case that is particularly relevant for the issue of residential co-parenting, as it actually deals with a practical residential arrangement in which the child alternates between the homes of both parents, and therefore should be discussed more extensively, is *Zaunegger v. Germany*. In *Zaunegger* the prohibition of discrimination also played a role.[32] In this case a father wanted to have joint parental responsibilities (*elterliche Sorge*) with the mother over their daughter who was born during their cohabitation. Under German law married parents have the right and the duty to exercise parental responsibilities over a minor child, but joint parental responsibilities for parents of children born out of wedlock can only be obtained through a joint declaration (*gemeinsame Sorgerechtserklärung*), marriage, or a court order which requires the consent of both parents.

---

28 ECtHR, *Lebbink v. the Netherlands*, Appl. No. 45582/99, 1 June 2004, para. 36.
29 ECtHR, *McMichael v. the United Kingdom*, Appl. No. 16424/90, 24 February 1995, para. 86.
30 ECtHR, *Hoppe v. Germany*, Appl. No. 28422/95, 5 December 2002, para. 48; ECtHR *Johansen v. Norway*, 17383/90, 7 August 1996, para. 78.
31 ECtHR, *Salgueiro Da Silva Mouta v. Portugal*, Appl. No. 33290/96, 21 December 1999, paras. 35-36.
32 ECtHR, *Zaunegger v. Germany*, Appl. No. 22028/04, 3 December 2009, paras. 8-12.

As the mother was withholding her consent, despite the parents having a factual residential co-parenting arrangement, the domestic authorities denied the father's application.[33]

The father alleged before the European Court of Human Rights that the German law applied the right to family life in a discriminatory fashion, first by automatically granting sole parental responsibilities to the unmarried mother and making an application for joint parental responsibilities dependant on her consent.[34] Second, there was different treatment in comparison with married or divorced fathers, who are able to retain joint parental responsibilities following divorce or a separation from the mother.[35] The Court agreed with the father that there had been a difference in treatment, but considered it justified for the protection of the child's interests to attribute parental responsibilities over the child born out of wedlock initially to the mother in order to ensure that there is at least one person at birth who can act for the child in a legally binding way.[36] However, even if it may be justified in some cases to deny an unmarried father participation in parental responsibilities, the idea that joint parental responsibilities against the will of the mother of a child born out of wedlock is prima facie not in the child's interests could not be justified.[37]

This should also be seen in the light of the Court's conviction that biological and social reality should prevail over a legal presumption, especially in cases concerning family relations.[38] The Court hinted that in circumstances as in the present case, where the father was a de facto residential co-parent of his daughter, the reasons for denying him parental responsibilities will have to be particularly weighty as it will have to be proven that granting him parental responsibilities would be manifestly contrary to the interests of the child. Following the Court's judgement, the German *Bundesverfassungsgericht* declared Articles 1626a and 1672 of the German Civil Code unconstitutional for violating the constitutional guarantee of family life.[39]

In *Zaunegger* the legal situation did not represent the factual situation. The opposite situation, in which the legal reality is not supported by the actual reality, is also possible. This is the case when the parents have an official residential co-parenting arrangement or joint parental responsibilities, but one parent is prevented from exercising his or her rights by the other parent (or he or she is not exercising his or her rights

---

33 *Ibid.*
34 *Ibid.*, paras. 32-33.
35 *Ibid.*, para. 43.
36 *Ibid.*, paras. 49 and 55. After all: mater semper certa est.
37 *Ibid.*, paras. 56 and 59.
38 ECtHR, *Kroon v. the Netherlands*, Appl. No. 18535/91, 27 October 1994, para. 40.
39 BvR 420/09, 21 July 2010.

because he or she does not want to). In such cases the Court has ruled that it is not sufficient for domestic authorities to grant parental rights; they should also ensure that the rights can be and are enforced.[40] The Member States therefore do not only have the negative obligation not to interfere with family life, but also the positive obligation to ensure effective respect for family life.[41] However:

> 'In relation to the State's obligation to take positive measures, the Court has held that in cases concerning the implementation of the contact rights of one of the parents, Article 8 includes a parent's right to the taking of measures with a view to his being reunited with his child and an obligation on the national authorities to facilitate such reunion, in so far as the interest of the child dictates that everything must be done to preserve personal relations and, if and when appropriate, to "rebuild" the family; the State's obligation is not one of result, but one of means.'[42]

This indicates that as long as the Member State in question has actively taken all the necessary measures to ensure enforcement, there has not been a violation, even if these measures have failed in maintaining or rebuilding the family life.

While the ECHR protection of family life is mostly associated with the protection of the parent-child relationship, the Court has also made it clear that it is important to act consistently with the child's wishes where possible. However, the case law shows that states enjoy a wide margin of appreciation with regard to the degree of consultation with children and the weight to be attached to the children's opinion in reaching decisions on family matters.[43] In cases of contact, the child's wishes are important, but the domestic authorities should not base a refusal to grant access to the child solely on the negative attitude of a child. The child's age and maturity should be taken into account when deciding what significance should be attached to the child's opinion. The Court has not yet explained what should determine a child's maturity. It is also unclear whether a refusal by domestic authorities to take into account the view of a child who has reached a suitable age and maturity would violate the child's right to family life or the child's freedom of expression.[44]

---

40 See for example: ECtHR, *Dąbrowska v. Poland*, Appl. No. 34568/08, 2 February 2010.
41 ECtHR, *Hokkanen v. Finland*, Appl. No. 19823/92, 23 September 1994, para. 55.
42 ECtHR, *P.K. v. Poland*, Appl. No. 43123/10, 10 June 2014, para. 86.
43 U. KILKELLY, *The Child and the European Convention on Human Rights*, 1999, pp. 117-118.
44 *Ibid.*, p. 119.

Relevance for co-parenting
The findings in this section lead to the conclusion that while the ECHR and the case law on Article 8 do not prescribe (residential) co-parenting as such, they do make it more difficult for Member States to deprive parents of parental responsibilities and contact with their children. The child's interests are also important, and in many cases decisive, in matters touching upon family life. The bond between parent and child is something that should be protected as much as possible, sometimes requiring positive action by the domestic authorities. The recent case law has also shown that an established practice of residential co-parenting should give the co-parent without legal rights the opportunity to apply for parental responsibilities.

2.2.5. CONVENTIONS: EXERCISE OF CHILDREN'S RIGHTS AND CONTACT

In 1996 and 2003, the Council of Europe adopted two new conventions concerning the exercise of children's rights and contact: the European Convention on the Exercise of Children's Rights and the Convention on Contact Concerning Children.[45] Although these conventions contain more detailed provisions and provide more protection than their predecessors, their influence in Europe is nonetheless limited, even questionable, because the number of signatories to and ratifications of the conventions remain very limited: 20 ratifications of the European Convention on the Exercise of Children's Rights and 9 ratifications of the Convention on Contact Concerning Children.[46] Out of the three countries that this book describes only Belgium has signed, though not yet ratified, the Convention on Contact Concerning Children. None of the three countries have signed or ratified the European Convention on the Exercise of Children's Rights.[47]

Throughout the text of the Convention on the Exercise of Children's Rights two very important family law notions are restated and anchored: the idea that in proceedings concerning children, their best interests should

45 *1996 European Convention on the Exercise of Children's Rights*, European Treaty Series 160; *2003 Convention on Contact Concerning Children*, European Treaty Series 192.

46 The states that have ratified the Convention on the Exercise of Children´s Rights are: Albania, Austria, Croatia, Cyprus, the Czech Republic, Finland, France, Germany, Greece, Italy, Latvia, Malta, Montenegro, Poland, Portugal, Slovenia, Spain, the former Yugoslav Republic of Macedonia, Turkey and Ukraine. The states that have ratified the Convention on Contact concerning Children are: Albania, Bosnia and Herzegovina, Croatia, the Czech Republic, Malta, Romania, San Marino, Turkey and Ukraine.

47 See for the most recent status of the two conventions the Council of Europe website: conventions.coe.int (last visited 29 April 2015).

be the primary consideration as well as the right of children to be informed and express their view in proceedings affecting them.

The obligation to consider the best interests of the child applies to all the parties concerned, meaning that while a treaty can only bind the States Parties directly, it can and does state that the parents, generally speaking, should also consider their child's best interests and that the national judicial authority should take decisions in the best interests of the child.[48]

Article 3 provides that those children who are considered by internal law as having sufficient understanding should – in proceedings affecting them – receive all relevant information and be given the opportunity to express their views. Children should be able to participate in such proceedings whether directly or through a special representative and should be assisted, if needed, in expressing their views.[49] The holders of parental responsibilities (usually the parents) should help the child – even if they are not the legal representatives of the child – to understand the proceedings, the information and to express his or her views.[50] The judicial authority should give due weight to the views expressed by the child before taking a decision.[51]

The Convention on Contact Concerning Children stresses that a child and his or her parents have the right to obtain and maintain regular contact with each other. Contact for the purposes of the Convention is broadly defined; not only is staying with or meeting the non-resident parent covered by the term contact, but also any form of communication between the parent and the child and the provision of information to the parent about the child or to the child about the parent is included in the definition.[52] One can see this inclusion as both limiting and extending the rights of the non-resident parent, depending on how it is interpreted. Limiting, as it could create the danger that the non-resident parent will only be given information about the child or allowed to correspond, but not actual contact, as correspondence is also seen as 'contact' under the Convention; extending, if the interpretation would allow for correspondence and information *in addition* to regular meetings with the child.

The most important provision of the Convention on Contact is to be found in Article 4 which states that a child and his or her parents have the right to obtain and maintain regular contact with each other and that such contact may only be restricted or excluded in case a restriction or exclusion

48 See more specifically the preamble, Paragraph 2 of Article 1 and Paragraph 6 of Article 6 of the European Convention on the Exercise of Children's Rights.

49 Paragraph 2 of Article 1, Articles 3-6 and Article 10 of the Convention on the Exercise of Children's Rights.

50 *European Convention on the Exercise of Children's Rights Explanatory Report*, para. 22.

51 Article 6, subsection c of the Convention on the Exercise of Children's Rights.

52 Article 2, subsection a of the Convention on Contact Concerning Children.

is necessary in the best interests of the child. Contact is therefore seen as very important for both the child and the parents and practical obstacles, such as for example the fact that the parents do not live in the same state, are not sufficient to restrict or deny such contact.

In decisions on contact the child's best interests are important, even decisive, when deciding to restrict or exclude contact, and the notion of the best interests of the child reappears in the text of the Convention on multiple occasions.[53] The child is not merely the object of decisions on contact; he or she – if having sufficient understanding – also has the right to receive all relevant information, to be consulted and to express his or her views. These views, wishes and feelings of the child should be given due weight by the authority that takes the decisions on contact.[54] But also, should the child become older and express his or her wishes against the enforcement of the contact arrangement, then his or her views should be respected.[55] Other than against the child's best interests or wishes, the text of the Convention urges the States Parties to do all that they can to enforce contact orders.

While the maintenance of regular contact is not at all the same as joint (exercise of) parental responsibilities, regular contact could lead to the sharing of care for the child or children and greater co-operation between the parents. One could say that by promoting contact between (both) parents and child despite practical obstacles, the Convention on Contact sends out a positive message for more intensive co-operation between the parents that may result in a positive attitude towards joint parental responsibilities.

Relevance for co-parenting

The application of the Convention on the Exercise of Children's Rights to the issue of joint parental responsibilities and residential co-parenting would mean that the question of how the child's residence, the care for the child and the contact with the child after the separation of the parents should be devised, must be answered taking into account the best interests of the child and the child's views. These types of decisions are not up to the parents to decide as they deem fit. The legal procedures have to be child-oriented instead of parent-oriented.

---

53 The Preamble, Articles 4, 6, 7 and 8 of the Convention on Contact Concerning Children.

54 Article 6 of the Convention on Contact Concerning Children.

55 *Convention on Contact Concerning Children Explanatory Report*, para. 32.

2.2.6. THE EU CHARTER

While most European Union laws deal with harmonization and cross-border issues, an important exception to this is the Charter on Fundamental Rights of the European Union (the Charter).[56] The Charter is a relatively recent addition to European Community law, having been adopted in December 2000, but only gaining binding force through the entry into force of the Lisbon Treaty on 1 December 2009.[57] The Charter contains human rights provisions and has been strongly influenced by other (binding) human rights instruments such as the ICCPR, the CRC and the ECHR with some overlapping provisions. An important difference between these international instruments and the Charter is the monitoring. As the Charter is now a binding EU instrument its provisions can be relied upon directly before the national courts of the Member States and before the European Court of Justice. This is more individualized protection than most (binding) human rights treaties offer. It will be interesting to see whether this will encourage more Europeans to invoke these rights. So far, it is too early to come to any conclusions as the Charter has only been binding for a brief period of time. The human rights set out within the Charter are presented as common (European) values.

The two Charter articles that have the potential to influence parenthood (in the future) are Article 24, which deals with the rights of the child, and Article 7, which lays down the right to respect for private and family life.

Paragraph 3 of Article 24 provides that 'every child [should] have the right to maintain on a regular basis a personal relationship and direct contact with both his or her parents, unless that is contrary to his or her interests'. This provision is based on Paragraph 3 of Article 9 of the CRC, but unlike this paragraph, Article 24 of the Charter applies to all children instead of children who are separated from their parents. Also, 'a personal relationship and direct contact' are factual instead of legal notions.

Paragraph 2 of Article 24 is a restatement of Paragraph 1 of Article 3 of the CRC and prescribes that in all actions relating to children the child's best interests must be a primary consideration. Like the CRC, the Charter does not explain what those best interests are exactly.

Another notion that has been borrowed from the CRC is the right of children to express their views and the obligation to take these views into consideration in matters concerning them.[58] However, unlike the CRC, the

---

56 *2000 Charter of Fundamental Rights of the European Union*, 2000/C 364/01.

57 *2007 Treaty of Lisbon amending the Treaty on European Union and the Treaty establishing the European Community*, Official Journal 2007/C 306/01.

58 Paragraph 1 of Article 24 of the Charter and Paragraph 1 of Article 12 of the CRC.

Charter does not grant the child the explicit right to be heard in proceedings concerning him or her.

Apart from the rights of the child, the Charter also protects the family. Article 7 provides that 'everyone has the right to respect for his or her private and family life, home and communications'. This provision is an exact replica of Paragraph 1 of Article 8 of the ECHR. However, Article 8 of the ECHR has a second paragraph that sets out the possible exceptions to the right. Article 7 of the Charter does not have a similar system of exceptions. Does this mean that the right to respect for private and family life is unconditional? This is unlikely, but because the Charter is such a new instrument, there has not yet been any case law to either disprove or confirm this right's status.

Relevance for co-parenting

When it comes to the interpretation of the above articles it will be interesting to see whether the domestic courts and the Court of Justice of the European Union (ECJ) are going to use the interpretation that has already been established in CRC and ECHR case law concerning similar provisions or whether they will devise a completely new line of interpretation. It would be premature to draw any conclusions at this stage, but considering that the ECJ has a long history of using other international instruments (including the ECHR) in the reasoning for its decisions, it is likely that the ECJ, at the very least, will not completely ignore the already established interpretation. This means that it is unlikely that the Charter will be interpreted so as to prevent or discourage joint (exercise of) parental responsibilities or residential co-parenting.

2.2.7. BRUSSELS II BIS REGULATION

When it comes to European Union legislation in the field of family law, it is mainly concerned with *cross-border implications* and the unification of private international law rules. The Brussels II bis Regulation on jurisdiction, recognition and enforcement of judgments in matrimonial matters and matters of parental responsibility is the most well-known and far-reaching private international law instrument in this area.[59] This Regulation sets out rules on jurisdiction, recognition and enforcement of judgments concerning, among other things, parental responsibility. Where it deals with the same issues as the 1996 Hague Convention, the Brussels

---

[59] *2003 Council Regulation (EC) No. 2201/2003 concerning jurisdiction and the recognition and enforcement of judgments in matrimonial matters and the matters of parental responsibility, repealing Regulation (EC) No. 1347/2000*, Official Journal L 338, 23/12/2003, pp. 0001-0029.

II bis Regulation applies when the child concerned has his or her habitual residence on the territory of a EU Member State or when the case concerns the recognition and enforcement of a judgment delivered in a court of a EU Member State on the territory of another Member State.[60]

The Brussels II bis Regulation applies to the 'attribution, exercise, delegation, restriction or termination of parental responsibility as well as to the rights of custody and access'.[61] This means that it will also apply in (cross-border) cases on the joint exercise of parental responsibilities and residential co-parenting. The Brussels II bis Regulation does not repeat the definition of *parental responsibility* from the 1996 Hague Convention; instead it defines parental responsibility as 'all rights and duties relating to the person or the property of a child which are given to a natural or legal person by judgment, by operation of law or by an agreement having legal effect' including the rights of custody and the rights of access.[62]

The hearing of the child also plays an important role in the application of the Regulation as can be seen in Paragraphs 19 and 20 of the Preamble, Articles 23 subsection b, Paragraph 2 subsection c of Article 41 and Paragraph 2 subsection a of Article 42. The Regulation frequently mentions the best interests of the child as being an important or primary consideration as well.[63]

The Brussels II bis Regulation mainly provides clarity on what to do in cross-border situations or what rights a parent has when the other parent moves to another Member State with the child. In the latter case the arrangement need not necessarily be changed (for example, when the move is just across the border and the distance between both parents and the child's school is still reasonable for the child to alternate between the parents), as a judgment (including a residential arrangement) delivered in one Member State shall be recognized in other Member States - unless one of the exceptions of Article 24 is applicable - and the Recommendation even provides rules on when such a judgment can be enforced (in other Member States).[64]

Relevance for co-parenting

The Brussels II bis Regulation is most likely only relevant in co-parenting situations where the parents either live in different countries, both move to another country while already in the possession of a binding parental responsibilities arrangement or residential arrangement or when such an

---

60 Article 61 of the Brussels II bis Regulation.

61 Article 1 subsection b and Article 2 subsection a of the Brussels II bis Regulation.

62 Paragraph 7 of Article 2 of the Brussels II bis Regulation.

63 See Paragraph 1 subsection b of Article 12 and Paragraph 1 of Article 15 of the Brussels II bis Regulation.

64 Chapter III of the Brussels II bis Regulation.

arrangement exists and one of the parents relocates to another (Member State) country with or without the child.

2.3. NON-BINDING INSTRUMENTS

In this section non-binding instruments are discussed. These instruments, although not binding, have a strong persuasive effect, because they have been drafted by renowned national experts and are often based on extensive research. A close link also often exists between the non-binding instruments and the legislature of international or European organizations, because many of the experts involved in the drafting of these instruments are employed by these organizations. The weakness of these instruments is their non-enforceability.

Three of the instruments discussed below, the Recommendation on Parental Responsibilities, the White Paper and the Draft Recommendation on the rights and legal status of children and parental responsibilities, originate from the Council of Europe; while the last one, the CEFL Principles, was drafted by the Commission on European Family Law, an independent, international, academic initiative. All of the instruments contain substantive law and are therefore discussed chronologically.

2.3.1. 1984 RECOMMENDATION ON PARENTAL RESPONSIBILITIES

The Recommendation on Parental Responsibilities was adopted by the Committee of Ministers of the Council of Europe on 28 February 1984 and was at that time the first international instrument dealing specifically with parental responsibilities.[65] The Recommendation sets out the way parental responsibilities should be allocated in different situations, when the competent authority should take measures if parental responsibilities are misused and what some of the responsibilities entail. Parental responsibilities are defined as 'a collection of duties and powers which aim at ensuring the moral and material welfare of the child, in particular by taking care of the person of the child, by maintaining personal relationships with him [or her] and by providing for his [or her] education, his [or her] maintenance, his [or her] legal representation and the administration of his [or her] property'.[66]

---

65 1984 Recommendation No. R (84) 4 on Parental Responsibilities.

66 Principle 1 subsection a of the Recommendation on Parental Responsibilities.

When taking a decision relating to the attribution or exercise of parental responsibilities or a decision that affects the essential interests of the child the competent authority is required to consult the child involved with regard to the decision. This requirement only exists if the child's degree of maturity permits this.[67]

The Recommendation makes a distinction between married, divorced and non-married parents when it comes to the exercise of parental responsibility. Married parents should have joint parental responsibilities for the child of their marriage.[68] When they decide to separate the competent authority requested to intervene should divide the exercise of the responsibilities between the two parents. The competent authority can only provide that the responsibilities should be exercised jointly if the parents consent to this, and in general the competent authority should take account of any agreement concluded between the parents, unless this is contrary to the interests of the children.[69]

When children are born out of wedlock and a legal filiation link is established with regard to both parents, domestic law can *only* provide that the parental responsibilities should be exercised jointly by both parents if they live together or if an agreement to this extent has been concluded between them.[70] This is the case even if the joint exercise of parental responsibilities would have been in the best interests of the child in a particular case. This is surprising as in Principle 2 it is stated that any decision by the competent authority concerning the attribution of parental responsibilities or the way in which these responsibilities are exercised should be based primarily on the interests of the child.

Not only does the Recommendation set out the different possible ways in which the parental responsibilities should be allocated, but it also provides guidelines as to their exercise. Thus Principle 10 explains that where parental responsibilities are exercised jointly by both parents, any decision affecting the interests of the child should be taken with the agreement of both and in case of disagreement the competent authority should try to reconcile the parents insofar as the interests of the child so require. When reconciliation is not possible it is up to the competent authority to take the appropriate decision. Here one can see the best interests of the child being given priority over the individual wishes of the parents.

---

67 Principle 3 of the Recommendation on Parental Responsibilities.
68 Principle 5 of the Recommendation on Parental Responsibilities.
69 Principle 6 of the Recommendation on Parental Responsibilities.
70 Principle 7 of the Recommendation on Parental Responsibilities.

Relevance for co-parenting

The main conclusion that can be drawn from the provisions of the Recommendation on Parental Responsibilities is that joint parental responsibilities after parental separation cannot be allocated against the parents' wishes, not even if it is in the best interests of the child (although one can question whether it could ever be in the child's best interests to force disputing parents into a co-parenting arrangement). The inability of the competent authority to choose joint parental responsibilities without the parents' consent/prior agreement could be seen as an obstacle to the joint exercise of parental responsibilities, and by extension to residential co-parenting, especially in situations where contact between the parents is reasonable and parental responsibilities could be exercised together in harmony, but one of the parents still refuses to consent.

2.3.2. THE WHITE PAPER

For over a decade the Recommendation on Parental Responsibilities remained the only instrument regulating parental responsibilities. Then, in 1997, the Council of Europe's Committee of Experts on Family Law decided to request the preparation of principles on the legal status of children, to be included in an international instrument. This led to the drafting of the White Paper on principles concerning the establishment and legal consequences of parentage (the White Paper). Due to the low number of comments from the Council of Europe Member States and the fact that the national legislation in this field was then still in the process of development, it was eventually decided to adopt and publish this document as a Report instead of an official Recommendation.[71] It is now being replaced by the new Draft Recommendation.[72]

The White Paper sets the joint attribution and exercise of parental responsibilities as the point of departure, because it is seen as the ideal situation for the child.[73] It is presented as the norm and any departure therefrom is seen as an exception, justified only by the best interests of the child.

Parental responsibilities are defined in Principle 18 as 'a collection of duties and powers, which aim at ensuring the moral and material welfare

---

[71] Council of Europe Committee of experts on Family Law, *Report on principles concerning the establishment and legal consequences of parentage – 'The White Paper'*, 23 October 2006, CJ-FA (2006) 4 e; Council of Europe European Committee on Legal Co-operation, *'White Paper' on principles concerning the establishment and legal consequences of parentage*, 15 January 2002 (adopted 11-14 May 2004), CJ-FA (2001) 16 rev.

[72] More on this in the next section.

[73] Paragraph 66 of the White Paper.

of children, in particular: care and protection, maintenance of personal relationships, provision of education, legal representation, determination of residence and administration of property'. This is essentially a restatement of Principle 1 subsection a of the Recommendation on Parental Responsibilities 1984, so the old definition is retained.

Principle 19 states that parental responsibilities should in principle belong jointly to both parents and when, by the operation of law, only one parent is allocated parental responsibilities, the other parent should be able to acquire them, unless it is against the best interests of the child. The lack of consent or opposition by the parent having parental responsibilities should not as such be an obstacle to the acquisition of parental responsibilities by the other parent.

Not only should the parents both *have* parental responsibilities, they should also have the equal right to *exercise* these responsibilities and should preferably do so *together*. Just as the allocation, the exercise of parental responsibilities is subject to the child's best interests and if those interests so require, the exercise of parental responsibilities may be divided between the parents or limited to one of the parents, based on the decision of a competent authority or on an agreement concluded between the parents.[74]

Parents may *only* be deprived – partly or totally – of parental responsibilities or of the exercise thereof in exceptional circumstances determined by the law and only upon a decision by a competent authority made in the best interests of the child. Such decisions, once made, should be reviewed periodically.[75]

Because the underlying idea of the principles is that the joint exercise of parental responsibilities is in the best interests of the child, no distinction is made between married and unmarried couples or between legitimate and illegitimate children.[76] This is a clear departure from the Recommendation on Parental Responsibilities which did make a distinction based on the legal status of the parents' (previous) relationship.[77] To remove any doubt, in Principle 22 it is specifically stated that the dissolution or annulment of a marriage, the separation of the parents or the termination of the cohabitation should not *as such* affect the right of a parent to exercise parental responsibilities. However, in exceptional situations the competent authority may rule – after the relationship of the parents has changed – that parental responsibilities should be exercised differently if the automatic continuation of joint parental responsibilities is clearly shown to be contrary to the best interests of the child.[78]

74 Principle 20 of the White Paper.
75 Principle 24 of the White Paper.
76 Paragraph 66 of the White Paper.
77 See section 2.3.1 of Chapter 2.
78 Paragraph 66 of the White Paper.

As a final note on the provisions of the White Paper: the child is not simply a subject that should be cared for. The child has a voice of their own. When exercising parental rights and responsibilities the child should have a right to express his or her views and due weight should be given to the views expressed by the child according to his or her age and maturity.[79] The same must be done by the competent authority when taking a decision relating to parental responsibilities.[80]

Relevance for co-parenting
The White Paper's strong promotion of the joint exercise of parental responsibilities can be seen as very favourable to the joint exercise of parental responsibilities as well as residential co-parenting, as the joint exercise of parental responsibilities creates a favourable legal and practical climate for such a residential arrangement.

2.3.3. DRAFT RECOMMENDATION

In 2009 steps were taken to revive the idea of a new instrument on (among other things) parental responsibilities; Nigel Lowe then wrote a report proposing a New European Convention on Family Status. This proposal was part of a study into the rights and legal status of children being brought up in various forms of marital or non-marital partnerships and cohabitation.[81] This resulted in a Draft Recommendation on the rights and legal status of children and parental responsibilities.[82] The Draft Recommendation has not yet been adopted, and after 2011 there has not been any news or change in its status. Its future is therefore highly questionable. However, the Draft Recommendation is still discussed here as it reflects the most recent European position on parental responsibilities.

The Recommendation was meant to provide minimum standards for issues concerning the rights and legal status of children and parental responsibilities.[83] There are many similarities between the Draft Recommendation and the White Paper.[84] This is easily explained as both documents originate from the same organization, concern the same or

79 Principle 21 of the White Paper.
80 Paragraph 2 of Principle 25 of the White Paper.
81 N. LOWE, *A study into the rights and legal status of children being brought up in various forms of marital or non-marital partnerships and cohabitation*, 21 September 2009, CJ-FA (2008) 5.
82 Council of Europe Committee of Experts on Family Law, *Draft Recommendation on the rights and legal status of children and parental responsibilities*, 27 May 2010, CJ-FA-GT3 (2010) 2 rev. 2.
83 Preamble to the Draft Recommendation.
84 For a discussion of the White Paper see section 2.3.2 of Chapter 2.

similar issues and the Draft Recommendation was drafted within a relatively short period of time after the White Paper. Another source of inspiration for the Draft Recommendation has been the Principles of European Family Law Regarding Parental Responsibilities by the Commission on European Family Law (the CEFL Principles).[85] Many of these Principles were either literally copied by the Draft or slightly amended and then used in the Draft.

The Draft uses the same definition of parental responsibilities as the Recommendation on Parental Responsibilities 1984 and the White Paper, but adds the word 'including' to the definition when listing the different responsibilities to highlight the intention not to make the list exhaustive.[86] The Draft gives an indication of for what objective parental responsibilities should be utilized: the holders of parental responsibilities should care for, protect and educate the child to promote the child's personality in a manner consistent with his or her evolving capacities. The child should not be subjected to violence or treatment that could endanger his or her - mental or physical - health.[87] It is also stated explicitly and separately in Article 27 that parents should be under a duty to maintain the child.

Parental responsibilities should in principle belong to each parent and the dissolution, termination or annulment of the parents' marriage or other formal relationship, or their legal or factual separation should not *as such* constitute a reason for terminating parental responsibilities (by operation of law).[88] This is not an absolute obligation as can be seen by the words 'in principle' and Paragraph 2 of Article 30 which provides that if only one parent has parental responsibilities by the operation of law, states should make procedures available for the other parent to have an opportunity to acquire parental responsibilities, unless it is against the best interests of the child. The state is therefore able to exclude certain parents from having and exercising parental responsibilities. The explanatory memorandum clarifies that this exception concerns *totally unfit* parents and gives rapist fathers as an example. The sole lack of consent or opposition by the parent who has parental responsibilities is not enough to refuse to grant parental responsibilities to the other parent.[89]

Just as parental responsibilities can be acquired by the parent previously not having them, they can come to an end or a parent can be deprived of them. Parental responsibilities usually end when the child reaches majority

---

85 More about the CEFL principles in section 2.3.4 of Chapter 2.

86 Art. 21 of the Draft Recommendation; Principle 1 subsection a of the Recommendation on Parental Responsibilities 1984; Principle 18 of the White Paper. For a discussion of the Recommendation on Parental Responsibilities 1984 see section 2.3.1 and for a discussion of the White Paper see section 2.3.2 of Chapter 2.

87 Article 31 of the Draft Recommendation.

88 Paragraph 1 of Article 23 and Paragraph 3 of Article 23 of the Draft Recommendation.

89 Paragraph 2 of Article 23 of the Draft Recommendation.

or the age of emancipation.[90] The domestic, competent authority may also, in exceptional circumstances, decide to partly or totally deprive the parent of parental responsibilities.[91] Exceptional circumstances may include the commission of criminal offences against the child or the mental illness of the parent.[92] Considering that the Draft's preamble states that the best interests of the child are a primary consideration in all actions concerning children, parents should *only* be deprived of parental responsibilities if it is in the best interests of the child. Also, a (partial) deprivation of parental responsibilities does not have to be permanent. When such deprivation is no longer justified parental responsibilities should be restored.[93]

The Draft gives more elaborate directions as to the exercise of (joint) parental responsibilities than any other international instrument. Article 37 explains that not only should the holders of parental responsibilities have an equal right and duty to exercise such responsibilities; they should - where possible - exercise them jointly. For the joint exercise of parental responsibilities it is imperative for the parents to be able to make decisions together. Agreement between parents is strongly encouraged, but each holder of parental responsibilities has the right to act alone with respect to daily matters.[94] The consent of the other parent is then presumed.[95] Decisions concerning *important* matters should be taken jointly.[96] Paragraph 2 of Article 38 gives an example of such matters: changing the child's school or the child's place of residence. In urgent cases, however, national law may determine that certain important decisions may be taken by a holder of parental responsibilities acting alone. The other holder(s) of parental responsibilities should be informed about these decisions without undue delay.

In cases where the parents cannot reach agreement either parent may apply to the competent authority. The competent authority should promote the reaching of an agreement, but where an agreement cannot be reached, the competent authority should decide how or by whom the parental responsibilities should be exercised taking into account the best interests of the child and the child's wishes (if the child is sufficiently mature).[97]

Another unique (for an international instrument) feature of the Draft is that it regulates how the residential arrangements of the child and changes

---

90 Article 25 of the Draft Recommendation.
91 Article 27 of the Draft Recommendation.
92 Explanatory memorandum.
93 Article 28 of the Draft Recommendation.
94 Paragraph 1 of Article 30 of the Draft Recommendation.
95 Explanatory memorandum.
96 Paragraph 2 of Article 30 of the Draft Recommendation.
97 Article 29 of the Draft Recommendation.

thereto should be made. It is (or it should be) the norm that the child lives with both parents.[98] However, when the holders of parental responsibilities are living apart, they should agree upon with whom the child resides. If a joint holder of parental responsibilities then wishes to change the child's residence within or outside the jurisdiction, he or she should inform the other holder of parental responsibilities in advance. If the other holder of joint parental responsibilities objects to the change of the child's residence, he or she may apply to the competent authority for a decision. It is then for the competent authority to decide whether the move can take place taking into account the child's best interests and wishes; the child's right to maintain personal relationships with the other holder of parental responsibilities; the ability and willingness of the holders of parental responsibilities to co-operate with each other; the personal situation of the holders of parental responsibilities; the geographical distance and accessibility; and the free movement of persons.[99]

Relevance for co-parenting
The Draft clearly determines that the joint exercise of parental responsibilities as well as residential co-parenting during the parents' relationship should be the norm, but leaves many possibilities to depart from this norm, especially if a departure would be in the best interests of the child. Agreement between the parents is strongly encouraged. The parents can of course agree that there should not be a joint exercise of parental responsibilities or residential co-parenting. It is then unlikely that they will be forced into one. The domestic competent authority is given quite a strong position as the deciding body when the holders of parental responsibilities cannot come to an agreement. The competent authority's main responsibility seems to be to ensure that the best interests and wishes of the child are respected and given primary consideration in these types of decisions.

2.3.4. CEFL PRINCIPLES

Finally, the Principles of European Family Law regarding Parental Responsibilities drafted by the Commission on European Family Law (the CEFL Principles) deserve a special mention in this chapter even though they do not originate from an official European (or international)

---

98 Explanatory memorandum.
99 Article 32 of the Draft Recommendation.

legislative organization.[100] It is nevertheless important to mention the CEFL Principles here, because Nigel Lowe is a member of the CEFL and has relied heavily on the CEFL Principles in the Draft Recommendation on the rights and legal status of children and parental responsibilities. The CEFL Principles were devised by comparing national legislation, taking into account international instruments, and searching for common ground as well as looking into the future. The CEFL Principles suggest how (European) family law should evolve and progress. Later the Principles were tested by applying them to the national systems of Estonia, Malta, Romania, Scotland, Denmark, England and Wales, and Turkey.[101] The CEFL Principles are also the most extensive and progressive principles on parental responsibilities – in the sense that they regulate more issues and in more detail than other instruments.

The CEFL Principles make a strong case in favour of parental equality judging from Principle 3:11, which states that parents having parental responsibilities should have an equal right and a duty to exercise such responsibilities and, whenever possible, they should exercise them jointly. According to Principle 3:10 these parental responsibilities should not be affected by parental separation.

The decision making on daily matters, important decisions, urgent decisions and the power of the national competent authority to decide in cases where the holders of parental responsibilities cannot reach an agreement have been discussed in detail in the previous section when discussing the Draft Recommendation on the rights and legal status of children and parental responsibilities. The CEFL Principles were slightly rephrased in the Draft Recommendation, but the meaning has remained the same.[102]

The CEFL Principles, however, have a couple of additional provisions that did not make it into the Draft Recommendation. These provisions regulate the exercise of parental responsibilities in more detail. As such, Principle 3:15 provides that subject to the best interests of the child, parents may agree that one of the parents may exercise parental responsibilities alone. This decision can also be taken by the competent authority. Parents, who have joint parental responsibilities, may also, subject to the best interests of the child, agree in general on the exercise of

---

100 K. BOELE-WOELKI et al., *Principles of European Family Law Regarding Parental Responsibilities*, 2007.

101 J. MAIR & E. ÖRÜCÜ (eds), *Juxtaposing Legal Systems and the Principles of European Family Law on Parental Responsibilities*, 2010.

102 Daily matters, important and urgent decisions: Principle 3:12, corresponding with Article 30 of the Draft Recommendation; Disagreement on exercise: Principle 3:14, corresponding with Article 29.

parental responsibilities and the way in which this should be done. Such agreements may be scrutinized by the competent authority.[103]

The provisions on termination, discharge and restoration of parental responsibilities are (again) very similar to those in the Draft Recommendation, although instead of stating that the competent authority *can,* in exceptional circumstances, deprive a holder of parental responsibilities of this possibility, the CEFL Principles provide when the competent authority *should* do so (namely where the behaviour of the holder of parental responsibilities causes a serious risk to the person or property of the child).[104]

The goal of the exercise of parental responsibilities is care, protection and education.[105] This has been adopted by the Draft Recommendation, but the more practical prohibition of corporal punishment and humiliating treatment has been replaced with a more vague prohibition of violence and harmful treatment.[106]

When it comes to the rights of the child, Principle 3:37 explains that the hearing of the child should occur in all proceedings concerning parental responsibilities and if the competent authority decides not to hear the child it should give specific reasons to justify its decisions. The Principles also clarify where and how the hearing of the child should be done.

For residential co-parenting Principle 3:20 on residence is very important as it explicitly provides for an alternating residence as an option after parental separation. This option may either be chosen by the parents or through a decision of a competent authority as long as it is in the best interests of the child. When deciding, the competent authority should take into account the age and opinion of the child, the ability and willingness of the holders of parental responsibilities to co-operate with each other in matters concerning the child, their personal situation and the distance between the residences of the holders of parental responsibilities, as well as the distances between these residences and the child's school.[107] This Principle proved inspirational for the Norwegian Child Law Commission when designing the 2010 law reforms. An alternating residence may now be imposed by the competent authority when 'special reasons so indicate'.[108]

---

103 Principle 3:13 of the CEFL Principles.

104 Principle 3:32 of the CEFL Principles.

105 Paragraph 1 of Principle 3:19 of the CEFL Principles, corresponding with Paragraph 1 of Article 31 of the Draft Recommendation.

106 Paragraph 2 of Principle 3:19 of the CEFL Principles, corresponding with Paragraph 2 of Article 31 of the Draft Recommendation.

107 Principles 3:20 and 3:21 of the CEFL Principles, corresponding with Article 32 of the Draft Recommendation.

108 T. SVERDRUP, 'Equal parenthood: recent reforms in child custody cases' in *The International Survey of Family Law*, 2011, p. 305.

Relevance for co-parenting

The CEFL Principles clearly encourage the joint exercise of parental responsibilities and they state that residential co-parenting is one of the residential arrangements that national legislation should at least allow. Paragraph 2 of Principle 3:20 does not decide whether residential co-parenting should be the rule or the exception, but it does present it as a viable option, one that should be considered.[109]

2.4. COMPARATIVE SYNTHESIS

The various international instruments and their relevance have been described in the previous sections. In themselves, their influence is limited: to see the bigger picture, it is important to consider the relation between them; the differences and the similarities; the developments and changes over time; and their influence on national law.

2.4.1. DIFFERENCES BETWEEN BINDING AND NON-BINDING INSTRUMENTS

There are many differences between the instruments and their provisions. The greatest difference is between binding and non-binding instruments. The first difference is that binding instruments tend to contain general ideas and broad notions such as the protection of the family (including the protection of the relationship between the parent and the child); the best interests of the child; the right of the child to know and be cared for by both parents; and the right of the child to be heard in proceedings concerning him or her. Non-binding instruments contain more specific rules, such as detailed prescriptions on the circumstances in which a parent can be deprived of parental responsibilities.

Similarly, binding instruments tend to be more 'conservative', meaning that their provisions usually contain general notions on which there is already some sort of consensus in the Member States. The non-binding instruments, on the other hand, tend to be more progressive, introducing new notions and terminology and proposing further-reaching rules. As an example one can take the introduction and definition of parental responsibilities in the 1984 Recommendation on Parental Responsibilities.[110]

---

109 K. BOELE-WOELKI et al., 2007, p. 135.

110 See section 2.3.1 of Chapter 2, The Hague Convention and Brussels II bis only introducing the term, which was more narrowly defined over a decade later.

To date, where binding instruments have concentrated mainly on the legal aspects of parentage, such as the attribution of parental responsibilities and official contact arrangements, non-binding instruments have begun to regulate the more practical issues such as the (joint) exercise of parental responsibilities. This is not very surprising, first because legal bonds are easier to define and regulate and because where care and residence are ongoing, legal arrangements have to be established only when a major change in circumstances occurs. Rules relating to legal bonds are therefore easier to impose and monitor.

While binding and non-binding instruments are both intended to apply to states, the non-binding instruments focus more on children's rights than on the rights of the parents. They are drafted to ensure that the child's best interests are considered. The *binding* instruments focus more on the state and its role in making and enforcing rules concerning the parents or guaranteeing parents' rights.

2.4.2. RECURRING NOTIONS AND VISIBLE TRENDS

Despite differences between the instruments, certain notions recur in the body of international and European instruments and trends in family law become visible. This section lists and explains the most important notions that have been shown to recur throughout the various international instruments discussed in this chapter: the best interests of the child. This section also highlights visible trends and movements within these notions.

2.4.2.1. Best interests of the child

A legal principle that can be found in multiple provisions of different international instruments is that of the best interests of the child.[111] It is the idea that when decisions or actions must be taken that concern children, their best interests should be a primary consideration. This means that the best interests of the child do not have to be decisive, but have to be at least considered first. In all decisions and actions it should first be considered what course of action is in the best interests of the child. Only thereafter can the interests of the parents and other considerations be taken into account. In exceptional circumstances it is therefore possible that the parents' interests outweigh those of the child's.

Of the international instruments discussed, Paragraph 1 of Article 3 of the CRC is the oldest provision containing the notion of the best

[111] This notion can be found in all international instruments either directly in the provisions or indirectly in explanatory reports or case law.

interests of the child.[112] Ever since then, the notion has often been restated in many different other instruments. The notion has not changed much over time, but its influence has grown and it has become the key notion in (international) legislation concerning children.

The notion of the best interests of the child is not only used in itself or to explain how certain decisions or actions must be taken, but also to justify exceptions. For example, Principle 20 of the White Paper provides that parents should have an equal right to exercise parental responsibilities and, whenever possible, should exercise them together, *unless the best interests of the child otherwise require*.[113]

The child's position has also changed over the years, from an object of parental rights to an autonomous party in the process. Where, at first, the child was a pawn in a tug of war between the parents, now he or she is the main player. At least, that would be the ideal situation if the new rules are applied correctly.

The provisions that have been strengthened over the years give the child a voice. The child has the right to express his or her views and in case of proceedings concerning the child, he or she has the right to be heard.[114] There is a catch, however: only children who are considered to be sufficiently mature enjoy these rights.[115] No minimum age is set to enjoy these rights; instead the maturity of the child is decided on the basis of the facts of the case and the child in question. This, of course, gives the national legislator and the national competent authority a great deal of leeway to apply the provisions very restrictively should they want to do so.

2.4.2.2. *Respect for family life*

Even before international law started to specifically concern itself with children, children's rights and the child-parent relationship had already been protected, because the two oldest binding international instruments, the ECHR and the ICCPR, protected family life.[116]

While the provisions themselves are too broad and general to say anything about children's rights, parental responsibilities, or even anything directly on the parent-child relationship, they have generated a large body of case law. The case law expanded and adapted to a changing society and the emerging needs. From the notion of the protection of family life it has

---

112 See section 2.2.2 of Chapter 2.

113 See section 2.3.2 of Chapter 2.

114 All of the discussed instruments except for the very general instruments: the ICCPR and the ECHR contain one or more provisions on the child's right to express his or her views or the child's right to be heard.

115 See for example Articles 4 and 6 of the Convention on Contact, section 2.2.5.

116 See sections 2.2.1 and 2.2.4 of Chapter 2.

derived the right to regular contact between children and their parents and the right of an unmarried father to apply for joint parental authority despite the mother's refusal, something that the organisations could not have been able to foresee at the time of drafting both instruments.

2.4.2.3. *Right to maintain a relationship with both parents*

It is an established presumption in international law that it is in the best interests of the child to gain and maintain a good relationship with both parents. For this reason most instruments contain provisions to the effect that states should allow parents to at least have (regular) contact with their children.

The basis of these kinds of provisions lies in the CRC, more specifically in Articles 7 and 9.[117] The main idea is that the child should know and be cared for by both parents when possible and should not be separated from his or her parents against his or her will. Should separation occur, usually in the case of divorce or the breakdown of the relationship, there should at least be regular contact between parent and child. The EU Charter has recently restated this notion, but in general there has been a move away from the idea of regular contact and towards an equal or joint exercise of parental responsibilities especially in European instruments.[118] This is very likely because 'contact' and 'a good relationship' are very vague terms and allow for large discrepancies in interpretation between national systems.

2.4.2.4. *Parental responsibility*

Because of the vagueness and the minimum protection of such terms as contact and parental authority the more recent international instruments and also some national laws prefer the term parental responsibilities (or parental responsibility). This term in general encompasses more rights and duties than parental authority. Not only parental rights, but also *duties* are included and the term has both legal and practical implications.

Because parental responsibilities have more practical implications than contact and parental authority, the first international instrument on parental responsibilities – the Recommendation on Parental Responsibilities 1984 – was very cautious in the allocation of parental responsibilities, making the joint (exercise of) parental responsibilities dependant on parental agreement.[119]

---

117 See section 2.2.2 of Chapter 2.

118 See for a discussion of the EU Charter section 2.2.6 of Chapter 2.

119 See section 2.3.1 of Chapter 2.

However, nowadays the main idea seems to be that parental responsibilities should as a rule belong to both parents jointly. Neither the separation of the parents, nor the refusal of consent by one of the parents should be a sufficient obstacle for awarding joint parental responsibilities to the parents. Once the parents jointly hold parental responsibilities, it is also preferable that they exercise them together, especially in the case of important decisions concerning the child.[120] This presumption of joint parental responsibility is also evident from the fact that the new instruments make depriving parents of parental responsibility by law very difficult and only possible if the child's best interests require this.

The distinctions that used to exist between married and unmarried, as well as divorced or separated parents have disappeared. The relationship between the parents is no longer important, the best interests of the child are. Even after separation the original situation (which was the joint exercise of parental responsibilities) should continue, unless there is a necessity related to the best interests of the child to change this situation.

This all means that in general there is a change in attitude towards parents, especially visible in European instruments, from providing the minimum rules on parental authority and contact to regulating the exercise of parental responsibilities. It is no longer the parents who are the main holders of rights, but the children. They have the right to care and contact. The parents have the duty to provide this care and an obligation to seek contact.

2.4.3. SUMMARY

Within the international framework, a movement can be discerned from a parent-oriented allocation of parental authority towards a child-oriented joint exercise of parental responsibilities. Where in the past international law was very reluctant to interfere in national family law, the new international legislation is introducing increasingly specific and substantive rules. These new rules are clearly in favour of joint parental responsibilities after parental separation and the joint exercise thereof.

None of the instruments discussed forbid the joint exercise of parental responsibilities or residential co-parenting outright, nor can any of the discussed instruments be interpreted as forming an obstacle to national legislation that allows these care arrangements. However, it can be inferred from the notion of the best interests of the child that national legislation that would prescribe either the joint exercise of parental responsibilities or residential co-parenting in *all* post-separation cases could be in conflict

---

[120] See sections 2.3.2, 2.3.3 and 2.3.4 of Chapter 2.

with international law. This makes sense, considering, for example, that residential co-parenting in cases where there is violence or neglect (from one of the parents) would be very detrimental to the child's well-being. There is no obstacle, though, to establishing joint parental responsibilities or residential co-parenting as the norm, as long as there is enough room for exceptions in cases where such arrangements would be detrimental to the child's well-being.

Parenting-centred legislation within the international law framework needs to be child-centred, in the sense that the child's best interests need to be considered and the child's voice needs to be heard. While the child's views by no means need to be decisive, it is important that the child is included in the process, especially when decisions are made concerning his or her residence.

Besides the protection of the child, international law also prescribes parental equality. This, however, should be seen in the light of non-discrimination on the basis of marital status, rather than an equal sharing of the child's time. This means that international law has stopped making distinctions between divorced and formerly cohabiting parents. Both types should be eligible for joint parental responsibilities.

International law did not want, until very recently, to meddle in the residence arrangements of the child after parental separation. Only the most recent, non-binding instruments – the Draft Recommendation and the CEFL Principles – have tentatively ventured in this direction.[121] The new international instruments only make some minimal rules on residence and do not really speak in favour or against residential co-parenting. They only include it as a possibility.

As a general conclusion to this chapter it can be stated that international law in its current form does encourage the joint exercise of parental responsibilities, but it would be going too far to state that the joint exercise of parental responsibilities, especially in combination with residential co-parenting, is prescribed in all or most cases. This gives national legislators the freedom to adopt new rules or to amend old ones in order to make the joint exercise of parental responsibilities and residential co-parenting the norm (or not), should they wish to do so.

---

121 See sections 2.3.3 and 2.3.4 of Chapter 2.

CHAPTER 3
THE ENGLISH LEGAL SYSTEM

3.1. HISTORY OF THE MAIN LEGAL AND SOCIETAL DEVELOPMENTS

The English[1] law concerning children, and especially parent-child relationships, has undergone a rigorous change in the last 25 years. The most important piece of legislation that signified this change was the Children Act 1989, which came into force on 14 October 1991.[2] Since the enactment of the Children Act 1989, English family law has become more concerned with the extend to which arrangements between parents, irrespective of their relationship to each other, meet the best interests of their child or children, while in the past the main focus used to be on the horizontal relationship between adults.[3] It symbolises the shift in policy emphasis away from marriage and spousal relationships toward parenthood and parent-child relationships.

The Children Act 1989 introduced the term 'parental responsibility', before that many different terms to describe parental responsibilities and parental authority were used, often inconsistent with each other and sometimes outdated or misleading.[4] The use of parental responsibility has been suggested by the Law Commission in preparation of the Children Act 1989.[5]

---

1 Where this chapter and the rest of this book mentions England or English law, England and Wales/the law applicable to England and Wales is meant; this includes law which applies to a larger region than England and Wales, such as UK law.

2 *An Act to reform the law relating to children; to provide for local authority services for children in need and others; to amend the law with respect to children's homes, community homes, voluntary homes and voluntary organisations; to make provision with respect to fostering, child minding and day care for young children and adoption; and for connected purposes* (*Children Act 1989*), 1989 Chapter 41, available online through the UK government website: www.legislation.gov.uk (last visited 29 April 2015). This act governs England and Wales as well as Scotland and Northern Ireland.

3 C. SMART, 'Children and the Transformation of Family Law', in J. Dewar & S. Parker eds., *Family Law: processes, practices, pressures; Proceedings of the Tenth World Conference of the International Society of Family Law*, 2003, p. 224.

4 R. WHITE et al., *A guide to the Children Act 1989*, 1990, p. 9.

5 Law Commission, *Family Law review of Child Law: Guardianship and Custody*, Law Com No 172, London: HMSO 1988, para. 2.4.

3.1.1. PARENT-CHILD RELATIONSHIP

The commencement of the Children Act 1989 coincided with the rise of the Fathers' Rights Movement. Men were becoming more vocal in their claims as fathers rather than as husbands or breadwinners. While before divorce or separation from the partner had often meant the loss of the children as well, less and less fathers were willing to accept this as the norm.[6] This has led to the growth and establishment of UK charities such as Families Need Fathers,[7] The Fatherhood Institute,[8] and the civil rights group Fathers 4 Justice.[9]

Prior to the Children Act 1989 there was a presumption that the best thing for children post parental separation was for the parent with custody to (re-)marry and to create a new nuclear family.[10] Gradually the idea that 'parenting across households' was not only possible, but could be successful became more popular. Now some authors even point out the *positive* effects being parented in two households can have on children as it exposes them to a wider range of childhood experiences and new challenges.[11]

3.1.2. CHILDREN'S RIGHTS

Parallel to the growing emphasis on the parent-child relationship, another movement within the family law can be perceived. It is the idea that children should be seen as autonomous beings with wishes and needs of their own, instead of the generic child without a voice. A milestone in this development was the House of Lords decision in the *Gillick* case,

---

6 See B. FEATHERSTONE's articles 'Taking Fathers Seriously' in the *British Journal of Social Work*, Vol. 33, 2003, pp. 239-254 and 'Fathers Matter: A Research Review' in *Children and Society*, Vol. 18, 2004, pp. 312-319 for an in depth exploration of the contemporary developments in men's lives in relation to fathering and the attitude towards it.

7 A registered UK charity which provides information and support to parents of either sex. Founded in May 1974. See their website for more information and publications: www.fnf.org.uk (last visited 29 April 2015).

8 A charity founded in 1999, focusing on research on fathers, fatherhood and different approaches to engaging with fathers by public services and employers. See their website for more information and publications: www.fatherhoodinstitute.org (last visited 29 April 2015).

9 A father's rights group founded in 2001 which campaigns against a perceived bias of the courts against fathers in post-separation cases. Because of their extreme ways of protesting, they often are seen as controversial in the media and even by other father's organizations. See their website for more information: www.fathers-4-justice.org (last visited 29 April 2015).

10 C. SMART, 2003, p. 230.

11 *Ibid.*, pp. 227-228.

which concerned the question whether a doctor can ever, lawfully give contraceptive advice or treatment to a girl under the age of 16 without her parents' consent.[12] The judgement contains a couple of important, general statements about parental rights and children's autonomy.

Lord Fraser of Tullybelton stated that:

> 'parental rights to control a child do not exist for the benefit of the parent. They exist for the benefit of the child and they are justified only in so far as they enable the parent to perform his duties towards the child, and towards other children in the family.'[13]

He considered as unnatural, a situation where a child is completely under the control of the parents and has no voice or rights before he or she reaches the age of 18, and once he or she reaches majority suddenly attains all rights and freedoms. The reality is that children slowly gain more rights and freedoms as they grow up and the parents gradually relax their control and this reality should be reflected by law.[14]

In the same decision Lord Scarman clarified that the time had come to break with the precedent that gave parents complete control over their children. While parental rights do exist and remain in force up to the child reaching majority, they are derived from parental duty and exist only so long as they are needed for the protection of the person and property of the child. Parental rights yields to the child's right to make his or her own decisions when he or she reaches *a sufficient understanding and intelligence* to be capable of making up his or her own mind on the matter requiring decision.[15] The 'sufficient understanding' criterion has been subsequently taken on board within multiple Children Act 1989 provisions, which will be discussed in more detail later on in the chapter.

3.1.3. SHARED RESIDENCE

When it comes to shared residence, just as big a change has taken place over the last two decades. Originally, the case law had established that shared care and residence could not be granted. In *Riley v Riley*, a 1986 case, the Court of Appeal commented that a divorce court order approving an arrangement by which a child was to spend every other week with each of her parents, should never have been made in the first place, even though the arrangement had been working well for three years prior to the

---

12 *Gillick v West Norfolk and Wisbech Area Health Authority*, [1986] 1 AC 112 (HL).
13 *Ibid.*, p. 170.
14 *Ibid.*, p. 171.
15 *Ibid.*, pp. 183-186.

original order and for five years after it had been made. The paramount interests of the child were, according to the court, that she should have a settled home and, where nothing could be said against either parent, that home should be with the mother.[16]

By the time discussion started on the new Children Act in late 1980s, this negative attitude towards residential co-parenting was somewhat watered down. Shared residence orders[17] were deemed appropriate by the advisory Commission only in cases where it was more realistic to describe the division of the time the child spends with his or her parents as more or less equal, than to say the child resides with one parent and has frequent contact with the other. Such situations were seen by the Commission as very rare and therefore, Parliament agreed, shared residence orders should only be made in very rare cases where residence was genuinely shared.[18]

Since the coming into force of the Children Act 1989 in 1991, the approach that no shared residence order was to be made, unless there was equally shared residence in practice has been maintained in general, emphasizing that a shared residence order is not about parental equality, but about where the child is to live.[19] However, as early as the mid 1990s, some courts have started to depart from this policy, making shared residence orders in a myriad of cases, not all of them reflecting genuine situations of residential co-parenting and a normative model of equal shared parenting post separation has become firmly entrenched in the minds of a few policy makers and legal practitioners.[20] The UK coalition government's agreement in 2010 stated explicitly that it will 'encourage shared parenting from the earliest stages of pregnancy – including the promotion of a system of flexible parental leave' and 'conduct a comprehensive review of family law in order to increase the use of mediation when couples do break up, and to look at how best to provide greater access rights to non-resident parents and grandparents'.[21]

In 2010, the House of Commons had put forward the Shared Parenting Orders Bill, which proposed to amend the Children Act 1989 to explicitly mention the court's power to make shared parenting orders and 'to create a legal presumption that such orders enhance the welfare of the child

16 *Riley v Riley*, [1986] 2 FLR 429.

17 Orders establishing the child's residence with both parents.

18 P. HARRIS & R. GEORGE, 'Parental responsibility and shared residence orders: parliamentary intentions and judicial interpretations', *Child and Family Law Quarterly*, Vol. 22, No. 2, 2010, p. 156.

19 See for example *D v D (Shared Residence Order)*, [2001] 1 FLR 495; *Re A (Shared Residence)*, [2001] EWCA Civ 1795; and *Re A (Children) (Shared Residence)*, [2003] 3 FCR 656.

20 See for an in-depth discussion of residence orders section 3.4.1 of Chapter 3.

21 *The Coalition: Our programme for government*, HM Government, 20 May 2010, p. 20. Available online through the Cabinet Office website: www.cabinetoffice.gov.uk (last visited 29 April 2015).

unless certain exceptions apply'.[22] However, this Bill failed to complete its passage through Parliament before the end of the session, and therefore will make no further progress.

As of yet there are no large-scale UK studies which focus specifically on shared parenting time.[23] However, different family studies contain some indicators on what the current situation is. Shared residence has not really been defined in the studies, legislation or case law. Usually the broad definition of shared care based on 30/70 to 50/50 division of overnights is used. Shared residence remains relatively uncommon in England.[24]

A UK study on contact problems in separated families conducted by the Gingerbread and Nuffield Foundation in 2009 showed that out of all separating or divorcing parents, only 9-12% opt for shared residence, meaning in this particular study, that the child or children spend at least three overnights a week with each parent or up to around half a year with each parent. The authors of the study note that this figure is actually unexpectedly high and should be tested further.[25]

3.2. BACKGROUND OF THE LAW CURRENTLY IN PLACE

The Children Act 1989 has not only introduced the concept of parental responsibilities, it was built around it. The Act had been met with much praise from policy makers, authors and practitioners alike. Where previous legislation on children and the parent-child relationship was scattered over different statutes and overall quite unintelligible, making it difficult for families to understand and use in court, the new Act was comprehensive and logical. It also brought with it the most far-reaching reforms of the law affecting children.[26]

---

22 Shared Parenting Orders Bill. Available online through the UK Parliament website www.parliament.uk (last visited 29 April 2015).

23 University of Oxford Department of Social Policy and intervention, *Family Policy Briefing 7. Caring for children after parental separation: would legislation for shared parenting time help children?*, Oxford 2011, p. 7. However, there exist some smaller empirical studies that provide some insight into the situation.

24 See Chapter 6 for a discussion of the available English empirical studies on residential arrangements, statistic figures, and psycho-social studies into residential co-parenting.

25 V. PEACEY & J. HUNT, *I'm not saying it was easy…: Contact problems in separated families*, Report, Gingerbread 2009, p. 17. Available online through the Gingerbread website: www.gingerbread.org.uk (last visited 29 April 2015). The study comprised of a quantitative, nationwide, face-to-face survey of 559 separated parents, followed by in-depth, qualitative interviews with a sub-sample of 41 families. More on this and other English and UK studies, see section 6.2.1.

26 P. HARRIS & R. GEORGE, 2010, pp. 151-153.

The Act applies to children and a 'child' is defined in Paragraph 1 of Section 105 as a person under the age of eighteen. However, some powers of the court and the parents cease to apply once the child reaches the age of sixteen.

By force of the Children Act 1989, the court has been given the power to make different types of orders, concerning children and their parents or guardians. The most important are the so-called *'Section 8 orders'*, which are contact orders, prohibited steps orders, residence orders and specific issues orders.[27]

Where a court is considering whether or not to make one or more orders with respect to a child under the Children Act 1989, including the Section 8 orders, it shall not make any of the orders unless it considers that doing so would be better for the child than making no order at all.[28] This applies in reverse as well: when deciding whether or not to discharge an existing order, the court must regard the child's welfare as its *paramount* consideration and be satisfied that discharging the order is better than not doing it.

This is a departure from the past. Before the Children Act 1989 there was a tendency to assume that when a case was brought before the court some order about the children should always be made. Now the primary responsibility for the upbringing of children is placed firmly with their parents and the courts should only interfere if the child is in danger of unacceptable risk. The intention of the Act and the powers given to the court within its provisions was to reduce the opportunity for conflict and litigation in the future.[29]

Since its coming into force, the Children Act 1989 has been amended and added to subsequently. Among the most important changes have been: the provisions enabling unmarried fathers who are registered as the child's father in the birth register to acquire parental responsibilities,[30] giving mothers' (female) civil partners rights equal to the mothers' husbands, and mothers' unmarried female partners similar rights to the rights held by the unmarried fathers,[31] as well as giving local authorities additional guidelines and powers to protect and care for children in need.[32]

---

27 Paragraph 1 of Section 8 of the Children Act 1989. These orders will be explained in depth in the following sections of this chapter. For now it is sufficient to know that a contact order establishes and regulates contact between the child and the non-resident parent, a prohibited steps order forbids a holder of parental responsibilities to exercise them in certain ways, a residence order establishes and governs the residence of the child, and a specific issues order decides a specific question concerning the child.

28 Paragraph 5 of Section 1 of the Children Act 1989.

29 P. HARRIS & R. GEORGE, 2010, pp. 153-155.

30 Section 111 of the Adoption and Children Act 2002.

31 Human Fertilisation and Embryology Act 2008.

32 Children Act 2004 and Childcare Act 2006.

3.3. JOINT PARENTAL RESPONSIBILITIES

For parents to set up any type of shared care arrangement after separation, it is important that they are recognised as legal parents and have the rights and duties needed for and associated with parenting. In the past this was done by granting one parent custody over the child and allowing the other parent contact. However, this creates an unequal division where one parent gains all rights and duties and the other parent can have contact, but not much say in how to raise the child.

With the coming into force of the Children Act 1989, the term 'custody' has been replaced with the term 'parental responsibility' and the idea that both parents should hold and exercise parental responsibilities together in harmony, consulting each other when making important decisions on the upbringing of the child.

3.3.1. PARENTAL RESPONSIBILITIES: MEANING AND CONTENT

The definition of parental responsibilities the way it is used in the English legal system is provided in paragraph 1 of Section 3 of the Children Act 1989. Parental responsibilities are 'all the rights, duties, powers, responsibilities and authority which by law a parent of a child has in relation to the child and his property'.[33]

This definition is rather vague and does not explain exactly what *kind* of rights, responsibilities and duties parents have. When advising on the Children Act 1989, the Law Commission had decided against a statutory definition of the rights and duties of parents, because those rights and duties strongly differ from case to case and from child to child.[34]

Some scholars have tried to explain what parental responsibilities mean. For instance, Eekelaar provides that:

> 'Parental responsibility may indicate that parents, rather than anyone else, are to have responsibility for making decisions about children. In other words the key role of the concept of parental responsibility is to stress that the state should not normally interfere with the decisions made by parents about children.'[35]

---

33 This definition is somewhat misleading as it seems to stipulate that only parents can hold parental responsibilities, which is not the case, as shall be explained in the next section.

34 J. HERRING, *Family Law*, Pearson Education Limited, 2011, p. 406.

35 J. EEKELAAR, 'Parental Responsibility: State of Nature or Nature of the State?', *Journal of Social Welfare and Family Law*, Vol. 13, 1991, p. 37.

In literature, attempts have also been made to identify the most important rights and duties enshrined within the concept of 'parental responsibilities'. A frequently cited list has been comprised by Lowe and Douglas in *Bromley's Family Law* and names rights and duties such as: bringing up the child, having contact with the child, protecting and maintaining the child, determining and providing for the child's religion and education, consenting to the child's medical treatment, administering the child's property and representing the child in legal proceedings.[36]

When it comes to parents' decision making powers, instead of asking: on which issues concerning the child can holders of parental responsibilities decide, it is easier to consider what limitations there are in place on the parental power to decide how to raise a child.[37] These limitations can lie within the realm of criminal law, for example, a parent who causes injury to his or her child as punishment, commits assault; or within the realm of private law, when the court makes a specific order prescribing or forbidding a certain action, the parent must abide by this order. It is also possible that the parent's power has been limited because the child has been taken into care by the local authority. When more than one person holds parental responsibilities, certain decisions can only be taken after consulting with the other holder or parental responsibilities or after obtaining consent from them.[38] Finally, older children, who are sufficiently mature, can make (some of the) decisions for themselves.[39] Still, the point of departure remains that each parent can exercise parental responsibilities on his or her own as he or she sees fit.

Arguably, the greatest duty parents have towards their children is to care for them, but the standard of that care is uncertain and diverse standards of parenting exist and should be tolerated.[40] Even so, parents who fail to provide *reasonable* care, who neglect their children or who fail to protect their children from abuse may have their children taken into care by the local authority or may be liable to criminal prosecution or liability in tort.[41]

Whether or not a person has parental responsibilities does not affect the child's right to succeed to their estate and is separate from any obligation they may have towards the child, for example, a parent may be liable to pay child support under the Child Support Act 1991, even though he does

---

36 N. LOWE & G. DOUGLAS, *Bromley's Family Law*, Oxford University Press 2007, p. 377.

37 J. HERRING, 2011, p. 407.

38 These limitations have predominately been set through case law. More on the exercise of joint parental responsibilities and the obligation of information in section 3.3.3 of Chapter 3.

39 See the discussion of the *Gillick* case and its impact earlier in this chapter.

40 Hedley J. in *Re L (Care: Threshold Criteria)*, [2007] 1 FLR 2050, para. 50.

41 J. MASSON et al., *Cretney's Principles of Family Law*, Thomson, Sweet and Maxwell 2008, p. 553; Section 31 of the Children Act 1989.

not have parental responsibilities.[42] This is also the case for stepparents where the child is 'child of the family'.[43]

3.3.2. ATTRIBUTION OF (JOINT) PARENTAL RESPONSIBILITIES

Section 2 of the Children Act 1989 sets out who has or can gain parental responsibilities over a child. Parental responsibilities and legal parentage are treated within the act as separate concepts and while whey often coincide - in the sense that legal parents are usually the holders of parental responsibilities - they are not synonymous.

Paragraph 5 explicitly states that more than one person may have parental responsibilities for the same child at the same time, but nowhere in the Act is it stated that there is a limit of two holders of parental responsibilities for the same child. It is therefore possible, although rare, that more than two people hold parental responsibilities over one child at any given time.[44] A person gaining parental responsibilities over the child does not cause any other holder of parental responsibilities over the same child to lose them.[45]

Still, it is of course possible that only one parent has parental responsibilities, though considering the law set out above, this should be expected to be rare. Sole parental responsibility is of course the sad consequence of one of the parents dying. It is as well possible that the father is not aware - or uncaring - of the mother's pregnancy and the subsequent birth of the child and never seeks to gain parental responsibilities. Joint parental responsibilities can change into sole parental responsibilities if one of the parents loses parental responsibilities, although this too is a rare occurrence.[46] Finally, lack of information can prevent persons from obtaining parental responsibilities. If the mother and her partner, be that partner male or female, have never been in a formal relationship and upon separation did not have any legal matters to resolve and have instead arranged the child's residence and contact with the non-resident parent privately, it is very possible that they never realised the necessity of the partner obtaining parental responsibilities.

---

42 Paragraph 4 of Section 3 of the Children Act 1989.

43 Sections 25 and 52 of the Matrimonial Causes Act 1973.

44 For example the (legal) parents and a stepparent. Legal parentage on the other hand is limited to two persons.

45 Paragraph 6 of Section 2 of the Children Act 1989.

46 See section 3.3.4 on discharge of parental responsibilities.

Not all parents gain parental responsibilities in the same way. Certain parents will gain parental responsibilities ex lege, while others will need a court order or a registration.

3.3.2.1. *The mother*

All mothers automatically (ex lege) gain parental responsibilities at the moment of birth.[47] For this purpose 'mother' means a woman who has given birth to the child, the biological mother.[48] This includes mothers who have become pregnant through assisted reproductive techniques.[49]

3.3.2.2. *The father*

The situation is different for the father. Fathers can only obtain parental responsibilities with the co-operation of the mother or through the court.[50] How they obtain parental responsibilities depends on their relationship with the mother of the child.

A father is only automatically granted parental responsibilities (ex lege) if he is married to the mother at the time of the child's birth (and he does not lose it upon divorce).[51] If the marriage takes place after the birth of the child, the father will also gain parental responsibilities for their child or children through Section 2 of the Legitimacy Act 1976 from the date of their marriage onwards. If the child was conceived by means of artificial insemination using the husband's sperm or embryos created using the husband's sperm, then the husband will automatically be the legal father of any child born as a result of the treatment and automatically gain parental responsibilities. If the child was conceived by means of artificial insemination not using the husband's sperm, he is still treated as the father, and thus given parental responsibilities, unless it is shown that he did not consent to the placing of the embryo or the sperm and eggs or to the artificial insemination.[52] The burden of proof is on the person claiming that he did not consent, but the clinic in which artificial insemination took place should, according to the code of conduct, ascertain whether the husband consents to the treatment and obtain a written record of the

---

47 Paragraphs 1 and 2 of Section 2 of the Children Act 1989.

48 Section 33 of the Human Fertilisation and Embryology Act 2008. It is the gestational care of the mother and not the genetic link which is crucial. See J. HERRING, *Family Law: issues, debates, policy*, Willan Publishing 2001, p. 129.

49 Paragraphs 1A and 2A of Section 2 of the Children Act 1989.

50 J. HERRING, 2011, pp. 354-355.

51 Paragraph 1 of Section 2 of the Children Act 1989. More about losing parental responsibilities in section 3.3.4 of Chapter 3.

52 Section 35 of the Human Fertilisation and Embryology Act 2008.

husband's consent. If the husband does not consent, the centre should take all practical steps to obtain written evidence of this.[53]

While there is debate over whether all fathers should automatically obtain parental responsibilities over their children, this is currently only the case for fathers who are married to the mother. An unmarried father can obtain parental responsibilities if he is registered as the father of the child on the birth certificate, which can only be done if he and the mother agree, or later, if he enters into a parental agreement with the mother.[54] In practice, the second option is rarely used due to widespread ignorance about the concept of parental responsibilities.[55] In cases where the mother does not want the father to have parental responsibilities and withholds consent, the father can apply to the court and ask for a parental responsibility order.[56] Such an order replaces the mother's consent and grants the father joint parental responsibilities together with the mother.

The court may not make a parental responsibility order of its own motion. Case law has provided three factors that should be considered as *a starting point* in deciding whether or not to make a parental responsibility order upon request. The court should take into account: the degree of commitment which the father has shown towards the child, the degree of attachment which exists between him and the child and the reasons for applying for the order.[57]

3.3.2.3. *Mother's female partner*

The law on the acquisition of parental responsibilities is similarly applied to the mother's female partner as is it is to the father. Mother's female partner who at the time of the artificial insemination of the mother was in a civil partnership with her or married to her automatically gains parental responsibilities over the child, unless she did not consent to the artificial insemination.[58] Again the burden of proof lies with the person who claims that they did not consent, but the clinic in which artificial insemination took place should, according to the code of conduct, ascertain whether the civil partner or wife consents to the treatment and obtain a written record of the civil partner's or wife's consent. If the civil partner or wife does not consent, the centre should take all practical steps to obtain written

53 See Legal Paternity after Sperm Donation on www.alternativefamilylaw.co.uk and Paragraph 6.3 of the Human Fertilisation and Embryology Act guidance on www.hfea.gov.uk (last visited 29 April 2015).
54 Paragraph 2 of Section 2 and Paragraph 1 of Section 4 of the Children Act 1989.
55 S. HARRIS-SHORT & J. MILES, *Family Law: texts, cases, and materials*, Oxford University Press, 2011, p. 662.
56 Paragraph 1 subSection c of Section 4 of the Children Act 1989.
57 S. HARRIS-SHORT & J. MILES, 2011, p. 663.
58 Section 42 of the Human Fertilisation and Embryology Act 2008.

evidence of this.[59] Just like in case of fathers marrying the mother after the child is born, if the female partner enters into a civil partnership with the mother or marries the mother after the birth of the child, she will gain parental responsibilities through Section 2A of the Legitimacy Act 1976 from the date of civil partnership or marriage onwards.

A woman who is neither the wife, nor the civil partner of the mother can also obtain parental responsibilities if she is registered as the parent of the child on the birth certificate. Again, this can only be done if both the female partner and the mother consent, if she enters into a parental responsibility agreement with the mother, or if she applies to the court and obtains a parental responsibility order.[60]

3.3.2.4. (Other) non-parents

The last category of people who may hold parental responsibilities are (other) non-parents. This category encompasses a large variety of people, from non-biological genetic parents to guardians. Because this book's focus lies on parents, the law surrounding non-parents will only be discussed briefly. One thing all non-parents have in common is that they never gain parental responsibilities ex lege, they will need an order.

If a child is born as a result of a surrogacy arrangement the commissioning parents, at least one of whom must be a genetic parent, will be able to apply to the courts for a parental order.[61] The commissioning parents can be husband and wife, civil partners, or persons who are living as partners in an enduring family relationship and are not within prohibited degrees of relationship in relation to each other.

A step-parent, meaning a person who is married to or in a civil partnership with a parent with parental responsibilities, is in a similar legal position as an unmarried partner of the mother. A parent or parents with parental responsibilities may by agreement with the step-parent provide for the step-parent to have parental responsibilities for the child; or the court may, on the application of the step-parent, make a parental responsibility order.[62] This means that if the child's parents are separated and have entered into new formal relationships, it is theoretically possible for a child to have four persons who have parental responsibilities for him or her.

---

59 See Legal Paternity after Sperm Donation on www.alternativefamilylaw.co.uk and Paragraph 6.6 of the Human Fertilisation and Embryology Act guidance on www.hfea.gov.uk (last visited 29 April 2015).

60 Sections 2 and 4ZA of the Children Act 1989.

61 Section 54 of the Human Fertilisation and Embryology Act 2008. 'Parental order' in this case means an order providing for a child to be treated in law as a child of the applicants.

62 Paragraph 1 of Section 4A of the Children Act 1989.

When the parents are deceased, untraceable, (temporarily) unfit to care for the child or it is for some other reason better that a third person makes legal decisions or cares for the child or children, non-parents and even local authorities as an entity can acquire parental responsibilities, as well as legal guardians.[63]

A special category of non-parents who become parents and gain parental responsibilities over the child are persons adopting a child. By means of an adoption order the adopting person or couple become the legal parents and automatically gain parental responsibilities.[64]

3.3.2.5. Overview

Below, the different means of obtaining parental responsibilities discussed in this section are set out in an explanatory table.

Table 1

Persons eligible for PR	PR automatically granted	PR through legal agreement with mother	PR through court order
Mother	x		
Mother's husband	x*		
Mother's civil partner/wife	x*		
Unmarried father		x	x
Female partner not in formal relationship with mother		x	x
Adoptive parents			Adoption order
Non-parents			x

* Unless there was no consent to artificial insemination.

3.3.3. EXERCISING (JOINT) PARENTAL RESPONSIBILITIES

Where more than one person has parental responsibilities for a child, each of them may act alone and without the other in fulfilling those responsibilities.[65] *Having* joint parental responsibilities does not necessarily

63 Sections 5, 14A and 33 of the Children Act 1989.
64 See for the rules on adoption and the adoption process the Adoption Act 1976.
65 Section 7 of the Children Act 1989.

mean that they are or should be jointly *exercised*. While the holder of parental responsibilities may not surrender or transfer any part of those responsibilities to another, he or she may arrange for some or all of it to be exercised by one or more persons acting on his behalf.[66] The idea behind this provision is primarily to encourage parents, whatever their relationship with each other is, to agree among themselves on the best (practical) arrangements for the child, which, however, are not legally binding.[67] Delegation will not absolve a holder of parental responsibilities from any liability for failure on their part to meet any part of their parental responsibilities for the child concerned.[68] Disposition of parental responsibilities is not possible.

There is no hierarchy among the holders of parental responsibilities; each parent can exercise them alone, in most cases even without obtaining the consent of the other holder of parental responsibilities or without consulting him or her.[69] There are, however, a few exceptions to the rule that there is no need to consult or to gain consent from the other holder of parental responsibilities.

First of all a holder of parental responsibilities can prevent that the child or children are taken from him or her by withholding consent to adoption,[70] objecting to the child being accommodated in local authority accommodation,[71] objecting to the granting of a passport to the child or children,[72] withholding consent if the other parent (or any other person) seeks to remove the child from the jurisdiction,[73] or, if this has already happened without his or her consent, by invoking child abduction rules.[74] Second, he or she can have a say in important events of his or her child's or children's life, for example, by giving or withholding legal authorisation for medical treatment,[75] withholding consent to change the

66 Paragraph 9 of Section 2 of the Children Act 1989.

67 R. WHITE et al., *A guide to the Children Act 1989*, London Butterworths 1990, p. 14.

68 Paragraph 11 of Section 2 of the Children Act 1989.

69 J. HERRING, 2011, p. 411.

70 By virtue of Section 16 of the Adoption Act 1976 the consent of all parents with parental responsibilities and all guardians is needed to free a child for adoption.

71 Section 20 of the Children Act 1989. All holders of parental responsibilities need to be asked to give their consent to the accommodation of the child in local authority accommodation and any holder of parental responsibilities who is willing and able to provide accommodation for the child or arrange that accommodation is provided, may object to the accommodation of the child in local authority accommodation.

72 Children's applications guidelines available online through the Home Office website: www.homeoffice.gov.uk (last visited 29 April 2015).

73 Section 13 of the Children Act 1989.

74 Sections 1 and 2 of the Child Abduction Act 1984; Article 8 of the Convention on the Civil Aspects of International Child Abduction.

75 Even overriding the child's refusal of treatment, see *Re W (A Minor) (Medical Treatment: Court's Jurisdiction)*, [1993] Fam. 64.

child's surname,[76] being consulted about changing the child's school,[77] giving consent to the marriage of a child aged 16 or 17,[78] withdrawing the child or children from sex education or religious classes and making representations to schools concerning the child's or children's education.[79] Finally, the holder of parental responsibilities can appoint a legal guardian for the child or children.[80]

3.3.3.1. *Court's procedural powers to restrict and regulate the exercise of parental responsibilities*

The court can restrict or regulate the exercise of (joint) parental responsibilities by issuing one or multiple Section 8 orders. It can make Section 8 orders with respect to the child, either upon an application of an entitled person (including parents, guardians and partners of parents) or of its own accord, when it is deemed necessary.[81] The making of a Section 8 order usually happens when the parents cannot reach an agreement on care arrangements or residential arrangements. For instance, when there is a dispute on where and with whom the child should live, the court can issue a residence order that establishes the child's (main) residence.[82] No new Section 8 orders should be made with respect to a child who has reached the age of sixteen, unless the circumstances of the case are exceptional.[83] The court may not only make a Section 8 order, it may also give directions as to how a Section 8 order is to be carried out, impose conditions to be complied with, specify the period for which the order or any provision in it is to have effect and make any provisions as the court thinks fit.[84] There are various possible orders to fit different situations.

3.3.3.1.1. Contact orders

If the child lives with one parent only, a contact order can be issued that requires the person with whom the child lives, or is to live, to allow the child to visit, to stay or to have contact with the person named in the order.[85]

---

76 Section 13 of the Children Act 1949, supplemented by *Re PC (change of Surname)*, [1997] 2 FLR 730.
77 *Re G (A Minor) (Parental responsibility: Education)*, [1994] 2 FLR 964.
78 Section 3 of the Marriage Act 1949. All parents with parental responsibilities and all guardians must consent.
79 Education Act 1996.
80 Section 5 of the Children Act 1989.
81 Section 10 of the Children Act 1989.
82 Paragraph 1 of Section 8 of the Children Act 1989. More on residence orders and development of their use in section 3.4.1.
83 Paragraph 7 of Section 9 of the Children Act 1989.
84 Paragraph 7 of Section 11 of the Children Act 1989.
85 Paragraph 1 of Section 8 of the Children Act 1989.

This type of order is usually not issued when the parents harmoniously exercise their joint parental responsibilities, but it can be useful in cases where the communication between the parents is difficult and there is a real danger that the resident parent shall obstruct contact with the other parent. Contact orders may either be drawn up in general terms, to permit reasonable contact, or they may define the duration, frequency, times and location of the contact.[86] In fact, orders may even be so detailed as to include the costs of gifts for the child or children and the contents or messages sent to the child or children.[87]

When the difficulty lies not in residence or contact, but in certain specific issues, the court can either issue a prohibited steps order or a specific issues order.[88] Although, the court should not make a prohibited steps order or a specific issue order if the same result can be achieved by making a residence or contact order.[89]

3.3.3.1.2. Prohibited steps orders

Applied to a situation where the parents have joint parental responsibilities and a prohibited steps order has been made in favour, or more accurately against, one of them, it restricts the exercise of parental responsibilities thus, that the holder of parental responsibilities may not take a certain action specified in the order, which normally lies within his or her abilities as holder of parental responsibilities, without the consent of the court. Such an order works as a pre-emptive obstacle to prevent one parent from doing something against the other parent's wishes, for example, preventing the child's surname to be changed[90] It is an order meant to prevent unwanted action from one of the parents in the future and can be very specific. In *Clayton v Clayton*, for example, a prohibited steps order was made to prevent the father to publish the story of him taking his daughter to Portugal and the consequent abduction proceedings.[91]

3.3.3.1.3. Specific issue orders

A specific issue order can be obtained where it is not a certain action that needs to be prevented, but where the parents cannot agree on a certain issue and ask the court to make the decision for them. Specific issue orders are as varied as the families that are engaged in the proceedings. Religion

---

86 J. MASSON et al., 2008, p. 599.
87 *A v L (Contact)*, [1998] 1 FLR 361.
88 Paragraph 1 of Section 8 of the Children Act 1989.
89 Paragraph 5 subsection a of Section 9 of the Children Act 1989.
90 *Dawson v Wearmouth*, [1999] 1 FLR 1167.
91 *Clayton v Clayton*, [2007] 1 FLR 11.

often plays a part in requests for a specific issue orders. In *Re J (Specific Issue Orders: Child's Religious Upbringing and Circumcision)* for instance, the father, a (non-practising) Muslim, asked the court for a specific issue order requiring the surgical circumcision of his five-year-old son despite opposition from the child's (non-practising) Christian mother. In this case, the father's request was denied, as was his appeal, because for male circumcision the consent of both parents was needed and as the child had a mixed heritage and a mostly secular lifestyle, the judge saw no reason to substitute the mother's consent with a specific issues order.[92] Here the emphasis lay on the religious and not the medical aspect, because circumcision was not seen as having any particular medical benefit or detriment for the child. Important was that both parents were non-practising. It would be interesting to see if the decision would have been different if the father was a practising Muslim and the mother was not religious. Would the father's wish to raise his child according to his religion have a greater weight then?

Another example of something the parents often have a difficulty agreeing on by themselves is vaccination of their children. In the combined case of *Re C & F* (*Children*) fathers who had parental responsibilities over their daughters wanted to see them receive a range of immunisation appropriate to their age. The mothers, with whom the girls lived the majority of time opposed this because they did not believe in its necessity. The judge examined each disease against which immunisation was sought and found that immunisation was in the best interests of the children involved. He also stated that:

> 'The opposition of the mothers is of considerable concern. Both mothers and fathers have equal rights before the court. [...] The parent with whom a child is living, whether mother or father, does not have greater rights than an absent parent who is entitled to be consulted on major decisions in the child's life. But the court does attach importance to the bond between a child and the parent with whom they are living and will take care to safeguard and preserve it in the best interests of the child. [...] Where a course proposed is beneficial for a child but may cause damage to that relationship, the court will balance the issue with care. It may prevent a course otherwise beneficial to the child being ordered. This is especially where the proposal is for invasive medical intervention to which that parent is opposed compelling evidence is required.'[93]

Despite these considerations, the court held that the impact on the mothers in this case was not such as to prevent immunisation and that the children's best interests should prevail over the mother's opposition.

---

[92] *Re J (Specific Issue Orders: Child's Religious Upbringing and Circumcision)*, [2000] 1 FCR 307.
[93] *Re C (A Child) (Immunisation: Parental Rights)*, [2003] EWHC 1376 (Fam), paras. 377-379.

The court therefore made the specific issue order to allow immunisation without the mothers' consent.

Something that deserves attention in this case is that the court has used the argument of the children's health to override the mothers' consent. But the same health argument cannot be used to override the consent of *both* parents with parental responsibilities. If the mothers and fathers had agreed not to vaccinate their children, the court would not interfere with their decision. This shows the English courts' reluctance to interfere in family business, unless they are specifically asked to make a decision.

3.3.3.2. Care arrangements

The above-mentioned case law aside, in practice, where litigation is concerned, only about 10% of separating parents involve the courts in the process of making arrangements concerning the child or children.[94] These parents are likely to have not a single, but multiple problems.[95] Most parents come to some sort of mutual agreement. This means that in most post-separation situations arrangements are made without Section 8 orders, even without the direct involvement of the court. Separating parents are legally encouraged to make some basic arrangements for the children, though.

When filing for divorce, civil partnership dissolution, (judicial) separation or nullity of marriage, the applicant must fill in and submit the 'Statement of arrangements for children' together with their divorce petition if he or she or their partner has a child or children who are under 16, or under 18 and at school, college or training for a trade, profession or vocation.[96] The form asks for information to be provided on where the child or children live, how the contact with the non-resident parent is arranged, who will care for the child or children on a day to day basis, the educational institute(s) of the child or children and if this is going to change because of the separation, if the child or children have any special health needs and if there have ever been any court proceedings concerning the child or children. The petitioner is asked if the arrangements have been made in mutual agreement and if not, why not, and if the petitioner would be willing to reach an agreement with the ex-partner directly, through alternative dispute resolution or through court. A copy of this form is sent to the respondent and he or she is asked to say whether or not they agree with the arrangements

---

94 University of Oxford Department of Social Policy and intervention, *Family Policy Briefing 7. Caring for children after parental separation: would legislation for shared parenting time help children?*, Oxford 2011, p. 2.

95 V. PEACEY & J. HUNT, 2009, p. 8.

96 See for the explanation of the procedure and the relevant forms the UK Government website: www.direct.gov.uk (last visited 29 April 2015).

within. If they do not agree they can send the court their own 'Statement of arrangements for children'.[97] If the parents do not come to a mutual agreement, possibly after alternative dispute resolution, only then a court hearing will follow.

However, according to the 2003 Office for National Statistics study only 50-60% of the parents had agreed arrangements and around three in ten were dissatisfied with the current position.[98] If these figures are correct and 10% of parents choose to litigate and 50-60% of the parents have made arrangements on their own, it is unclear what happened with the remaining 30-40% of the parents who had neither agreed arrangements, nor had asked the court for an order. It is likely that these are the parents who had never been in a formal relationship and had no dealings with the court about their relationship's aftermath, nor about their children, but one cannot say this with certainty.

3.3.4. DISCHARGE OF (JOINT) PARENTAL RESPONSIBILITIES

Parental responsibility orders or agreements end automatically once the child reaches the age of 18 years or is adopted.[99]

Otherwise, once acquired, it is difficult, in some cases even impossible, to lose parental responsibilities. A holder of parental responsibilities does not lose them upon divorce, separation, when another person acquires them or when a local authority obtains a care order. Nor may a holder of parental responsibilities surrender or transfer those responsibilities to another person voluntarily without the intervention of a court.[100]

> 'In contrast to unmarried fathers, who, having acquired parental responsibility in one of the ways specified in [Section 4 of the Children Act 1989], can be divested of it by court order […], a father who was married to the child's mother cannot lose parental responsibility, unless the child is subsequently adopted.'[101]

This means that parental responsibilities gained *ex lege* cannot be discharged. They can, however, be restricted, in the sense that the holder of parental responsibilities is prevented from exercising them. For example, in the 2014 *P v D* case, in which the father of three girls, one of whom

---

97 See the D185 Children and divorce/dissolution leaflet form the HM Courts and Tribunals Service. Available through the Her Majesty's Courts and Tribunals Service website: hmctsformfinder.direct.gov.uk (last visited 29 April 2015).

98 V. PEACEY & J. HUNT, 2009, p. 8.

99 Paragraph 7 of Section 91 of the Children Act 1989; Paragraph 3 of Section 12 of the Adoption Act 1976 and Paragraph 2 of Section 46 of the Adoption and Children Act 2002.

100 Paragraph 9 of Section 2 of the Children Act 1989.

101 *P v D*, [2014] EWHC 2355 (Fam), para. 107.

still a minor, had been violent and abusive towards the mother and the youngest child's sisters, causing the youngest severe emotional harm, the court made a prohibited steps order prohibiting the father from taking any steps in the exercise of his parental responsibilities in respect of his minor daughter.[102]

In cases where parental responsibilities were not gained ex lege or the discharge proceeds an adoption, a discharge is only possible if the court so orders. Such an order can be made upon an application of any person with parental responsibilities over the child in question or of the child himself or herself, but only if the child has been given leave to make this application by the court in the first place.[103] Only a child who has sufficient understanding to make an application will be given leave and before applying for leave they have to contact and instruct a solicitor themselves.[104]

An example of a recent case in which the mother asked for the termination of parental responsibilities was *Re DW (A Child) (Termination of Parental Responsibility)*. In this case the child's parents had not been married, but the father had parental responsibilities over the boy through the registration on the birth certificate. The father later was convicted of sexually abusing two of the mother's daughters from a previous relationship. The court decided that this had cause his son extreme emotional harm, even though his father had not (physically) abused him, and was sufficient ground for the termination of parental responsibilities.[105] The father appealed, but the ruling was upheld.[106]

3.4. CHILD'S RESIDENCE

When parents decide to separate it is their responsibility to make arrangements on where their children should live. If their relationship had been formalised and they need to apply to court for its dissolution, they have to submit their planned arrangements together with their application for dissolution.[107] When the parents cannot agree or want to make their decisions legally binding by obtaining a court order, they can ask the court to intervene and decide the issue.

---

102 *Ibid.*

103 Section 4 of the Children Act 1989.

104 Paragraph 2 of Section 96 of the Children Act 1989; J. FORTIN, *Children's Rights and the Developing Law*, Cambridge University Press 2009, p. 257. See for more discussion on children's independent procedural rights in section 3.5 of Chapter 3.

105 *Re DW (A Child) (Termination of Parental Responsibility)*, [2013] EWHC 854 (Fam).

106 *Re DW (A Child) (Termination of Parental Responsibility)*, [2014] EWCA Civ 315.

107 See section 3.3.3.2 of Chapter 3.

3.4.1. ASSIGNING OR CHOOSING RESIDENCE

When the court is asked to make a decision with regard to where the child or children should live after parental separation, it may make a residence order. A residence order is one of the Section 8 orders and may either be made upon request or when the court considers it necessary to make such order, in the course of family proceedings in which a question with respect to the child's welfare arises.[108]

> 'When any family court decides with whom the children of separated parents are to live, the welfare of those children must be its paramount consideration [...]. This means that it must choose from the available options the future which will be best for the children, not the future which will be best for the adults.'[109]

Once the parents separate, each continues to have parental responsibilities even if a residence order has been made in favour of one of them. They still have equal rights and duties before the law.[110] The only thing the residence order is designed to signify is devising where the child lives. If the child (mainly) lives with one parent, the residence order is made in favour of that parent. If the child stays roughly the same amount of time with both parents, a shared residence order is made in favour of both parents.

It is specifically mentioned in Section 13 of the Children Act 1989 that a residence order does not give the holder the right to change the child's last name or remove the child from the United Kingdom for longer than a month. To do either of those things the written consent of every person who has parental responsibilities over the child or the leave of the court is needed.

A residence order can be applied for and made in favour of someone who does not hold parental responsibilities. In such a situation the court should also make an order granting this person parental responsibilities.[111] In such circumstances two orders are made simultaneously: a parental responsibility order and a residence order. This way the resident parent will always have the necessary legal rights and duties to care for the child or children in daily life.

Additional conditions can be attached to a residence order. In *Re D (Residence: Imposition of Conditions)* for instance, children were returned to live with their mother under the condition that the children should not be

---

108 Section 10 of the Children Act 1989.

109 Baroness Hale of Richmond in *Holmes-Moorhouse v Richmond-Upon-Thames LBC*, [2009] 1 FLR 904, para. 30.

110 Although of course, the practical situation is less equal as the resident parent is usually the one making the day-to-day decisions.

111 Section 12 of the Children Act 1989.

brought into contact with the mother's partner who was in prison at the time of judgment, but was likely to be released soon.[112]

3.4.2. SHARED RESIDENCE

A residence order may also be made in favour of two or more persons who do not live together, which is usually the case after parental separation. Such order may specify the periods during which the child is to live in the different households concerned.[113] Such orders are commonly known as shared residence orders.[114]

In recent years, the attitude towards the (shared) residence order has changed and the parents, especially fathers, have started to see it as the legal recognition of *parental equality* instead of the legal establishment of the practical residential situation of the child or children (what it was originally devised to be). Now parents have started to apply for a shared residence order even if there is no shared residence in practice and the child lives for most of the time with one parent only.[115]

The first indications of the rise of the new approach - making a shared residence order in a situation where there is no equal division of time - came in the mid-1990s from Ward LJ. It started with a very unusual case that had little to do with recognising equality of parents. In this case the child had been raised by the mother and her new husband. Her husband was not the child's biological father, but was seen and accepted by the child as such. After the marriage broke down a shared residence order was made, because the original plan was that the child would stay one week with the mother and one week with the (ex-)step-father. In practice, the child resided mainly with the mother. The mother sought to change the shared residence order into a sole residence order in favour of her. However, that would mean that the step-father would also lose parental responsibilities over the child, which were given to him in lieu of making the shared residence order. The court considered it beneficial for the child that he had good contact with his step-father and that the step-father would continue to hold and exercise parental responsibilities over the child, even though there was no practical shared residence. An exception had to be made for the benefit of the child's welfare.[116]

---

112 *Re D (Residence: Imposition of Conditions)*, [1996] 2 FCR 820.
113 Paragraph 4 of Section 11 of the Children Act 1989.
114 J. HERRING, 2011, p. 480.
115 S. HARRIS-SHORT, 'Resisting the march towards 50/50 shared residence: rights, welfare and equality in post-separation families', *Journal of Social Welfare & Family Law*, Vol. 32, No. 3, 2010, pp. 258 and 260.
116 *Re H (Shared Residence: Parental Responsibility)*, [1995] 2 FLR 883 (CA).

The next step was making a shared residence order in cases where there was a genuine fear that if the order would not be made, the resident parent would attempt to exclude the other holder of parental responsibilities from the children's lives. For example, in *Re F (Shared Residence Order)* the mother moved with the child to the other side of the UK while the father remained where he lived and a shared residence order was made to be sure the mother would not use a sole residence order to push the father away.[117] In this case the choice was made to make a shared residence order instead of letting the father have (joint) parental responsibilities and extensive contact. Wilson J admitted that 'to make a shared residence order to reflect the arrangements here [...] is to choose one label rather than another [...] *But labels can be very important*'. (emphasis added).[118] This seems to imply that the label 'parental responsibilities' is somehow less important than the label 'holder of shared residence' or 'resident parent'.

The 2001 ruling in *Re D (Children) (Shared Residence Orders)*, in which Hale LJ noted that there should be no constraint on the making of shared residence orders by the addition of 'gloss' to the wording of the legislative provisions, has subsequently been interpreted to mean that shared residence orders should not be regarded and treated as unusual, nor that it is necessary to show some positive benefit to the child before the making of the order can be justified.[119]

In the 2004 *A v A (Children) (Shared Residence)* case the parents had been fighting over their children for many years since their separation. They both had parental responsibilities, but the residence order had originally been made in favour of the mother. The father applied for a shared residence order because he felt that the mother was making unilateral decisions about the children's health and education. As a response, the mother prevented the contact between the father and the daughter. Eventually, because the mother continued to frustrate the contact, an interim order was made for the children to live with their father, which led to the practical situation that the children spent 50% of their time with the father and 50% with the mother. To maintain this practice, the judge made a shared residence order.[120] This case shows that the absence of co-operation and communication between the parents is not seen as an insurmountable

117 *Re F (Shared Residence Order)*, [2003] EWCA Civ 592.
118 *Ibid.*, para. 32.
119 See *Re D (Children) (Shared Residence Orders)*, [2001] 1 FCR 147; and the subsequent rulings in *Re W (A child)*, [2009] EWCA Civ 370 and *Holmes Moorhouse v. London Borough of Richmond upon Thames*, [2009] UKHL 7.
120 *A v A (Children) (Shared Residence)*, [2004] EWHC 142 (Fam).

obstacle for shared residence.[121] However, Justice Wall does caution that '[s]hared residence and an equal division of the children's time between their parents' houses is possible in this case because the parents live close to each other, and the children can go to school from either home.'[122]

Nevertheless, geographical proximity between the parents is not seen as a *necessity* for a shared parenting order as can be seen in cases such as *Re F (Children) (Shared Residence Order)* in which a shared residence order was made in favor of the parents of children aged five and four despite the fact that the parents were likely to come to live in different jurisdictions (the mother in Scotland and the father in England).[123] Thorpe LJ noted that '[t]he fact that the parents' homes are separated by a considerable distance does not preclude the possibility that the children's year will be divided between the homes [...] in such a way as to validate the making of a shared residence order.'[124] This idea was taken even further in *Re A (Temporary Removal from Jurisdiction)* when a 70/30 shared residence order was not changed or ended when the mother was granted leave to take the child abroad with her for two years, because shared residence was 'a formal recognition of an underlying reality, namely, that both parents have parental responsibility which they will continue to exercise'.[125] Here the court seems to use a shared residence order as a device for the recognition of joint exercise of parental responsibilities.

Some scholars have voiced their concerns on the way the courts have interpreted the meaning of a shared residence order in the last decade. They fear that by allowing this practice, the concept of parental responsibilities is being diluted as the status of holders of parental responsibilities is seemingly placed below that of persons in favour of whom a residence order has been made.[126]

As Harris and George point out:

> 'It is arguable that the courts are starting on the same road with shared residence as was seen with parental responsibility. Whereas parental responsibility was down-graded so as to be given to fathers who had no practical role to play in

---

121 This was confirmed by Lord Justice Thorpe in *Re R (Children) (Residence: Shared Care: Children's Views)*, [2005] EWCA Civ 542, who in para. 11 said that 'a harmonious relationship between the parents is not a prerequisite of a shared care order'. High levels of conflict *can*, however, be a reason to not make a shared residence order in combination with other arguments. See *Re B (Leave to Remove)*, [2006] EWHC 1783 (Fam).

122 *A v A (Children) (Shared Residence)*, [2004] EWHC 142 (Fam), para. 24.

123 *Re F (Children) (Shared Residence Order)*, [2003] EWCA Civ 592.

124 *Re F (Shared Residence Order)*, [2003] EWCA Civ 592, para. 21.

125 *Re A (Temporary Removal from Jurisdiction)*, [2004] EWCA Civ 1587, para. 26.

126 See for an example of this opinion the work of S. HARRIS-SHORT, especially her article 'Resisting the march towards 50/50 shared residence: rights, welfare and equality in post-separation families' in the *Journal of Social Welfare & Family Law*, Vol. 32, No. 3, 2010.

> their children's lives at all, now shared residence is being down-graded to give fathers who are involved, but not in a day-to-day care.'[127]

Others, however, are of the opinion that it was not allowing shared residence orders to be made despite there not being equally shared residence in practice that diluted the meaning of parental responsibilities. Instead, parental responsibilities had already been diluted and shared residence orders were being made to resolve the difficulty created by this dilution and represented the new way of giving separated parents equal authority. The rise of the shared residence orders is seen as linked to the perceived ineffectual nature of parental responsibilities.[128]

Some academics fear that should shared residence become a legal presumption, which is not yet the case in English law, it could undermine the child's welfare paramountcy.

> '[T]he court is duty bound to focus on the child's welfare including the child's "ascertainable wishes and feelings". The court therefore cannot start with any prior view of either parent's "rights". [...] A legal presumption of shared care risks shifting the emphasis away from the attributes of quality parenting towards arrangements determined by set amounts of time.'[129]

According to Harris-Short, even without a legal presumption it is possible that the court's messages about shared parenting and the desirability of shared residence can possibly fuel the popular and professional perceptions that 50/50 shared residence should be seen as the optimal or preferred solution in the post-separation context.[130] These cases are still too few and too recent to say with confidence that this is indeed what is happening or going to happen in the future.

Whether these fears are justified remains to be seen, because despite the changing views towards residential co-parenting, it is still relatively rare within the English society. According to the two studies conducted in the recent years, the Gingerbread and Nuffield Foundation research and the *Understanding Society* survey, only about 9-12% of separated parents have shared care in practice and an even smaller group practice 50/50 residential co-parenting.[131] It is therefore unlikely to expect that residential co-parenting will become the prevailing post-separation arrangement any time soon, even despite the positive legal conditions and political

---

127 P. HARRIS & R. GEORGE, 2010, p. 169.
128 *Ibid.*, p. 166.
129 P. NEWIS, *Firm Foundations: Shared care in separate families: building on what works*, Gingerbread 2011, p. 5.
130 S. HARRIS-SHORT, 2010, p. 258.
131 See section 6.3.1.

climate. As can be read in Chapter 6 there can be other practical obstacles to residential co-parenting other than rules and general opinion.

3.4.3. CHANGING RESIDENCE

Nothing in the English legislation precludes parents to ask the court to change or end an existing order, or issue a new one. However, the courts have stressed the importance of maintaining the status quo for children if possible, as changing children's schools and housing can cause further disturbance. The court will therefore usually confirm the existing arrangements if the children have a settled life with one parent, unless there are really good reasons for change.[132] In *Re B (A Child)* it was considered preferable to keep the arrangement in which a four-year-old boy lived with his maternal grandmother instead of making a residence order in favour of his father to preserve the situation in which the child had lived virtually his whole life and was used to.[133] In *Re B (T) (A Minor) (Residence Order)* one of four children had been living for a while with the father, while the other children lived with the mother. Then both mother and father applied for a residence order for all the children to live with her, respectively him. The request was denied. The court considered that because the households were near each other and there was sufficient contact between the siblings and between the children and both parents, there was no reason to change the existing arrangements.[134]

The situation is different when one of the parents wants to relocate for whatever reason and take the child or children with him or her. In such cases an order, either preventing the relocation or approving it and making different residential arrangements, is often inevitable.

3.4.3.1. Relocation within the UK

When a resident parent wants to move from one place to another within the UK and bring the child along, theoretically he or she is free to do so; there are no automatic restrictions within English law.[135] However, when multiple people hold parental responsibilities for the child, a decision

---

132 J. HERRING, 2011, p. 500. See for example *Re B (A Child)*, [1998] 1 FCR 549 and *Re H (Children) (Residence Order)*, [2007] 2 FCR 621.

133 *Re B (A Child)*, [2009] UKSC 5.

134 *Re B (T) (A Minor) (Residence Order)*, [1995] 2 FCR 240.

135 R. GEORGE, 'Practitioners' views on children's welfare in relocation disputes: comparing approaches in England and New Zealand', *Child and Family Law Quarterly*, Vol. 23, No. 2, 2011, p. 180.

to relocate the child can interfere with contact between these holders of parental responsibilities and the child.

The holders of parental responsibilities who disagree with the relocation of the child can then discuss the issue with the resident parent and if they cannot agree, take the matter to court. It is often the other parent who objects to relocation, out of fear that his or her contact with the child will deteriorate or become impossible due to the move. Whether this outcome is inevitable depends strongly on the factual situation. If the objecting parent only has infrequent contact with the child mainly on weekends, this contact can continue even if the child moves further away with the resident parent. This is of course more problematic if the child is so young that he or she cannot travel on their own of if the contact parent does not have the money to finance (part of) the travel expenses. Additionally, if the child is to commute between the resident parent and the contact parent, the contact parent is likely to be more dependent on the co-operation of the resident parent to make sure the child will indeed do so, by putting him or her on the train or bus and by providing him or her with tickets.

When the original arrangement is one of shared residence, the relocation of one of the resident parents can render the arrangement practically undoable. For example, if the original arrangement consisted of the child switching residence twice or thrice a week and the mother relocates to another county a few hours away from the other resident parent and takes the child with her, it cannot be expected from the child to spend so much time travelling each week. Even if the arrangement is changed into a one week with one parent, the other with the other parent, problems arise with regard to the child's school attendance.

Relocation can be prevented by a court order. The person opposing the relocation can seek a prohibited steps order to prevent the move or, if a residence order is in force, seek to have conditions imposed on the residence order.[136] However, case law shows that judges only consider making restrictions on relocation within the UK in 'truly exceptional cases'.[137] This means that usually relocation within the UK is allowed by the courts, even if the other parent is against it.

The type of order does not affect the approach taken. This was confirmed in the 2009 case of *Re L (Internal Relocation: Shared Residence Order)* in which a mother wanted to relocate with her daughter from London to Somerset in pursuit of a job offer, but was denied this change in the shared residence order, because according to the judge the mother's motive in seeking to relocate was to weaken the link between her daughter and the father and undermine the shared residence order, possibly with the

---

136 Section 8 and Paragraph 7 of Section 11 of the Children Act 1989.

137 *Re B (Prohibited Steps Order)*, [2008] 1 FLR 613, para. 7.

intention of renewing an application to relocate abroad (which had been denied previously). The judge noted that a distinction ought to be made between a case where the parent with a residence order in his or her favour wished to relocate and a case where there was a shared residence order. The mother appealed and while the appeal itself was dismissed, the court did correct the assumption about the special status of a shared residence order. It clarified that the correct approach was not to distinguish the case, but to look at the underlying facts in welfare terms, bearing in mind the tension which might well exist between the freedom to relocate, which any parent had to enjoy, against the welfare of the child, which might indicate against relocation.[138]

3.4.3.2. Relocation outside the UK

The situation is significantly different, in legal terms, when it comes to relocation outside of the UK. Where a residence order is in force with respect to a child, no person may remove the child from the United Kingdom without either the *written* consent of every holder of parental responsibilities or the leave of the court.[139] This provision also applies to the person in whose favour the residence order has been made, with the slight alteration that the resident parent may take the child abroad for a period of less than one month.[140] A resident parent can thus not freely relocate to a country outside of the UK and take their child or children with them. They either need to get the written consent from the other holder(s) of parental responsibilities - who will usually be the other parent or, in case of shared residence, the other resident parent - or go to court. They can apply for leave to remove the child from the UK, either temporarily or permanently, under Paragraph 1 of Section 13 of the Children Act 1989;[141] apply for a specific issue order;[142] or apply for a new residence order to be made or the order in force to be terminated.

While domestic relocation is usually allowed, there is no presumption either way in cases of international moves. Especially in cases where each parent shares a significant amount of child-care all factors are balanced on the facts.[143] For example, in the 2004 case of *Re Y (Leave to Remove from Jurisdiction)*, an American mother sought leave to take her five-year-old

---

138 *Re L (Internal Relocation: Shared Residence Order)*, [2009] 1 FLR 1157.

139 Paragraph 1 subsection b of Section 13 of the Children Act 1989. See also Section 1 of the Child Abduction Act 1984.

140 Paragraph 2 of Section 13 of the Children Act 1989.

141 Paragraph 1 of Section 13 of the Children Act 1989.

142 Section 8 of the Children Act 1989. However, the Court of Appeal seems to strongly prefer the route of leave through Section 13 instead of an application for a specific issue order. See *Dawson v Wearmouth*, [1998] Fam 75, paras. 80-82.

143 R. GEORGE, 2011, p. 180.

child to live with her and her family in the United States. She and the child's father had a harmonious shared care arrangement, but she felt isolated in Wales and had better employment prospects in the United States. The court refused her application, because it considered that a move would be detrimental to the child's welfare as it would be disruptive for the child, who was equally close to both parents, settled in his life and doing well at school.[144]

On the other hand, in a case where the mother was the primary carer and resident parent, had re-married and wanted to join her new husband and her family members with her two children in Australia, she was allowed to do so. Because according to the Court of Appeal the emotional and psychological wellbeing of the primary carer was a valid consideration and carried great weight in an assessment of the welfare of the children.[145]

3.5. CHILDREN'S PROCEDURAL RIGHTS

Under English law, children do not have a *legal right* to be consulted over the arrangements to be made for their future.[146] However, their best interests are very important in family law proceedings and they are not voiceless. If the matter is important enough and the child is mature enough he or she can, in exceptional circumstances, initiate proceedings or be a party to the case In most other circumstances they can let their voice be heard in a different way.

When making Section 8 orders, or in issues dealing with special guardianship orders the court should have regard in particular to the ascertainable wishes and feelings of the child concerned; the child's physical, emotional and educational needs; the likely effect on the child of any change in his or her circumstances; the child's age, sex, background and any characteristics which the court considers relevant; any harm the child has suffered or is at risk of suffering; how capable each of the parents, and any other person in relation to whom the court considers the question to be relevant, is of meeting the child's needs; and finally, the range of powers available to the court under the Children Act 1989 in the proceedings in question.[147] This list is not exhaustive and could be best categorised as the minimum of necessary considerations.

The ascertainable wishes and feelings of the child concerned is therefore one of the factors the court should take into account when deciding whether

---

144 *Re Y (Leave to Remove from Jurisdiction)*, [2004] 2 FLR 330.
145 *Re B (Leave to Remove: Impact of Refusal)*, [2005] 1 FLR 239.
146 J. FORTIN, 2009, p. 240.
147 Paragraph 3 of Section 1 of the Children Act 1989.

to make, vary or discharge a Section 8 order. The more mature the child is the more weight should be place on his or her wishes.[148]

Additionally, Article 12 of the Convention on the Rights of the Child requires the State Parties to 'assure to the child who is capable of forming his or her own views the right to express those views freely in all matters affecting the child, the views of the child being given due weight in accordance with the age and maturity of the child' and for this purpose, the child should be provided the opportunity to be heard in any judicial and administrative proceedings affecting him or her.

It is important though, that before weight is attached to the views of the children in question, the court ensures that they are not repeating what one of the parents has told them to say. In *Re M (Intractable Contact Dispute: Court's Positive Duty)* the teenaged children's opposition to contact with their mother was not given weight, because they have been force-fed malignant stories about their mother by their father for many years.[149]

The difficulty with the ascertainable wishes and feelings of the child concerned is that these wishes and feelings are usually not gained directly from the child. If the case makes it to court, which happens, as has been stated in previous sections, in only 10% of all separation cases, the court usually either relies on the parents' assessment of what is in the child's best interests or on the welfare report prepared by the Centre for Family Research, which includes an account of the child's wishes and feelings.[150] The court can, but is not obliged, to ask for a welfare report to be made.[151]

Relying on the parents' assessment of what the children´s wishes are and what is in the child's best interests seems a hardly adequate substitute for hearing the child, especially if the child is old and mature enough to express his or her feelings. Parents in post separation cases, while undoubtedly wanting to do what is best for their child, are unlikely to view their ex-partner with much fondness and could project those feelings on what they think is best for their child. There is little objectivity and the court will have to instead weigh the views of one parent against the other. The parents' retelling of the child's views does not quite satisfy the CRC's requirements in cases where the child is old and mature enough to present his or her wishes and feelings, especially when one considers that the English family law does contain provisions which make it possible for a child to express his or her wishes and feelings, either directly, through

---

148 See *B v B (M v M) (Transfer of Custody: Appeal)*, [1987] 2 FLR 146; *Re T (Abduction: Child's Objections to Return)*, [2000] 2 FLR 193 and *re R (A Child) (Residence Order: Treatment of Child's Wishes)*, [2009] 2 FRC 572.

149 *Re M (Intractable Contact Dispute: Court's Positive Duty)*, [2006] 1 FLR 627.

150 J. FORTIN, 2009, p. 248.

151 Section 7 of the Children Act 1989.

representation or by means of a welfare report, but these provisions are not always used.

Not only are there provisions for children to make their voices heard in proceedings concerning them, the court may make a child a party to proceedings if it considers it is in the best interests of the child to do so.[152] Then the child is given his or her own guardian and solicitor.[153] In such cases usually the guardian, and not the child, instructs the solicitor. A child may conduct proceedings without a children's guardian if he or she has obtained the court's permission or the solicitor considers that the child is able, having regard to the child's understanding, to give instructions in relation to the proceedings and has accepted instructions from that child to act for that child in the proceedings (if the proceedings have begun, the solicitor is already acting).[154] However, as Butler-Sloss LJ has stated in *Re M (Family Proceedings: Affidavits)*:

> 'it is not the practice in the Family Division to allow children to intervene in family proceedings between their parents, and for very good reason. It is not fair on children that they should be dragged into the arena, that they be asked specifically to choose between two parents, both of whom they love, and they ought not to be involved in the disputes of their parents.'[155]

Besides being a party to a case concerning them, children can even be granted leave by the court to apply for a Section 8 order. In that case they have to contact and instruct a solicitor themselves and apply for leave.[156] A child can apply for leave to make an application for a Section 8 order, but the court may only grant leave if it is satisfied that the child has sufficient understanding to make the proposed application.[157] This is of course not an easy route for a child to take and assumes that the child knows his or her rights and can find and contact a solicitor. In such a case the child is treated as any other client by the solicitor, which means the solicitor is not obliged to provide any emotional support for the child or mediate between the child and his or her parents.[158] This can be problematic with the view of the legal proceeding's aftermath.

The Section 8 order does not always have to apply to the parent-child relationship. If a child wishes to have contact with his or her sibling, but his or her parents or carers forbid or obstruct it, he or she may, also

---

152 Paragraph 1 of Section 16.2 of the Family Procedure Rules 2010.

153 Paragraph 1 subsection c of Section 16.4 of the Family Procedure Rules 2010; *L v L (Minors) (separate representation)*, [1994] 1 FLR 156, para. 159.

154 Section 16.6 of the Family Procedure Rules 2010.

155 *Re M (Family Proceedings: Affidavits)*, [1995] 2 FLR 100, para. 103.

156 J. FORTIN, 2009, p. 257.

157 Paragraph 8 of Section 10 of the Children Act 1989.

158 J. FORTIN, 2009, p. 265.

with leave from the court, apply for a contact order with that sibling.[159] However, such contact will not be allowed if it could seriously detriment the wellbeing of the sibling with whom the contact is sought, which was for example the case in *Re S (Contact: Application by Sibling)*.[160] In a similar way, if the court is satisfied that the child has sufficient understanding to make an application it can grant leave for the child to request that someone with parental responsibilities should lose them by court order (keeping in mind that in section 3.3.4 it was explained that persons who have gained parental responsibilities ex lege cannot lose them).[161]

In the situation where a contact order has been made, but is not being applied satisfactory in practice, the child concerned, with leave from the court, can make an application for an enforcement order, or, if he or she has suffered financial loss due to the breach of the contact order, he or she can apply for financial compensation.[162] The child's evidence can be heard if the court is of the opinion that the child understands that it is his or her duty to speak the truth and that he or she has sufficient understanding to justify having his or her evidence heard.[163]

When it comes to monetary issues, children of any age may intervene in their parents' divorce proceedings and seek a financial order.[164]

3.6. ENFORCEMENT OF ARRANGEMENTS IN CASE OF NON-COMPLIANCE

In a perfect legal reality everyone abides by the arrangements they have agreed on and the orders they have been subjected to. Unfortunately the world we live in is far from that theoretic place. Agreements are often disregarded and obligations – including legal ones – not complied with. This is not different in the area of family law.

Only legal arrangements can be enforced. When looking at the residential post-separation arrangements this means orders, more specifically Section 8 orders. Arrangements such as those laid down in a Statement of arrangements for children are intentions and plans, not legally binding contracts.[165] They can, however, be used in arguments to obtain or

159 Paragraph 9 of Section 10 of the Children Act 1989.
160 *Re S (Contact: Application by Sibling)*, [1998] 2 FLR 897.
161 Paragraph 2 of Section 96 of the Children Act 1989.
162 Sections 11J and 11O of the Children Act 1989. More about enforcement, enforcement orders and financial compensation in section 3.6.
163 Sections 11J and 11O of the Children Act 1989. More about enforcement, enforcement orders and financial compensation in section 3.6.
164 *Downing v Downing (Downing Interfering)*, [1976] Fam. 288.
165 Discussed in section 3.3.3.2 of Chapter 3.

change an order. Once an order has been obtained, the compliance with it can be enforced.

Compliance with Section 8 orders can be enforced by fining persons in default or committing them to custody until the breach is remedied (but not longer than two months or two years if it is a High Court order).[166] However, a committal order is seen as the last resort and will very rarely be made in family law proceedings.[167] When enforcing compliance with court orders the courts may act by complaint or on its own motion.[168] It is important that the breach is committed with knowledge of the terms of the order and be wilful.[169] This can be complicated when the parent who is obliged by a contact or residence order to facilitate contact with the other parent is willing and does not obstruct the contact, but the child does not want to see or go with the contact parent. This has for example happened in *Re L-W (Children) (Enforcement and Committal: Contact)* where the court decided that in some of the instances of non-compliance the father had done everything to facilitate contact, but would not force his son to go with his mother against his will and should not be punished for that, especially not with committal.[170]

Where a residence order is in force and anyone is in breach of the arrangements settled by that order, the person in favour of whom the order has been made may, as soon as a copy of the order has been served to the person in breach, enforce the order under Paragraph 3 of Section 63 of the M1 Magistrates' Courts Act 1980 as if it were an order requiring the other person to produce the child.[171]

When the court makes a contact order with respect to a child, it may ask a family proceedings officer to monitor the compliance with the order. It depends on the circumstances of the case who or what should be monitored. It may be to make sure the resident parent does not obstruct the ordered contact or to make sure the contact parent fulfils his or her contact obligations. The officer can even monitor whether a certain condition, imposed by the order, is being adhered to. The monitoring cannot be unlimited, a period, not exceeding twelve months, should be specified.[172]

If the court is satisfied beyond reasonable doubt that a person has failed to comply with the contact order, it may make an *enforcement order* imposing on the person an unpaid work requirement, unless the court is satisfied that the person had a reasonable excuse for failing to comply with

166 J. MASSON et al., 2008, p. 643.
167 *A v N*, [1997] 1 FLR 533, para. 542.
168 Section 17 of the Contempt of Court Act 1981.
169 *P v W*, [1984] Fam. 32, para. 38.
170 *Re L-W (Children) (Enforcement and Committal: Contact)*, [2010] EWCA Civ 1253.
171 Section 14 of the Children Act 1989.
172 Section 11H of the Children Act 1989.

the contact order. The burden of proof in such situations is on the person claiming to have had a reasonable excuse. The court may not make an enforcement order of its own accord; either the resident parent, the contact parent, the individual subjected to a condition in the contact order or the child has to request it. It may make multiple enforcement orders, even in relation to the same person.[173]

The Children and Adoption Act 2006 has amended the Children Act 1989 to give the court another enforcement power. If an individual fails to comply with the contact order and the resident parent, the person in favour of whom the contact order has been made, or the child concerned suffers financial loss because of the non-compliance, the court may make an order requiring the individual in breach to pay the person wronged compensation in respect of his or her financial loss.[174] This was considered a less heavy-handed option than committal and better fitting remedy in certain cases.

Before making an enforcement order as regards a person in breach of a contact order, the court must be satisfied that making the order is necessary to secure the person's compliance, and the likely effect on the person of the enforcement order proposed to be made is proportionate to the seriousness of the breach of the contact order.[175]

Where an order requiring that a child should be handed to another is disobeyed, the court may authorise an officer of the court to enter the premises where the child is, if needed by force, and take the child and deliver him or her to the person in favour of whom the order has been made.[176] In practice the courts are reluctant to use this power, unless it is to return the child to the resident parent.[177]

In cases where there is non-compliance with a contact or residence order the difficulty often lies not with the lack of enforcement powers of the court, but with the desirability of enforcement in the light of the welfare of the child. On the one hand, preventing the child from having (regular) contact or residence with one of his or her parents where the child and that parent have that right is seen as harmful for the child. On the other hand, fining or committing the child's other parent can also have very harmful effects on the child. Courts do view breaches of contact orders very seriously and in case of severe obstruction have been known to use residence orders as a 'punishment'. In *Re C (Residence Order)* for example, a five-year-old girl had lived with her mother since she was one, and while the father had gained a contact order, the mother continued to frustrate

173 Section 11J of the Children Act 1989.
174 Section 11O of the Children Act 1989.
175 Paragraph 1 of Section 11L of the Children Act 1989.
176 Section 34 of the Family Law Act 1986.
177 J. MASSON et al., 2008, p. 644.

it to the effect that contact between father and daughter was almost non-existent. After multiple contact orders were ignored, the judge ordered the immediate transfer of the child's residence to the father.[178]

3.7. SUMMARY

The Children Act 1989 has shaped the current day English law on children, especially the law on the post parental separation arrangements concerning children and the court's powers of making orders to regulate the post separation arrangements. It has introduced parental responsibilities and given the courts the power to make Section 8 orders. The Children Act 1989 and the subsequent case law has also created a more favourable environment for residential co-parenting through the use of shared residence orders. However, attempts to create legal presumption in favour of shared residence have so far been unsuccessful.[179] In practice, the very limited research indicates that shared residence is still statistically quite rare, likely not exceeding 10% of all post separation arrangements.

Parental responsibilities are 'all the rights, duties, powers, responsibilities and authority which by law a parent of a child has in relation to the child and his property'.[180] The main duty of holders of parental responsibilities is caring for the child. Additionally they have all the rights, duties and authority to do so. Parental responsibilities are limited by legal provisions, the rights of others and the mature children's ability to make certain decisions for themselves.[181]

All mothers gain parental responsibilities ex lege at the birth of the child. Fathers and mother's female partners can obtain parental responsibilities ex lege, in case they are married to the mother or in a civil partnership with her; with the mother's approval by agreement with her; or by means of a court order. Most parents will therefore hold joint parental responsibilities.[182] Each holder of parental responsibilities may exercise them alone and there exists no hierarchy between the individual holders of parental responsibilities. However, when making important decisions about the child's life, consent needs to be obtained from all holders of parental responsibilities. This consent can in most cases be replaced by a court order.[183] Holders of parental responsibilities only lose them once the child turns 18 or, if the responsibilities were not gained ex lege, upon a

---

178 *Re C (Residence Order)*, [2007] 1 FLR 211.
179 See sections 3.1 and 3.2 of Chapter 3.
180 Paragraph 1 of Section 3 of the Children Act 1989.
181 See section 3.3.1 of Chapter 3.
182 See section 3.3.2 of Chapter 3.
183 See section 3.3.3 of Chapter 3.

court order requested by either a holder of parental responsibilities or the child in question.[184]

When parents separate they should make arrangements on where and with whom the child is to live. If they cannot come to an agreement, they can ask the court to make a residence order. The court may attach conditions to a residence order.[185] It may also make a shared residence order in favour of both parents. These type of orders have become less exceptional over the years.[186] While changing a residence order is possible, the courts tend to be reluctant to do so, unless an important change in circumstances requires this, preferring to maintain the status quo.[187] If a residence order is in force, a parent who wants to relocate with the child must ask the other holders of parental responsibilities or the court for permission. Relocation within the UK is usually permitted, unless the circumstances of the case are exceptional, while relocation abroad is decided upon the facts of the case and strongly depends on the welfare of the child.[188]

The ascertainable wishes and feelings of a child who is mature enough to understand the proceedings is one of the factors the court should take into account when deciding whether to make, vary or discharge a Section 8 order. Additionally children may in some cases apply to the court and be granted leave to petition a Section 8 order, its alteration or discharge or to intervene in their parents' proceedings.[189]

Finally, when there is no compliance with an order, various enforcement powers are available to the court, such as fines and imprisonment of the person in breach. However, enforcement can be difficult as it can harm the child for the benefit of whom the original order was made.[190]

---

184 See section 3.3.4 of Chapter 3.
185 See section 3.4.1 of Chapter 3.
186 See section 3.4.2 of Chapter 3.
187 See section 3.4.3 of Chapter 3.
188 See section 3.4.3 of Chapter 3.
189 See section 3.5 of Chapter 3.
190 See section 3.6 of Chapter 3.

CHAPTER 4
THE DUTCH LEGAL SYSTEM

4.1. HISTORY OF THE MAIN LEGAL AND SOCIETAL DEVELOPMENTS

The law tends to follow societal changes, especially in the field of family law, but does that with a certain delay. Over the years both society's views on what parenthood entails, as well as the practicalities of parenting have changed significantly.

When it comes to the post-separation provisions on parental responsibilities and residence in the Netherlands, the main legal changes have been realized in the last two decades. However, it was as early as 1984 when the highest Dutch court (*Hoge Raad*) allowed two parents to continue the joint exercise of parental responsibilities after divorce.[1]

4.1.1. 1984 CASE LAW

Back then the rule existed that after divorce one of the parents, in practice usually the mother, would be given parental authority (*gezag*) over the child. In the 1984 decision, the *Hoge Raad* considered that this legal provision entailed an interference with the right to respect for private and family life, as contained in Article 8 of the ECHR. Such interference can be justified if the best interests of the child would suffer because he or she would be exposed to the conflicts between the parents generated by the relationship breakdown. In the case at hand, the opposite was true: the parents both wanted to continue exercising parental authority jointly after divorce and said that they were able to do that in co-operation and harmony. The parents lived near each other and the child resided alternatively with both parents.[2] In such a case the court needed to evaluate whether the termination of joint parental authority would indeed be necessary to protect the best interests of the child.[3]

---

1 Hoge Raad, 4 May 1984, LJN AG4807, *NJ* 1985, 510.

2 So in this case the parents had a practical residential co-parenting arrangement.

3 Hoge Raad, 4 May 1984, LJN AG4807, *NJ* 1985, 510, para. 3.2.

In two subsequent decisions in 1986, the *Hoge Raad* elaborated on joint parental authority after separation and laid down certain conditions. In the first case the parents were cohabiting and had never been married, while in the second the parents were divorced and the mother had been granted sole parental authority. The parents in both cases wanted to jointly hold and exercise parental authority over their child.[4] The *Hoge Raad* decided that there was no legal basis to have joint parental authority *automatically* continue after divorce. However, joint parental authority could be assigned to the parents by a court order. For that to happen, it was considered paramount that the parents could, and were willing, to co-operate. Additionally joint parental authority could only be assigned to the legal parents of the child, upon both parents' request and according to their wishes, when it was probable that, despite the divorce, a good mutual understanding existed between the parents and they agreed upon and provided for the costs of raising the child and assigning joint parental authority would not be contrary to the child's best interests.[5] The lower courts subsequently followed this *Hoge Raad* decision.[6]

4.1.2. THE 1995 LAW REFORM

It took a decade before this judicial practice of granting separated parents joint parental authority was fully anchored within the Dutch legal system. On 2 November 1995 the Parental Responsibility and Access to Children Act (*Wet houdende nadere regeling van het gezag over en de omgang met minderjarige kinderen*) of 6 April 1995 entered into force.[7] This Act changed the Dutch Civil Code so that it then provided that the parents could continue to exercise joint parental authority after divorce *upon a joint request*. A court order was necessary and the court could deny this request if there was a reason to believe that granting joint parental authority would be detrimental to the best interests of the child.[8]

Meanwhile, there was growing interest within politics, the media and research in the role of fathers as carers. Research into the increase in caring fatherhood in the 1990s showed that the amount of care provision by the fathers studied did not increase – nor did it decrease – and increasing

4 Hoge Raad, 21 March 1986, LJN AC9283, *NJ* 1986, 585; Hoge Raad, 21 March 1986, LJN AC9284, *NJ* 1986, 586.

5 Hoge Raad, 21 March 1986, LJN AC9283, *NJ* 1986, 585, paras. 3.4 and 3.6; Hoge Raad, 21 March 1986, LJN AC9284, *NJ* 1986, 586, paras. 3.3-3.5.

6 C.G. JEPPESEN DE BOER, *Joint parental authority: a comparative legal study on the continuation of joint parental authority after divorce and the breakup of a relationship in Dutch and Danish law and the CEFL principles*, Doctoral thesis, Intersentia 2008, pp. 36-37.

7 *Stb.* 240.

8 C.G. JEPPESEN DE BOER, 2008, pp. 37-39.

paternal care, where it occurred, proceeded very slowly.[9] When it came to mothers, research had shown that while Dutch mothers worked mainly in part-time jobs, there was a slow change in the direction of full-time jobs.[10] In the media, 'caring fatherhood' had become a much revisited topic of many discussions and educational programmes, promoted by groups who represent a 'caring fathers' movement.[11]

4.1.3. THE 1998 LAW REFORM

Making joint parental authority dependant on both parents' agreement in the 1995 Act gave the parent who had, or would expect to get, parental authority, usually the mother, the ability to block the other parent, usually the father, from gaining it by simply withholding consent. This issue was addressed when very shortly after the Act came into force, a legislative discussion on the possibility of its reform started.

This discussion resulted in another reform that entered into force in 1998.[12] This reform changed Book One of the Dutch Civil Code so that it contained a provision stating that joint parental authority *automatically* continues after divorce, unless the parents or one of the parents request the court to decide, in the best interests of the child, that parental authority should be allocated to one parent only.[13] The previous situation was reversed: where the parents first had to request to obtain joint parental authority, they now had to request if they wanted sole parental authority.

However, one of the parents could still prevent the other parent from *retaining* parental authority by triggering a conflict and claiming that poor communication between the parents would necessitate granting sole parental authority as a good mutual understanding was considered essential for joint parental authority.[14]

The judicial response to this practice was not to consider poor communication between the parents as a sufficient ground for granting

---

9 E. SPRUIJT & V. DUINDAM, 'Was there an increase in caring fatherhood in the 1990s? Two Dutch longitudinal studies' in *Social Behaviour and Personality*, 30(7), 2002, p. 694.

10 *Ibid.*, p. 683.

11 T. KNIJN & P. SELTEN, 'Transformations of fatherhood: the Netherlands' in B. Hobson, *Making men into fathers. Men, Masculinities and Social Politics of fatherhood*, Cambridge University Press, 2002, p. 170.

12 Act of 30 October 1997 (*Wet tot wijziging van onder meer, Boek 1 van het Burgerlijk Wetboek in verband met invoering van gezamenlijk gezag voor een ouder en zijn partner en van gezamenlijk voogdij*), *Stb.* 507.

13 Old Article 251(2) of Book One of the Dutch Civil Code.

14 C.G. JEPPESEN DE BOER, 2008, p. 40.

sole parental authority.[15] Poor communication as a ground for granting sole parental authority became exceptional and was only accepted by the courts when there was an 'unacceptable risk that the children would be torn or lost between the parents and where sufficient improvement could not be expected within a reasonable time.'[16] This 'torn or lost between the parents' (*klem of verloren*) criterion has become the leading consideration in cases where there is a dispute concerning the allocation of parental authority.[17] This, of course, can create another problematic situation: the situation in which divorced parents retain joint parental authority, but are unable to adequately exercise this authority due to severe communication problems. It is additionally questionable if such conflict-laden environments could be beneficial for the child or children involved.[18]

The 1998 reform in favour of joint parental responsibilities should be seen within the social and political context of promoting the increased involvement of fathers in the upbringing of their children. In the late 1990s, the Dutch government launched a media campaign to persuade fathers to become more involved in the upbringing and raising of their children.[19] In 2000, Parliament passed the Adjustment of Working Hours Act that contains the right for workers, of both sexes, to reduce or extend their working time, which encouraged the reconciliation of work and family care for both fathers and mothers.[20] Flexible working hours can help (separated) parents who have joint parental responsibilities over their child or children to combine work and care and to facilitate residential co-parenting.[21]

4.1.4. THE 2009 LAW REFORM

After the 1998 reform, discussions commenced on how the system in place could be improved and adapted to societal changes. Parental equality played a major role in these discussions, as well as the increasing popularity of alternating residence. Around that time the terminology also

---

15 M. ANTOKOLSKAIA, 'Shared residence from a Comparative Perspective: A Solomon's Judgment New-Style?' in *Private Law, national – global – comparative. Festgeschrift* für Ingeborg *Schwenzer zum 60. Geburtstag*, Stämpfli Verlag AG, 2011, p. 71.

16 Hoge Raad, 10 September 1999, LJN ZC2963, *NJ* 2000, 20, para. 9.

17 C.G. JEPPESEN DE BOER, 2008, p. 42.

18 See more on the positive and negative effects of different types of arrangements on children in section 6.4.

19 T. KNIJN & P. SELTEN, 2002, p. 168.

20 Adjustment of Working Hours Act (*Wet van 19 februari 2000, houdende regels inzake het recht op aanpassing van de arbeidsduur (Wet aanpassing arbeidsduur)), Stb.* 114.

21 For example, when both the mother and father work on the days that the child resides with the other parent and stay at home when the child is with them.

started to change; where, first, the discussion was limited to the delegation and exercise of parental *authority*, the focus had shifted to parental *responsibilities* (*ouderlijke verantwoordelijkheid*), a term that seems to put more emphasis on parental duties instead of parental rights.[22]

The first political attempt to regulate residential co-parenting legally, in fact, to give it a priority status over other forms of post-separation residence, was made on 16 April 2004, when the Member of Parliament Luchtenveld proposed an Act that would make an administrative divorce possible (a divorce without the interference of the court), that would introduce a compulsory parenting plan, and and that would divide the time the child spends with each parent equally between them.[23] The proposed Act suggested a new Article 377a of Book One of the Dutch Civil Code that would give a child whose parents both hold parental responsibilities over him or her the right to spend an *equal* amount of time with both parents. The child would reside with both parents on an alternative basis, with a maximum of seven days spent with one parent consecutively. While the proposed Article did allow the parents to make different arrangements in a parenting plan, it was nonetheless a very strong indication in favour of 50/50 residential co-parenting.

This proposal suffered severe criticism and was soon replaced by another, a proposition that removed any mention of the child's residence or an equal time share. Instead it simply stated that a child, over whom his or her parents hold parental authority, will still have the right to be cared for and raised equally by both his parents after their divorce.[24] The emphasis shifted from an equal time share to the necessity to make good arrangements for the children during parental separation and the importance of parenting plans. The proposal eventually resulted in the Promotion of Continued Parenting and Proper Divorce Act (*Wet bevordering voortgezet ouderschap en zorgvuldige scheiding*) which came into force on 1 March 2009.[25]

4.2. BACKGROUND OF THE LAW CURRENTLY IN PLACE

While the proposition itself did not clarify what was meant by equal care and upbringing by the child's parents, the explanatory memorandum of

22 This development was not limited to the Netherlands. As can be seen in Chapter 2.

23 Act on the termination of marriage without legal interference and the shaping of continued parenting (*Wet beëindiging huwelijk zonder rechtelijke tussenkomst en vormgeving voortgezet ouderschap*), also known as the Luchtenveld proposal (*voorstel Luchtenveld*).

24 Kamerstukken II 2003/04, 29 676, no. 2.

25 See the revised Explanatory Memorandum, Kamerstukken II 2004/05, 30 145, no. 3.

the proposal emphasized that the legal reform intended to bring about a change in attitude to divorce in the sense that a divorce should not alter the relationship of care between the parents and the child. 'Equality implies that both parents in principle have the equal duty and right, also in the amount of time they spend, to care for and raise their child.'[26] Although the proposal did allow parents to make arrangements to divide the care differently, in the explanatory memorandum it is stated that this should happen when it is practically difficult or impossible to divide the care equally. As examples the working schedules of the parents and the geographical distance between the homes are provided.[27]

The proposal additionally wished to see the disappearance of the need to establish a main residence by the courts, thereby removing the resident/non-resident parent distinction, which, according to the proposal, facilitates conflict and gives the resident parent power over the non-resident parent. While the parents are free to make their own arrangements and can choose to designate a main residence, they should only do this in agreement and voluntarily. When the court is asked to establish a main residence with one parent, it should only do so when strictly necessary and this should be extensively reasoned.[28]

This proposal also underwent a revision and amendments to give the courts more powers to make the arrangements in cases where disputes would arise between parents exercising joint parental responsibilities.[29] Additionally, the possibility of an administrative dissolution of a registered partnership, without the interference of a court, was made impossible for registered partners who held joint parental responsibilities over their children,[30] and the parents who were not married and who were not registered partners, but who held joint parental responsibilities over their children, were obliged to make a parenting plan.[31] Although, legally, both sets of parents are obliged to make a parenting plan at the time of separation, in practice their circumstances are somewhat different.[32]

However, the core of the new Promotion of Continued Parenting and Proper Divorce Act (*Wet bevordering voortgezet ouderschap en zorgvuldige scheiding*) remained that all separating parents should make arrangements

---

26 Kamerstukken II 2003/04, 29 676, no. 3, p. 11.

27 Kamerstukken II 2003/04, 29 676, no. 6, p. 12.

28 *Ibid.*, p. 5.

29 See Article I(K) and Article II(Ba) of the Promotion of Continued Parenting and Proper Divorce Act (*Wet bevordering voortgezet ouderschap en zorgvuldige scheiding*).

30 Article I(Ba) of the Promotion of Continued Parenting and Proper Divorce Act (*Wet bevordering voortgezet ouderschap en zorgvuldige scheiding*) and the eventual Article 80c(2) of Book One of the Dutch Civil Code.

31 Article I(Ga) of the Promotion of Continued Parenting and Proper Divorce Act (*Wet bevordering voortgezet ouderschap en zorgvuldige scheiding*) and the eventual Article 247a of Book One of the Dutch Civil Code.

32 See section 4.3.3.2 of Chapter 4 for an extensive discussion of parenting plans.

for the continued care of their children in parenting plans and that it is important for the development of a child that he or she continues to have contact with both his or her parents after parental separation and that the parents continue to be jointly responsible for the care and the development of the child.[33] The legal reform was subsequently implemented in the Dutch Civil Code and its relevant Articles were changed accordingly.

For all its turbulent and ambitious history, the 2009 law reform has *only* changed the law to *actively promote*, instead of prescribe, the joint exercise of parental responsibilities after parental separation and has remained ambiguous and vague about residential arrangements.

4.3. JOINT PARENTAL RESPONSIBILITIES

Parents retaining joint parental responsibilities after separation has become the legal norm in Dutch law.[34] This stems from the strong belief that children have the right to maintain contact with both parents even after parental separation and that parents remain responsible for the care, upbringing and development of their children.[35] While the exercise of these responsibilities is for the major part left for the parents to fill in according to their circumstances and wishes, thinking about the future of the children and making care arrangements is no longer (legally) optional. Rules have been made to guide and support parents in this difficult process.

4.3.1. PARENTAL RESPONSIBILITIES: MEANING AND CONTENT

Dutch legal provisions governing parental responsibilities still use different terms. When talking about parental responsibilities held or exercised by parents the old term '*gezag*' is often used which means parental authority. When parental responsibilities are held or exercised by a person other than a parent, the term '*voogdij*' (guardianship) is mainly used. However, both terms generally indicate the same rights and duties, and in the literature, preference is currently being given to

---

33 See the revised Explanatory Memorandum, Kamerstukken II 2004/05, 30 145, no. 3.

34 First through the 1998 reform, which made joint parental authority automatically continue after divorce and subsequently with the 2009 reform which changed joint parental authority into joint parental responsibilities and made sole parental responsibilities only possible in exceptional cases. See more about this historical development of Dutch family law in sections 4.1 and 4.2. See also the revised Explanatory Memorandum, Kamerstukken II 2004/05, 30 145, no. 3, p. 1.

35 Article 247(4) of Book One of the Dutch Civil Code and Revised Explanatory Memorandum, Kamerstukken II 2004/05, 30 145, no. 3, p. 1.

the term '*ouderlijke verantwoordelijkheid*' (parental responsibility) instead of both the previously mentioned legal terms. Therefore the term 'parental responsibilities' shall be used in this book to indicate the Dutch terms *gezag* and *ouderlijke verantwoordelijkheid*. The term guardianship will only be used when it is necessary to differentiate between parental responsibilities held by a parent and parental responsibilities held by a guardian.

Parental responsibilities are defined in Article 247(1) of Book One of the Dutch Civil Code as 'the duty and the right of a parent to care for and raise his or her minor child'. All minors are subjected to parental responsibilities.[36] A minor is a person who has not reached the age of 18, is not or has not been married or in a registered partnership and who has not been declared of age pursuant to Article 253ha of Book One of the Dutch Civil Code.[37] Parental responsibilities relate to the person of the child, the administration of his or her estate and his or her representation judicially and extra-judicially.[38] Paragraph 2 contains two examples of what is meant by care and upbringing: care and upbringing include the care and responsibility for the mental and corporal well-being of the child and the fostering of the development of his or her personality. It also contains the warning that parents in caring for and raising the child must not use mental or physical violence or any other degrading treatment.[39]

Paragraph 3 adds that the duty to promote the development of the relationship between the child and the other parent is part and parcel of a parent's parental responsibilities. This brings back the notion behind the recent law reform that it is important for the child to have a relationship with both parents and that the parents should work together to facilitate this. This notion is strengthened by Paragraph 4, which states that a child whose parents hold joint parental responsibilities over him or her retains the right to equal care and upbringing by both of them even after the parents have divorced, their registered partnership is dissolved or they have ceased to live together.

The above-mentioned definition is, admittedly, quite vague when it comes to explaining what the *exact* content of the rights and duties of parents with parental responsibilities is. However, it is 'generally assumed that they encompass the provision of and the competence to decide on matters concerning clothing, food, accommodation, medical treatment and education. Furthermore, it is assumed that parents should acknowledge

---

36 Article 245(1) of Book One of the Dutch Civil Code.

37 Article 233 of Book One of the Dutch Civil Code.

38 Article 245(4) of Book One of the Dutch Civil Code.

39 This paragraph also applies to the (legal) guardian and to the person who cares for and raises the child without having parental responsibilities over that child. See Article 248 of Book One of the Dutch Civil Code.

the increasing maturity and needs of the child to develop according to his or her own vision.'[40]

Case law on the specification and an explanation of parental responsibilities is extremely rare. Certain parental rights or duties only come up in court when there is a dispute about their exercise and the court is requested to solve the dispute. These disputes usually concern one parent trying to prevent the other parent from moving with the child, choosing a school for the child, or consenting to a medical procedure to be undergone by the child.[41]

Nevertheless, information on what the *parents themselves* consider to be part of their parental responsibilities can be found in parenting plans such as the care arrangements they allocate. Among such rights and duties are: treating the other parent with respect and not involving the child or children in any conflicts; providing daily care for the child or children while the child or children reside with them (daily care includes, among other things: physical care, a daily regime, bedtime arrangements and pocket money); making decisions on the child's or children's leisure activities, medical care and education; making sure the child or children are insured; overseeing the child or children's appearance (haircuts, making sure their clothing is appropriate, making decisions about possible tattoos and piercings (if the child is aged between 12 and 16)); taking the child or children on holiday.[42]

4.3.2. ATTRIBUTION OF (JOINT) PARENTAL RESPONSIBILITIES

Within the current Dutch system the general rule is that one or both of the *legal* parents hold and exercise parental responsibilities, although exceptions to this rule are possible. A child can have no *more than two legal parents*,[43] which in practice means that a child always has at least one legal mother and may have a legal father.[44] This is a legal choice, a choice

---

40 C.G. JEPPESEN DE BOER, 2008, p. 236.

41 All three of these examples and more will be discussed in more detail in section 4.3.3 of Chapter 4.

42 Information gained from empirical research into parenting plans. More about parenting plans and their contents in section 4.3.3.2.

43 See Article 204(1) subsection e of Book One of the Dutch Civil Code, which states that the recognition of a child is invalid if the child already has two legal parents and Article 207(2) subsection a of Book One of the Dutch Civil Code, which states that if a child already has two legal parents, legal parentage cannot be determined with regard to somebody else.

44 M. VONK, *Children and their parents. A comparative study of the legal position of children with regard to their intentional and biological parents in English and Dutch law*, Doctoral thesis, Intersentia, 2007, p. 53.

which has lost its biological roots. In today's society, where stepfamilies and same-sex families are a reality, children born and raised outside of wedlock no longer have a societal stigma, and non-parents can exercise parental responsibilities,[45] so the question can be posed as to the necessity of the two-parents rule. Is it not better to allow those who want to care for the child to do so, whether it is a single mother or two separated parents and their new partners? Can the idea of 'the more, the merrier' be applied to parents? So far, no propositions have been made to alter the idea that no more than two persons can become legal parents.

4.3.2.1. The mother

As mentioned above, legal parents exercise parental responsibilities. The legal mother of the child under Dutch law is the woman who gives birth to the child.[46] This is the so-called *mater semper certa est* principle. This means that upon birth, the woman who gave birth to the child immediately, ex lege, becomes the child's legal parent, but also the holder of parental responsibilities and is assumed to exercise these responsibilities. This is unless, for some reason, she is (temporarily) unfit to exercise parental responsibilities.[47] A birthmother cannot deny her parentage.[48]

The birthmother is, however, not the only woman who can gain legal motherhood. Since the entry into force of the Duo-mother Act (*De Duomoederwet*) on 1 April 2014, legal motherhood has become available for the wife, registered partner, or female cohabitant of the birthmother and, depending on the circumstances, legal parenthood can be gained ex lege, through recognition or a court order.[49] For structural and comparative reasons, these ways of gaining legal motherhood and parental responsibilities are discussed in section 4.3.2.3.

4.3.2.2. The father

The father gains legal parentage and parental responsibilities by operation of law upon the child's birth if he is the birthmother's husband or registered

---

45 As can be seen later in this section.
46 Article 198(1) subsection a of Book One of the Dutch Civil Code.
47 Article 253b of Book One of the Dutch Civil Code.
48 M. VONK, 2007, p. 54.
49 Act of 25 November 2013 (*Wet van 25 november 2013 tot wijziging van Boek 1 van het Burgerlijk Wetboek in verband met het juridisch ouderschap van de vrouwelijke partner van de moeder anders dan door adoptie*), *Stb.* 480.

partner.[50] The husband or registered partner being the father of the child is a legal presumption and does not necessarily confirm biological paternity. Like most presumptions, it can be rebutted. If the legal father is not the biological father of the child, the legal father, mother, or even the child can deny legal parentage.[51] After divorce, the legal father retains parental responsibilities and continues to exercise them jointly with the mother.[52] Such gained parental responsibilities can only be converted into sole parental responsibilities if this is in the best interests of the child or there is a substantial risk that the child will be 'torn or lost' between the parents and the situation is unlikely to be improved within a foreseeable time.[53]

After the dissolution of a registered partnership, the joint exercise of parental responsibilities also continues, even though this is not explicitly mentioned in the Civil Code.[54] This can be deduced from Article 253aa of Book One of the Dutch Civil Code which lays down provisions on the joint exercise of parental responsibilities applicable by legal parents who are former registered partners, including Paragraph 1 of Article 251a of Book One of the Dutch Civil Code, which makes it impossible to convert joint parental responsibilities into sole parental responsibilities upon separation other than because the best interests of the child require this or because of the 'torn or lost' criterion.

Not all children are born within formal relationships. Out of the 180,060 children born in 2011, 81,620 were born outside marriage.[55] That is over 45% of children. And this percentage continues to grow, with especially firstborns being more and more often born outside of marriage.[56]

---

50 Article 199 subsections a and b of Book One of the Dutch Civil Code. If the husband or registered partner dies before the child is born, even if the woman enters into a new formal relationship after his death and before the birth of the child, and the child is born within 306 days of his death, the deceased is still considered to be the legal father of the child in the eyes of the law. However, if the mother and her deceased partner were legally separated or were living apart prior to his death, the mother can deny his paternity and have this legally confirmed by a civil servant.

51 Article 200 of Book One of the Dutch Civil Code. However, the legal father and mother cannot deny the presumption of parentage if the father was aware of the pregnancy prior to the marriage and had not been deceived about the parentage by the mother. Time limits for denying legal parentage also apply.

52 Article 251(2) of Book One of the Dutch Civil Code.

53 Article 251a(1) of Book One of the Dutch Civil Code.

54 Article 253aa(2) of Book One of the Dutch Civil Code excludes Article 251(2) of Book One of the Dutch Civil Code from being applicable in this situation. However, this seems to have been an error and does not remove the meaning of this law from applying also in cases of joint parental responsibilities after the dissolution of a registered partnership.

55 Data from the Dutch Central Statistics Bureau. See the official website for more information: www.cbs.nl (last visited 29 April 2015).

56 The Dutch Central Statistics Bureau, 'Steeds meer kinderen buiten huwelijk geboren', *Cbs Webmagazine*, 26 February 2001, see the official website for the article: www.cbs.nl/nl-NL/menu/themas/bevolking/publicaties/artikelen/archief/2001/2001-0717-wm.htm (last visited 29 April 2015).

A legal father who is not married to the mother and is not in a registered partnership with her has joint parental responsibilities over their child if the parents have jointly requested this at the civil registry.[57] To jointly request joint parental responsibilities for a child, the parents have to fill in a form and submit it to a court in their district. On 1 September 2012 all courts became members of the Central Parental Authority Register (*Centraal Gezagsregister*).[58] In the register records are kept of who has parental responsibilities over minors. Originally the district courts kept their own public register.[59] Therefore it is now easy to look up who exercises parental responsibility over which children, even if the children or parents move.

Their request will be denied if either or both are incapable of exercising parental responsibilities, for example due to a mental illness or age, their parental responsibilities have been terminated, a guardian is exercising parental responsibilities or one of the parents is already exercising parental responsibilities jointly with someone else.[60] If one of the legal parents does not want to make a joint request, the other legal parent (either the mother or the father) can start a procedure and ask for joint or sole parental responsibilities. If one parent is exercising sole parental responsibilities, the request for joint parental responsibilities will only be denied if there exists an unacceptable risk of the child becoming 'torn or lost' between the parents (*klem of verloren*), or in other words, that the child would be very adversely affected by the joint exercise of parental responsibilities and this negative situation is unlikely to improve within a reasonable time; or denying the request for joint parental responsibilities is otherwise *necessary* in the best interests of the child.[61] This opportunity for the father to request joint parental responsibilities has been introduced to encourage children to be brought up by both parents, even if these parents are no longer, or never have been, together. While the provision is formulated as if the denial of a request for joint parental responsibilities will occur very rarely, the reasons for a denial are very vague. When will a child be adversely affected in an unacceptable way? What is a reasonable time period? In what circumstances will granting joint parental responsibilities be contrary to the best interests of the child?

Other than requesting joint parental responsibilities, the legal father can also ask the court to be granted *sole* parental responsibilities over his child or children. This means that the court would remove parental responsibilities from the mother and grant it to the father. The court will

57 Article 252 of Book One of the Dutch Civil Code.
58 See the Official website of the Dutch Courts: www.rechtspraak.nl (last visited 29 April 2015).
59 See the old Article 244 of Book One of the Dutch Civil Code.
60 Article 252(2) of Book One of the Dutch Civil Code.
61 Article 253c(2) of Book One of the Dutch Civil Code.

only grant this request if it considers that this would be in the best interests of the child.[62]

If, instead of the mother, a guardian is the sole holder of parental responsibilities or no one has yet been appointed as the holder of parental responsibilities and the legal father requests the court to be the sole holder of parental responsibilities instead, the court can only *deny* this request if granting it would neglect the best interests of the child.[63]

A man who is not married to the mother or in a registered partnership with her can become the legal father by recognizing (*erkennen*) the child at the civil registry or by a notarial deed.[64] This can be done prior to or after the birth. Such recognition is invalid if the man would not be eligible to marry the mother; if he is a minor at the time of recognition; if at the time of recognition he is already married to another woman; or if the child already has two legal parents. Additionally, if the child is younger than 16 years of age, the man will need the written consent of the mother, and if the child is 12 years or older, the man will also need the written consent of the child.[65]

In virtually all other circumstances the man who wishes to become the legal father of a child, but is not married to the mother, will need a court order. If he is the biological father of the child – not just the donor of biological material, unless a 'family life' exists between the donor and the child[66] – and wants to recognize the child as his own, but the mother or the child refuses to give consent, the court can substitute that consent with an order if the recognition will not disturb the relationship between the mother and the child or harm the best interests of the child.[67] It is not necessary for the biological father and the child to have had a 'family life' prior to the request.[68] Not only the man himself can apply for a court order recognizing him as the legal father of the child, the mother or the child can do so as well, even against the wishes of the man in question.[69]

Finally, a man becomes the legal father of the child and gains parental responsibilities ex lege through the act of adoption.[70]

---

62 Article 253c(3) of Book One of the Dutch Civil Code.
63 Article 253c(4) of Book One of the Dutch Civil Code.
64 Article 203 of Book One of the Dutch Civil Code.
65 Article 204(1) of Book One of the Dutch Civil Code.
66 Hoge Raad, 24 January 2003, LJN AF0205, NJ 2003, 386, para. 3.5.
67 Article 204 of Book One of the Dutch Civil Code.
68 Hoge Raad, LJN AB0032, *NJ* 2001, 571, para. 3.4.
69 Article 207 of Book One of the Dutch Civil Code. See also M. VONK, 2007, p. 57.
70 Article 199 subsection e and Title 12 of Book One of the Dutch Civil Code.

4.3.2.3. *Mother's female partner*

Both a marriage and a registered partnership are open to different-sex and same-sex partners. When it comes to parental responsibilities and legal parentage the birthmother's female partner has almost all the same rights and duties as the birthmother's male partner would have. This came about through the coming into force of the Duo-motherhood Act (*Wet van 25 november 2013 tot wijziging van Boek 1 van het Burgerlijk Wetboek in verband met het juridisch ouderschap van de vrouwelijke partner van de moeder anders dan door adoptie*) on 1 April 2014.[71] This act changed the legislation surrounding the ways in which a birthmother's female partner can become the legal partner, creating a presumption of parentage for female partners in a formal relationship with the birthmother if the child was conceived through the use of an anonymous donor and making the process of legal recognition easier for female partners who are not in a formal relationship with the birthmother.

The mother's wife or the mother's registered partner automatically exercises parental responsibilities over a child born within their formal relationship if she is also the legal mother.[72] If the child has been conceived through the use of the genetic material of an anonymous donor, the birthmother's wife or registered partner becomes the legal mother ex lege.[73] This is a legal presumption and her parentage can be denied by the birthmother if at the time of the conception they had already separated.[74] Either mother can also deny the parentage of the woman who is not the birthmother on the grounds that she is not the biological mother, unless this woman was aware of the existence of the pregnancy before their marriage or registered partnership or had agreed to the artificial insemination. Finally, the child can also deny the legal parentage of the mother.[75]

If the donor is not anonymous, there is no presumption of legal parentage for the birthmother's wife or registered partner and she does not automatically become a legal parent upon the child's birth. Instead she will have to legally recognize the child.[76] The same rules and exceptions for legal recognition apply to a woman as they do to a man. See section 4.3.2.2 of Chapter 4 for a more in-depth discussion of legal recognition.

---

71 2013, *Stb.* 480.

72 Article 251 of Book One of the Dutch Civil Code.

73 Article 198(1) subsection b of Book One of the Dutch Civil Code.

74 Article 253sa(1) of Book One of the Dutch Civil Code. Because, as mentioned above, a child only can have two legal parents under Dutch law.

75 Article 202a of Book One of the Dutch Civil Code. Because, as mentioned above, a child only can have two legal parents under Dutch law.

76 Article 198(1) of Book One of the Dutch Civil Code.

If the wife or registered partner of the birthmother has not (yet) recognized the child and is not (yet) the child's legal mother, she still automatically gains parental responsibilities over the child born into her formal relationship, *unless legal familial ties* already exist between the child and another parent.[77] Think in this case of the known donor recognizing the child prior to the birth.

A legal mother who is not married to the birthmother and is not in a registered partnership with her gains parental responsibilities through a joint request with the birthmother at the civil registry or through a court order.[78] The same rules apply to a legal mother requesting (joint) parental responsibilities as to a legal father.[79]

A woman who is not the legal mother and is not married to or in a registered partnership with the birthmother can become the legal mother by recognizing the child with the birthmother's and/or the child's consent or a court order substituting this consent.[80] Once again, the same rules and exceptions apply as to a man wishing to recognize his child.[81]

Finally, a woman will become the legal mother and gain parental responsibilities ex lege through adoption.[82]

4.3.2.4. *(Other) non-parents*

The last category of people who may want and may be awarded parental responsibilities are non-parents. There are three types of non-parents who are in distinctly different situations: the ex-partner of a parent, the step-parent and the guardian.

Two examples of the first category are: a man who is not married to or in a registered partnership with the legal mother, who is not the biological or legal father, but has for many years before the relationship terminated raised the child together with her and a single father and his same-sex partner. In these situations the unmarried ex-partner may wish to gain (joint) parental responsibilities over the child.

A step-parent – the person who is not the legal parent of the child, but is raising the child within a committed, formalized or not, relationship with a parent – is in similar circumstances: they are taking on the role of a parent, but they do not hold parental responsibilities and have no rights to exercise them. In such situations they may want to gain joint parental responsibilities.

---

77 Article 253sa(1) of Book One of the Dutch Civil Code.
78 Article 252 and 253c of Book One of the Dutch Civil Code, respectively.
79 See section 4.3.2.2 for an in-depth discussion of these rules and exceptions.
80 Articles 198(1) subsection c, 203, 204, and 207 of Book One of the Dutch Civil Code.
81 See section 4.3.2.2 for an in-depth discussion of these rules and exceptions.
82 Article 198(1) subsection e and Title 12 of Book One of the Dutch Civil Code.

These two categories of non-parents can request the court, jointly with the legal parent, to grant them parental responsibilities.[83] However, if the child has another legal parent, who does not hold parental responsibilities over the child, a request for joint parental responsibilities with a non-parent can *only* be granted if the legal parent has exercised sole parental responsibilities for three consecutive years prior to the request and he or she has cared for the child together with the non-parent for a year immediately prior to the request.[84] If the child already has two legal parents, both of whom are holders of parental responsibilities, the non-parent cannot gain parental responsibilities.

The final category of non-parents who can gain parental responsibilities is that of guardians. These are non-parents who are granted parental responsibilities when the child has no legal parents or the legal parents are unable or unsuitable to exercise parental responsibilities. Like the other non-parents, guardians gain parental responsibilities through a court order, often with the intervention of the Child Care and Protection Board (*Raad voor de Kinderbescherming*).[85]

4.3.2.5. Overview

Dutch law gives all parents who are actually willing to care for and raise their children plenty of opportunities to arrange or request joint parental responsibilities. As can be seen in the table below, no category of parents is barred outright from gaining (joint) parental responsibilities and as can be inferred from the information set out in this section, the main reasons for denying someone who is willing and able to exercise parental responsibilities are either that there are already two people who are exercising joint parental responsibilities over the child in question or that granting (joint) parental responsibilities to the requesting person would be detrimental to the child's best interests.

---

83 Article 253t(1) of Book One of the Dutch Civil Code.
84 Article 253t(2) of Book One of the Dutch Civil Code.
85 See for rules concerning guardianship in Title 14, Chapter 6 of Book One of the Dutch Civil Code.

Table 2

Persons eligible for PR	PR automatically granted	PR through a legal agreement with mother	PR through a court order
Mother	x		
Mother's husband	x		
Mother's wife	x*		
Mother's registered partner	x*		
Legal parent not in a formal relationship with birthmother		x*	x*
Partner who is not the legal parent		x*	
Adoptive parents			Adoption order
Non-parents			x

* Unless the child already has two holders of parental responsibilities.

4.3.3. EXERCISING (JOINT) PARENTAL RESPONSIBILITIES

An important issue to consider is that parental responsibilities give rights on paper only. It is a legal fact. Having joint parental responsibilities means that, legally, both parents are equally *allowed* and *qualified* to make decisions involved in the raising of their child or children. Dutch law does not distinguish between *having* joint parental responsibilities and *exercising* them, in the sense that the person or persons who hold parental responsibilities over a child are also presumed to be exercising these responsibilities and if they hold parental responsibilities jointly, they are presumed to jointly exercise them.[86] In practice, the resident parent has the power to frustrate the exercise of parental responsibilities by the non-resident parent, because he or she has control over the daily care of the child.

While Dutch law does not provide a detailed outline of how best to exercise parental responsibilities, there are a few rules on how parental responsibilities should be exercised, especially concerning who can be barred from actions that under normal circumstances would fall within the boundaries of parental responsibilities. These rules are likely to be of

[86] As a matter of fact, Dutch law does not even speak of *holding* or *acquiring* parental responsibilities, only of *exercising* them (*gezag uitoefenen*).

most use in situations where two separated parents jointly hold parental responsibilities.

As was set out earlier in this chapter, the 2009 law reform was intended to promote equal care after parental separation; however, neither the 2009 Act itself, nor the subsequent *Hoge Raad* case law has made it sufficiently clear what equal care exactly means or how the courts should evaluate and scrutinize residential and care arrangements which the parents make.

The rules governing the intricacies and practicalities of the exercise of parental responsibilities are scarce and only roughly set out the contents of parental responsibilities.[87] They speak about aspects of what it means to exercise parental responsibilities, such as the administration of the child´s property. When it comes to the child's property, parents who hold joint parental responsibilities shall jointly conduct the administration of the child's property and represent the child in civil law acts. However, if it appears that the other parent has no objections, one of the parents has the capacity to conduct the administration of the child's property and represent the child alone.[88] The parents must conduct this administration adequately; if they do not, they can be held liable for damages.[89] As yet, there has not been a sufficient amount of case law on the matter of the administration of a child's property by a parent to properly discuss this topic.

When the holders of joint parental responsibilities are exercising them in harmony, the law does not interfere in their dealings. The courts only become involved once problems arise. Disputes about the exercise of parental responsibilities may, upon a joint or individual request, be presented to the court. The court will take a decision which is most in line with the best interests of the child.[90]

Disputes can arise about all sorts of issues linked to the exercise of parental responsibilities. It can concern religion: in accordance with whose religion should a child be brought up, the mother's or the father's and linked to that, should the child be circumcised?[91] Or it can be about important medical decisions, such as whether or not the child should be vaccinated[92] or whether the child should see a therapist.[93] Choosing or

87 See section 4.3.1 of Chapter 4.

88 Article 253a(1) of Book One of the Dutch Civil Code.

89 Article 253j of Book One of the Dutch Civil Code.

90 Article 253i(1) of Book One of the Dutch Civil Code.

91 Hof 's-Hertogenbosch, 26 November 2002, LJN AF2655: the mother wanted her son to be circumcised; the father did not. The High Court chose not to allow the circumcision, because there were no indications that the child would suffer social isolation or a stigma (if he was not circumcised) and it was an unnecessary, irreparable medical procedure.

92 Rechtbank Haarlem, 15 April 2005, LJN AT4422: the mother was ordered to have her daughter vaccinated.

93 Rechtbank Alkmaar, 20 June 2005, LJN AT9598: the mother should have discussed this with the father before arranging therapy sessions for their daughter.

changing schools and other problems connected to the child's education can also be the source of disputes.[94]

If there are no disputes or the disputes are not sufficiently grave to commence legal proceedings, it is assumed that the resident parent can make day-to-day decisions concerning the upbringing and care of the child. However, the more important decisions, such as medical care and choices concerning education, require the parents' agreement.[95]

4.3.3.1. *Courts' procedural powers to restrict and regulate the exercise of parental responsibilities*

In settling disputes on the exercise of parental responsibilities, the court has various procedural powers. The court can make an order in which it divides the care duties and establishes the care arrangements; a residence order;[96] and an order which dictates how important information about the child is provided to the non-resident parent and to others.[97] It can even decide to temporarily deny a parent contact with the child if the child's interests so require.[98] It can also prevent a parent from exercising (a part) of his or her parental responsibilities. Finally, it can substitute a court order for parental consent. For example, a parent with parental responsibilities can give consent to the marriage of his or her child who is between 16 and 18 years of age,[99] but the agreement of the parent can be substituted by a court order.[100]

If the parents have already made care arrangements or an order exists establishing care arrangements, but the circumstances have changed, the court may make a (new) order upon the joint request of the parents, upon the request of one of the parents or upon the request of another party with a close relationship with the child.[101]

Legally, a parent who holds parental responsibilities jointly with another parent (or non-parent) cannot prevent the other party from exercising his or her parental responsibilities without obtaining a court order. To obtain this order, they would have to start a procedure based on Article 253a of Book One of the Dutch Civil Code.

---

94 See for example Hof 's-Gravenhage, 23 June 2010, LJN BN3877, Rechtbank Zwolle, 19 August 2004, LJN AQ7125 and Rechtbank 's-Hertogenbosch 9 June 2005, LJN AT7299.

95 C.G. JEPPESEN DE BOER, 2008, p. 246.

96 Article 253i(1) of Book One of the Dutch Civil Code.

97 Article 253a(2) of Book One of the Dutch Civil Code.

98 Article 253a(2) subsection a of Book One of the Dutch Civil Code.

99 Article 35(1) of Book One of the Dutch Civil Code.

100 Article 36 of Book One of the Dutch Civil Code.

101 Article 377e in conjunction with Article 253a(4) of Book One of the Dutch Civil Code.

4.3.3.2. *Parenting plans*

Since the 2009 law reform, a new, obligatory instrument has been introduced to make sure that separating parents think about the consequences of their separation for the children involved and make sound care arrangements. This instrument is the parenting plan.

Separating parents are obliged to make a parenting plan, which is a document in which the parents lay down important agreements about the care and upbringing of the child or children over whom they exercise parental responsibilities.[102] The document can be as extensive as they deem necessary, but has to contain *at least* a description of the following arrangements: the division of care; the manner in which the parents will inform each other and consult with each other about the person and estate of the child; and the financial arrangements for the child's care and upbringing.[103]

Empirical research conducted by the author in preparation for this book in which 200 parenting plans which had been approved by the courts had been gathered and analysed has shown that while there are large differences between parenting plans, most parents use templates provided on the internet or by their lawyers which they fill in and add to. This was clear from the identical or similar phrasing of certain provisions.

Among the 200 parenting plans consulted, the large majority of these plans contained provisions on who would hold and exercise parental responsibilities after separation, the residential arrangements and where the child would have his or her main residence, the financial arrangements, what to do in case the child needs medical care, the school choice or how that choice would be made in the future and how to go about sharing information from the school.

Some 78.5% of the consulted plans contained a provision on 'respectful parenting' in which both parents promised to treat each other with respect and not involve the child or children in their disputes or to say anything negative to the child or children about the other parent. Something of the whole intention of the parenting plan seems to be lost, however, when one considers that nearly every time a standardised text is used, the parents simply copy-pasted this from an exemplary parenting plan.

It was mentioned above that the parents are legally obliged to arrange the manner in which they will inform each other and consult with each other about the person and estate of the child. However, only 65% of the

---

102 For divorcing parents: Article 815(2) of the Code of Civil Procedures; for parents wishing to dissolve a registered partnership: Article 828 in conjunction with Article 815(2) of the Code of Civil Procedure; for unmarried parents: Article 247a of Book One of the Dutch Civil Code in conjunction with Article 815(2) of the Code of Civil Procedure.

103 Article 815(3) of the Code of Civil Procedure.

parenting plans contain a provision on the information obligation, and only 42.5% contain a provision that goes into detail on how and when this information exchange will take place. It is therefore interesting to see that the courts are apparently not in the habit of enforcing the obligation to arrange the information exchange where it is absent from a parenting plan.

Another observation that can be mentioned is that only roughly half of the parents seem to prepare for disputes and their resolution, or at least, only 54% of the parenting plans analysed contain a provision on dispute resolution. Also, if one considers that new partners are often the cause of tensions and disputes between the parents, is it interesting to see that only 13.5% of the parenting plans analysed contain a provision on new partners.

While the contents of a parenting plan are for the most part left to the parents to decide upon, the obligation to draw up a parenting plan is not purely theoretical in nature. When *married parents* wish to file for a divorce or *parents in a registered partnership* wish to have their partnership dissolved, they must hand in a parenting plan among other necessary documents or explain why they could not reasonably be expected to do so. They must also note any matters on which they are still in disagreement and why, and how the child or children have been involved in the process of making the parenting plan.[104] If the parenting plan is not handed in without a good reason or the parents cannot reach an agreement, the court may, and usually will,[105] delay in issuing the divorce or dissolution order so as to await a parenting plan and it may send the parents to mediation in order to come to an agreement.[106]

Parents who jointly hold parental responsibilities, but are not married or in a registered partnership, do not need a court order to end their relationship. Therefore one might think that the obligation to make a parenting plan can never be enforced in the case of parents in non-formalized relationships and if the parents do not encounter any problems for which they need the assistance of a court; this is indeed true. However, if separated holders of joint parental responsibilities request the court to make an Article 253a order – an order devising care arrangements, an order suspending contact, a residence order, or an order regulating the provision of information about the child – the court shall suspend the proceedings until the parents have drawn up and submitted a parenting plan, unless

---

104 Articles 815 and 828 of the Code of Civil Procedure.

105 See the LOVF 2010 note on parenting plans as discussed in J. ACKERMANS-WIJN, 'De nieuwe aanbevelingen van het LOVF met betrekking tot het ouderschapsplan', *EB* 2012/74, pp. 1-2.

106 Article 818(2) of the Code of Civil Procedure. See Hof Amsterdam, 18 January 2011, LJN BP1465 for an example of a case where the court declined to make a divorce order because the parents had not made a parenting plan.

the child's best interests require that the suspension should be dispensed with.[107]

Parents may, in an agreement or a parenting plan, allow for practical obstacles which arise due to their separation, but only for so far and so long as these obstacles exist.[108] These practical obstacles are usually connected with one of the parents needing to find a new place to live. As it is sometimes impossible to predict how quickly a residence can be found, how far it will be from the other parent's residence and therefore if the child will be able to easily commute between the residences, the parents can explain in the parenting plan how they would *preferably* like to divide the care for the child and what the preferred division of time the child spends with both parents will be, but that it strongly depends on the eventual residential arrangements of the parent who is seeking accommodation.

In some cases the parents are unable to draw up a parenting plan. This could be because there is no contact at all with one of the parents;[109] one of the parents is unreliable because of an addiction;[110] there is so much hostility between the parents that it is impossible for them to agree on anything; or some other reason.[111] If the court deems that it is *reasonable* that the parents could not provide a parenting plan, it can dispense with the obligation. This is up to the court's discretion.[112]

While the parenting plan itself does not have legal authority, the court may, upon the request of one or both parties, include the arrangements made by the parents within the order.[113] Additionally, while making a divorce order, the court may add to that order a decision on parental responsibilities, care arrangements, the child's residence, contact, the provision of information, or financial arrangements.[114] As part of the order, all these arrangements can (theoretically) be enforced in the same way as the order itself.[115]

The law only requires the parents to make a parenting plan and describes what kind of minimal arrangements it has to contain. The letter of the law does not explicitly give the court the authority to scrutinise the arrangements themselves if the parents are in agreement and it does not prescribe that the court should suspend the proceedings if the parenting

---

107 Article 253(3) in conjunction with Article 247a of Book One of the Dutch Civil Code.

108 Article 247(5) of Book One of the Dutch Civil Code.

109 Rechtbank Utrecht, 9 September 2009, Case No. 270441 / FARK 09-3982.

110 Rechtbank Utrecht, 29 December 2010, Case No. 292780 / FA RK 10-5355.

111 Such as, for example, the psychological problems of one of the parents which make communication impossible, see Rechtbank Groningen, 12 October 2010, LJN BO2900.

112 Article 815(6) of the Code of Civil Procedure.

113 Article 819 of the Code of Civil Procedure.

114 Article 827(1) subsection c of the Code of Civil Procedure.

115 More about the enforcement of arrangements in section 4.6.

plan is 'not good enough'. However, whether the courts having this power is something that was intended by the law reform is a disputed issue.

In practice the courts may and do scrutinise the parenting plans. If the parenting plan completely lacks any controllable arrangements or agreements or the parents have neglected to discuss the consequences of the seperation with the child or children over the age of six, the court will reject it.[116] For parenting plans concerning children over 14 years of age the requirements are more lenient in the sense that instead of comprehensive arrangements it is sufficient for the parents to agree that they will make arrangements in consultation with the child or children.[117]

Recently Tomassen-van der Lans has published a doctoral thesis on the regulation and functioning of parenting plans.[118] In this thesis she looks at how parenting plans work in practice. She found that when looking at parenting plans, the courts generally only marginally consider the arrangements made in them, especially when older children are involved, with an occasional stricter test in specific cases.[119] While both judges and lawyers stress that the obligation to involve children in the making of the parenting plan is an important one, they admit that it is very difficult to test this in practice.[120] She also found that the introduction of the parenting plan does not seem to influence the percentage of cases in which a new procedure is commenced within a few years. This percentage remains low, about 9%, with most new procedures commencing after the courts had to make a decision for the parents.[121] Perhaps this is unsurprising as resorting to the courts once again is expensive and cumbersome for parents.

4.3.4. DISCHARGE OF (JOINT) PARENTAL RESPONSIBILITIES

As explained earlier, only unmarried minors who have not been emancipated can be subjected to parental responsibilities. This means that once the child reaches the age of majority, marries or is emancipated by a court order, the holder or holders of parental responsibilities lose those responsibilities. Although if a legislative proposal currently being considered by the Dutch Parliament will be approved and becomes law, the child marrying as a reason for the parent or parents to lose parental

---

116 Rechtbank 's-Gravenhage, 13 January 2010, LJN BL1926, LJN BL1932 and LJN BL2081.

117 See the LOVF 2010 note on parenting plans as discussed in J. Ackermans-Wijn, 'De nieuwe aanbevelingen van het LOVF met betrekking tot het ouderschapsplan', *EB* 2012/74, p. 7.

118 M. TOMASSEN-VAN DER LANS, *Het verplichte ouderschapsplan: regeling en werking*, Doctoral thesis, 2015.

119 *Ibid.*, pp. 61-67.

120 *Ibid.*, pp. 67-68.

121 *Ibid.*, pp. 115 and 119.

responsibilities will disappear, because this Proposal will remove the possibility for a person between the ages of 16 and 18 to marry.[122] These are the 'normal' ways for a parent to lose parental responsibilities.

There are, however, additional ways in which a holder of parental responsibilities can lose these responsibilities, either willingly or unwillingly, ex lege or upon a court order. This discussion concentrates on the discharge of parental responsibilities during or after parental separation.

The law deals differently with parents who want themselves or the other parent to be discharged of parental responsibilities depending on their (previous) relationship with each other. While Article 251 of Book One of the Dutch Civil Code provides that parents continue to exercise parental responsibilities jointly after the divorce and the same is assumed to apply to parents whose registered partnership has been dissolved, Article 251a gives the Court the power, upon the request of one or both parents, to grant one of the parents sole parental responsibilities. The court may *only* do so if there is an unacceptable risk of the child or children being 'torn or lost' between the parents and this situation is not likely to change within a reasonable period of time, or if granting sole parental responsibilities to one of the parents would be necessary from the point of view of the best interests of the child. This is one of the new provisions created by the 2009 Act. What is interesting about this is that it not only presents an obstacle for a parent to forcibly gain sole parental responsibilities against the other parent´s will, it makes it just as difficult for a holder of parental responsibilities to *voluntarily* give them up.

As explained in section 4.3.2 unmarried parents need to actively do something to gain joint parental responsibilities. They either have to agree thereon or they have to request the court to make an order to that extent. Vice versa, if one of the holders of parental responsibilities wants to divest himself or herself of these responsibilities, or he or she wants to have sole parental responsibilities and thus wishes that the other holder would be deprived of them, a court order is required. Article 253n of Book One of the Dutch Civil Code gives the courts the authority to terminate joint parental responsibilities at the request of one or both parents if a change of circumstances has taken place. Such a change of circumstances in this case would be the separation of the parents.

Outside of the situations when the parents are separating or they have a disagreement, the courts can also discharge a holder of parental

---

122 *Wijziging van Boek 1 en Boek 10 van het Burgerlijk Wetboek betreffende de huwelijksleeftijd, de huwelijksbeletselen, de nietigverklaring van een huwelijk en de erkenning van in het buitenland gesloten huwelijken (Wet tegengaan huwelijksdwang)*, Kamerstukken II, 2012/13, 33 488, no. 2.

responsibilities from these responsibilities for reasons of child protection. If a parent is unsuitable or incapable of fulfilling the duty of care for the child or children, unless the best interests of the child preclude this, the court can discharge this parent from exercising parental responsibilities.[123] The court can only do so at the request of the Child Care and Protection Board (*Raad voor de Kinderbescherming*) or the Ministry of Justice[124] and only if the minor's development is severely endangered and the parent in question is not able to remedy this within an acceptable period of time, or if the parent is abusing his or her parental responsibilities.[125]

4.4. CHILD'S RESIDENCE

Article 12(1) of Book One of the Dutch Civil Code provides that 'the residency of a minor follows that of the person who exercises parental responsibilities over him or her'. In the case of sole parental responsibilities the situation is clear: the child is registered with the parent who exercises sole parental responsibilities. When the parents jointly exercise parental responsibilities, but do not have the same residence, which is usually the case with separated parents, 'the child's residence follows that of the parent with whom he or she has his or her actual abode or has stayed most recently'.[126] This article may suggest to the reader that a child can only have his or her (official) residence with *one* parent; however, this, in fact, is no longer the case.[127]

The *Hoge Raad* has confirmed the authority of the Dutch courts to establish a main residence when the parents exercise joint parental authority and cannot come to an agreement.[128]

4.4.1. ASSIGNING OR CHOOSING RESIDENCE

In principle, the parents are free to decide with whom the child should live. The residence of the child is part of the care arrangement which parents decide upon and include within the parenting plan they are obliged to

---

123 See Article 253aa(2) of Book One of the Dutch Civil Code which explicitly excludes these provisions from applying to registered partnerships.
124 Article 267(1) of Book One of the Dutch Civil Code.
125 Article 266(1) of Book One of the Dutch Civil Code.
126 Article 12(1) of Book One of the Dutch Civil Code.
127 This will be explained more thoroughly later on in this chapter.
128 Hoge Raad, 15 December 2000, LJN AA9042, *NJ* 2001, 123, section 3.3.2. of Chapter 3.

draw up upon their separation. If they cannot reach an agreement on with whom the child should live, they can ask the court to decide.[129]

But how should the court decide if each parent wants the child's main residence to be with him or her? Various (practical) reasons play a part in making this decision. If the parents have already been living separately for some time, the court will consider with which parent the child or children factually reside most of the time.[130] Additionally, the court takes note of which of the parents can provide the child or children with a more stable environment and which parent can spend more time caring for the child (a parent who has a part-time job can generally devote more time to caring for a child than a parent who works full time, which can be especially important for very young children).[131] Continued contact with (half-)siblings is another consideration and depriving a child of such contact is seen as not being in his or her best interests.[132] Taking into account the different specifics of each case, the court decides on the main residence which is in the best interests of the child.

4.4.2. SHARED RESIDENCE

A shared residence, or more accurately, residential co-parenting, was first employed in the Netherlands by a small group of parents on a completely voluntary basis. These parents had a very co-operative relationship with each other and the ability to arrange their households in a way in which a shared residence could be incorporated (flexible working times, the geographical proximity of the residences and any other adjustments which were needed). However, now that fathers (and fathers' rights organizations) are starting to see residential co-parenting less as an alternative way of arranging post-separation care, and more as an equality issue, the call for residential co-parenting arrangements, in less appropriate situations, has increased.[133]

While the 2009 law reform had as its goal to promote equal parenting, it is not clear what exactly is meant by this term. It seems that, on the

---

129 Article 253a of Book One of the Dutch Civil Code. Also see the discussion of the parenting plans in section 4.3.3.2 of Chapter 4.

130 Hof Arnhem, 10 January 2013, LJN BZ1896, para. 4.12; Hof 's-Gravenhage, 21 July 2010, LJN BN5758, para. 9. However, this is not necessarily always the deciding factor. See for example: Hof Amsterdam, 3 January 2012, LJN BV8225.

131 Rechtbank 's-Gravenhage, 1 April 2010, LJN BM3090, second para. under 'Hoofdverblijfplaats van de minderjarige en verdeling van de zorg- en opvoedingstaken'.

132 *Ibid.*

133 M. ANTOKOLSKAIA, *Solomo's oordeel nieuwe stijl: verblijfsco-ouderschap in België en Nederland. Over de rol van de wetenschap, invloed van de politiek, en nattevingerwerk in het wetgevingsproces*, TPR, 2010, pp. 1179-1243.

one hand, equal parenting by both parents no longer leaves much room for the classical arrangement of the mother being the resident parent and providing all the care, while the father has contact with the child or children for one weekend every fortnight. On the other hand, the Promotion of Continued Parenting and Proper Divorce Act (*Wet bevordering voortgezet ouderschap en zorgvuldige scheiding*) does not go as far as to prescribe residential co-parenting.[134] The fact that equal care does not presuppose a 50/50 residential co-parenting arrangement has also been confirmed by the *Hoge Raad*.[135]

In circumstances where there are no counter-indications or practical obstacles and one of the parents requests a residential co-parenting arrangement, the court has very few reasons to deny such a request. For example, the Hof 's-Hertogenbosch case in 2012 in which the parents lived in the same street and where the father could arrange to be at home during the time the child resided with him, and had requested to have his son stay with him every other week. The mother wanted to continue the residential arrangement they had already been exercising for 2½ years, which consisted of the child spending a larger period of time with her. Here the court agreed with the father and made an order for residential co-parenting.[136]

This, however, does not mean that the courts will *always* make an order in favour of residential co-parenting when requested. There can be different reasons for denying such a request. In a 2010 Rechtbank Groningen case the ex-female partner of the mother, who had regular (one weekend every two weeks) contact with the children born during her cohabitation with the mother, requested the court to make an order to the effect that every other week the children would reside with her. The holders of parental responsibilities had not made a parenting plan, mediation had failed and communication between them was problematic. The court considered that *good communication is necessary for well-functioning, intensive residential co-parenting*.[137] Such communication was found to be lacking in the case at hand and therefore no 50/50 residential co-parenting arrangement would be ordered. The main residence was determined to be with the birthmother because due to the fact that she worked shorter hours, she would be more available to care for the children, but contact with the other

134 F. SCHONEWILLE, 'De Wet bevordering voortgezet ouderschap en zorgvuldige scheiding is een feit: exit klassieke omgangsregeling!', *WPNR* 2009, 6800.

135 Hoge Raad, 21 May 2010, LJN BL7407, para. 3.7.3. and earlier by the Hof 's-Gravenhage, 20 January 2010, LJN BL2337, para. 10.

136 Hof 's-Hertogenbosch, 21 February 2012, LJN BV6414.

137 Rechtbank Groningen, 6 April 2010, LJN BM 3955, third para. under: 'Verdeling van de zorg- en opvoedingstaken en hoofdverblijf'.

mother was increased from one weekend a fortnight to a period of five days consecutively every two weeks.

The reason or reasons for denying a request for residential co-parenting can be case-specific or child-specific. For some children a regular change of residence can be too much of a burden and therefore a residential co-parenting arrangement would be not in their best interests. This can be seen in, for example, the 2011 Hof 's-Gravenhage case which dealt with a child with leukaemia, who was undergoing chemotherapy.[138]

While residential co-parenting where the child resides with both parents is possible and encouraged, legally speaking, a child is *registered* at one address only and even within a 50/50 residential co-parenting regime cannot be registered with both parents. So far there has only been one case, in 2006, dealing with this practical discrepancy in which the judiciary did not see this as a problem or an obstacle for residential co-parenting.[139]

When more than one child is involved in a shared residence arrangement, the parents usually register one child as being resident with one parent and the other(s) as being resident with the other parent, while in practice they have an arrangement where all the children spend part of the week with one parent and the rest of the time with the other. This is mainly done for tax and child-support reasons. The courts support this structure and even make orders to this extent.[140]

4.4.3. CHANGING RESIDENCE

If the parents want to change the residential arrangement, for example changing the amount of days the child spends with a parent per week, because of a change of circumstances such as the child changing schools or one of the parents changing jobs and they do so in mutual agreement, there is no need for them to involve the judicial system. Theoretically their practical arrangement no longer reflects the parenting plan, but as the document is intended to have the parents working together and thinking of the children during the difficult period of separation, it has still served its purpose. Why would parents spend time and money on having a court approve an agreement they do not have a dispute over? Because residential arrangement orders are mainly issued upon parental request, often in order to decide a dispute, there is no legal requirement for the parents to start a procedure to legally change the residential arrangement when there is no dispute.

---

138 Hof 's-Gravenhage, 9 February 2011, LJN BP6275, para. 10.
139 Hof 's-Gravenhage, 18 October 2006, LJN AZ209.
140 See for example Hof Amsterdam, 4 May 2010, LJN BM3895.

When there *is* a dispute, one or both parents can request the court to make a residence order pursuant to its power to resolve disputes over the exercise of parental responsibilities.[141]

Sometimes residential arrangements which have worked well for a certain period of time, become difficult or impossible to maintain because of changing circumstances or because the children become older and their needs change. A residential arrangement of one week with the mother and one week with the father had been working well in the 2010 Hof 's-Hertogenbosch case, up until the point when the oldest child had to go to school. Because the parents lived too far from each other for the child to attend the same school and for them to maintain the residential co-parenting arrangement, the arrangement was changed to the child's main residence being with the mother, despite the fact that both parents were willing and able to care for their child, because the mother worked part-time and therefore had more time to provide the necessary care.

When the courts are asked to decide if the child's residence should be changed, the general opinion is that, in principle, it is in the child's best interests for his or her residence to remain unchanged. Only if the child's best interests *strongly point against* the child's continuous residence with the resident parent is there a reason to change the child's main residence. For that to be established, the residential parent has to seriously fail in taking care of the child. A mere change of circumstances is not sufficient. This was decided, for example, by the Hof Leeuwaarden in a case in which the parents had agreed, after their divorce, to share the care for their children and for that reason to remain living near each other, so that the children could spend every other weekend with the father. However, the mother decided to move to another province with the children. The court in Assen allowed the move. The father appealed and requested that the children's main residence should be established with him. The Hof denied the appeal, because there were no indications that the mother had failed in her care for the children, but a more extensive contact order was made to compensate for the fact that the move had limited the father's contact with his children.[142]

Most parenting plans contain a clause which obliges the residential parent who plans on moving with the child to inform the other parent a few months in advance. This period of time gives the other parent sufficient time and opportunity to prevent the move and to commence Article 253a proceedings before the move takes place.[143] Such proceedings – in which a parent either tries to prevent the other parent from relocating with the

141 Article 253a of Book One of the Dutch Civil Code.
142 Hof Leeuwaarden, 4 November 2010, LJN BO3724.
143 Article 253a of Book One of the Dutch Civil Code.

child, tries to reverse the relocation, or wants to have the child's residence changed as a reaction to the relocation – are the most common type of dispute when it comes to disagreements about the exercise of joint parental responsibilities. A parent may wish to relocate within the Netherlands or to move to another country. Either way, this is likely to have an impact on the exercise of joint parental responsibilities, especially in the case of a residential co-parenting arrangement, although this impact is arguably larger when the child is taken abroad. The case law on relocation does not follow a checklist or strict rules; instead the courts consider each case according to its particular facts. However, it can be said that usually, when there is no residential co-parenting and the intended move is within the Netherlands, the court will allow this move.[144] It is the case law on relocation as part of residential co-parenting and a relocation to another country which is strongly casuistic and difficult to predict.

4.4.3.1. *Relocation within the Netherlands*

Most cases that deal with relocation within the Netherlands concern the resident parent wanting to move with the children far away, or at least further away, from the other parent usually because they have found a new partner, a new job opportunity, want to be closer to their family, want to make a fresh start, or a combination thereof. When the parents have a residential co-parenting arrangement this will become impossible or very difficult to maintain. The question is then: is it in the best interests of the child to move with the residential parent and to partake in the positive effects the move has on that parent (a new family, a better job with potentially more financial security, emotional well-being) or is it in the best interests of the child to remain in his or her trusted environment, including extensive contact with the other parent, despite any negative effects this might have for the parent who wants to move, but is not allowed to? And if the second option is applicable, should the child's or children's best interests trump the interests of the parent who wants to move?

A relocation combined with the discontinuation of a residential co-parenting arrangement removes the child or children from a familiar environment and diminishes the contact with one of the parents. It is therefore perceived as not being in the best interests of the child and cannot easily be justified by the desire of one of the parents to start a new life at a different location.[145]

---

144 W. SCHRAMA & M. VONK, 'On the move: staat voortgezet gelijkwaardig ouderschap aan verhuizing in de weg?', *FJR* 2009, 82, para. 2.1.

145 See Rechtbank Dordrecht, 19 September 2012, LJN BX9134.

Even if the relocation would not make the residential co-parenting arrangement impossible, the court may still deny the request to move if the move and the subsequent longer time it will take for the child or children to travel between the parents and their school will negatively impact their well-being and the relocation is not strictly necessary.[146]

However, the opposite is also possible: the court will allow the relocation even though it will make the previous residential co-parenting arrangement impossible and reduce the time the child or children will spend with the other parent. For that the relocation has to be deemed *necessary* by the court. Indications that a move is necessary are, for example, the fact that the resident parent is financially reliant on his or her new partner whom he or she wants to join and the existence of children from a new relationship whose best interests must also be taken into account. Additionally, the courts will consider the preparedness of the parent who wants to move to stimulate contact with the other parent, for example by having the child or children spend more holidays with the other parent or to make sure that there is regular contact by telephone or computer.[147]

4.4.3.2. Relocation abroad

A relocation outside the Netherlands is arguably even more disruptive for (especially young) children than one within the Netherlands: a different culture, a different language, and probably much more limited contact with the other parent. Therefore, it is less likely that such a move will be allowed by the courts, even if there is no residential co-parenting, than a move within the Netherlands. Reasons which may be considered sufficient for a relocation within the Netherlands are unlikely to be seen as being sufficient to allow a relocation abroad, for instance the inability to find appropriate work in the Netherlands.[148] The argument that the parent had come to the Netherlands to be with the other parent and now that the relationship has broken down has no family or social ties that bind him or her to the Netherlands has also proven to be insufficient to allow him or her to move with the child to his or her country of origin.[149]

Cases in which a relocation abroad has been allowed by the courts are quite rare. The child's best interests, but also the child's wishes play a very important role. Therefore, in a 2012 Rechtbank Breda case a move to the UK was allowed because the 13-year-old son had explicitly stated that he

---

146 See for example Rechtbank Zwolle, 20 June 2011, LJN BQ9836, para. 4.6.

147 See Rechtbank Arnhem, 10 October 2012, LJN BY7647.

148 Hof 's Gravenhage, 29 February 2012, LJN BW7358; Rechtbank 's-Gravenhage, 28 July 2010, LJN BN3236; Rechtbank Maastricht, 27 October 2010, LJN BO1950.

149 Hof 's-Gravenhage, 11 May 2011, LJN BR3529; Rechtbank Haarlem, 10 November 2010, LJN BO6046.

wanted to live with his mother and would like to move to the UK with her. Her move was also necessary because she would join her current partner there and she had a job opportunity.[150]

4.5. CHILDREN'S PROCEDURAL RIGHTS

Within the Dutch legal system, when it comes to proceedings concerning parental responsibilities or residential proceedings the child fulfils both a passive role as the one whose best interests need to be considered and protected, and an active role as the recipient of procedural rights. The child has different rights when it comes to familial ties, parental responsibilities or residence. Children of 12 years of age or older additionally even have several rights they can employ to instigate a procedure or to become party to an already ongoing procedure.

Under Dutch law children have different procedural rights that concern issues surrounding parental separation, which can roughly be separated into three categories: the right to be heard, the right to become a party in the proceedings concerning them and the right to initiate proceedings themselves.

According to Article 809 of the Code of Civil Procedure the courts *must* provide children of 12 years of age and older with the opportunity to allow their voice be heard in proceedings concerning them, with the exception of cases of minor importance and disputes concerning child support. The courts *may* hear younger children if they consider this to be necessary.[151] To make the children aware of their right to be heard and to inquire if they want to make use of this right, the court usually sends a letter asking the child if he or she would like to talk to the judge; if he or she would like to write his or her opinion on the matter; or if he or she does not want to do either. The child has to sign the letter and return it. This is important, because it ensures that the child has received the letter and has been made aware of his or her rights.[152]

The court is not solely responsible for considering the child's wishes. In case of parental separation, when the parents are obliged to make a parenting plan, children aged six years or older must be involved in the process and the parents have to briefly explain in their request for a

---

150 Rechtbank Breda, 4 December 2012, LJN BY7479.

151 L. PUNSELIE, 'De positie van de minderjarige in het civiele proces', *Actuele ontwikkelingen in het familierecht. UCERF reeks*, 2010, p. 82.

152 Information gathered by means of empirical research at Rechtbank Utrecht and Rechtbank Arnhem. See also L. PUNSELIE, 2010, p. 83.

court order how they have been involved.[153] The wording 'involved' is used because it applies to children of all ages, but very young children cannot really be consulted or actively involved in discussions about care arrangements. All that parents can do with very young children is to explain what is going on in an age-appropriate manner. This wording, however, does make the requirement vague and lawyers who help parents draw up parenting plans have admitted that they are not quite sure how to check whether the parents have actually talked to their children about the parenting plan and the care arrangements or if it is even their task to check this.[154] Most parenting plans contain the following default sentence: 'The children have been involved in the process of drawing up this plan'.[155]

The right to be heard does not mean that children can make choices or demands as to the eventual care arrangements. The only circumstance when the child, of 12 years or older, actually has to give his or her consent is when a person wants to legally recognise him or her as their child, although the child's consent can be substituted by a court order.[156]

Outside of simply being heard, children can also become involved in the proceedings which concern them if there is a conflict between the interests of one or more holders of parental responsibilities. These children, although they are considered to be interested parties (*belanghebbenden*),[157] cannot represent themselves. Instead, the court will appoint a special representative to represent the child (*bijzondere curator*), both judicially and extra-judicially, if it considers that this is necessary in the best interests of the child, having regard to the nature of the conflict of interests. The court can do this of its own motion or at the request of an interested person.[158] The conflict of interests must be substantial; not every disagreement between a child and the holders of parental responsibilities over him or her warrant the appointment of a representative.[159]

Finally, there are a few possibilities for a child to initiate proceedings him/herself. A child of 12 years or older, or a child who is younger than this and is able to make a reasonable assessment of his or her situation, may, in the case of his or her parents' divorce, petition the court to make an order granting parental responsibilities to one of his or her parents,

---

153 See the LOVF 2010 notie on parenting plans as discussed in J. ACKERMANS-WIJN, 'De nieuwe aanbevelingen van het LOVF met betrekking tot het ouderschapsplan', *EB* 2012/74, pp. 5-6.

154 Interviews with legal practitioners conducted in the course of this PhD research have shown this.

155 Empirical research (parenting plans) gathered in the course of this PhD research show this.

156 Article 204 of Book One of the Dutch Civil Code.

157 Hoge Raad, 4 February 2005, LJN AR4850.

158 Article 250 of Book One of the Dutch Civil Code.

159 E. MINK, 'De procespositie van de minderjarige in de civiele procedure', *FJR*, 2012/41, p. 2.

instead of the ex lege continuation of joint parental responsibilities.[160] In 2011 the question arose before the Rechtbank Alkmaar whether this right to petition for sole parental responsibilities also allows the child to petition for a change to his or her *residence*. In this case the child's parents had divorced in 2007 and the child's main residence had been established with the mother. Then, three years later, the child had written a letter to the court requesting that his residence should be changed to that of his father. The court appointed a special representative (*bijzondere curator*) to represent him and that representative requested the court to change the child's main residence to that of his father. The court confirmed that Article 251a(4) of Book One of the Dutch Civil Code was intended to also cover issues of the exercise of parental responsibilities, and this included questions of residence. While, at face value, the article seems to only deal with a change from joint parental responsibilities to sole parental responsibilities, according to the court there is no reason why the child should be able to petition for something as far-reaching as a change in parental responsibilities, but not for other issues connected to parental responsibilities. The court sought confirmation of this position in the Explanatory Report of the 2009 Act. In this case the court made a residence order changing the child's main residence to that of his father.[161]

A child of 12 years or older, or a child who is younger than this and is able to make a reasonable assessment of his or her situation, may also informally write a letter to or telephone the court to request it to listen to his or her wishes concerning an existing care arrangement[162] or to petition the court to make a contact order.[163] A child has the right of contact with both his or her parents, but also with other persons with close legal familial ties to him or her.[164]

It is very rare that a child makes use of his or her right to directly approach the court. Most children are unlikely to be aware of their right to do so and even if they are, it is still a major step to involve the court in a dispute with their parents. While it is rare, it does occasionally happen that children initiate proceedings. In a 2011 Rechtbank Groningen case a girl petitioned the court to change the contact order, after many conflicts between her parents. The court heard all parties and while it did not change the contact order, it did order that the family, and especially the girl herself, should receive help from the Youth Care Agency to help in the communications between them.[165]

---

160 Article 251a(4) of Book One of the Dutch Civil Code.
161 Rechtbank Alkmaar, 16 February 2011, LJN BQ1141.
162 E. MINK, 2012, p. 4.
163 Article 377g in conjunction with Article 377a of Book One of the Dutch Civil Code.
164 Article 377a(1) of Book One of the Dutch Civil Code.
165 Rechtbank Groningen, 9 August 2011, LJN BS8007.

In another case, a 13-year-old girl whose residence was with her mother moved in with her father after conflicts with the mother and she petitioned the court to make an order assigning her residence with her father. However, before the application was heard the petition was revoked. The parents had talked to her and with each other and they had decided on 50/50 residential co-parenting.[166]

Finally, for the sake of completion it should be mentioned that the child does not only have rights, he or she also has two duties under Dutch law. He or she must take into account - meaning respect - the powers vested in the parent or guardian within the framework of the exercise of parental responsibilities and the interests of other members of his or her family.[167] Additionally, a child who resides with a parent (or parents) has the duty to contribute to the housing costs if he or she has an income.[168]

4.6. ENFORCEMENT OF ARRANGEMENTS IN CASE OF NON-COMPLIANCE

Orders deciding on or regulating parental responsibilities, care arrangements, residence or other matters concerning the care and upbringing of the child are legally binding, therefore they can be enforced. There are four different enforcement mechanisms available for the courts to use: a penalty in the form of a sum of money, a criminal conviction, a (temporary) reversal or a change of parental responsibilities or residence and, finally, placing the child under the supervision of the Child Care and Protection Board (*Raad voor de Kinderbescherming*).[169]

First of all, if the parenting plan or certain arrangements have been made part of the court order, the process server can gain a title of execution.[170] For this the arrangements need to be clear and to be able to be converted into a monetary sum, which will be the case with financial arrangements - for example, if it is arranged in the parenting plan that one of the parents must pay certain expenses and fails to do so - but other arrangements might prove difficult if not impossible to express in monetary terms.

It is more likely that a fine will be imposed on a parent after the other has petitioned a court to make an enforcement order because the parent has acted in breach of the arrangements. When a parent then breaches the enforcement order, he or she can be fined.

---

166 Rechtbank Arnhem, 21 November 2011, Case No. 222527/FARK 11-12655.
167 Article 249 of Book One of the Dutch Civil Code.
168 Article 253l of Book One of the Dutch Civil Code.
169 Kamerstukken I 2007/08, 30 145, no. C.
170 See Article 430 and further of the Code of Civil Procedure.

Imprisonment is very unlikely to be used as an enforcement mechanism for not abiding by care or contact arrangements as it is likely to worsen the conflict between the parents and to adversely impact the well-being of the child or children.[171] However, in 2009, the Leeuwaarden court sentenced a mother who had constantly refused to abide by the contact arrangement and frustrated contact between the father and the child to 100 hours of community service.[172]

In certain circumstances the change in or a reversal of parental responsibilities or residence can be used as an enforcement mechanism. This is done in cases where the resident parent continues to violate care or contact arrangements. In practice this, aside from a fine, seems to be the only enforcement mechanism that is used in disputes concerning contact and care arrangement disputes. For example, in a tragic 2010 case, the parents held joint parental responsibilities over their seriously ill seven-year-old daughter. The mother, however, frustrated all contact between the father and the daughter. Neither mediation nor fines helped to change the situation and finally the court awarded sole parental responsibilities to the father. The Dutch Supreme Court cautioned that such a change of parental responsibilities is only appropriate as an ultimum remedium.[173]

When the reversal concerns the (main) residence of the child instead of parental responsibilities it is usually not explicitly addressed as an enforcement mechanism, but as an adjustment to changed circumstances. To illustrate this: in a 2011 Hof 's-Gravenhage case the parents had a well-functioning residential co-parenting arrangement where the child would stay for one week with the father and one week with the mother. The child's main residence was with the mother. The mother then decided to move to a different town and took the child with her, thereby rendering co-parenting impossible. The court noted that the mother had acted selfishly and had disregarded the child's best interests by moving. The court ordered the child's main residence to be with the father from then onwards and that the child should be returned to the father and the environment she was used to.[174] While this is not strictly a case of enforcement, the judgement does convey a value judgement on the behaviour of the mother.

Placing the child under the supervision of the Child Care and Protection Board (*Raad voor de Kinderbescherming*) is another far-reaching mechanism which can be employed to enforce care, contact or residence arrangements. It is only exercised when the child's interests and well-being are (under threat of being) harmed by the lack of care being shown by the holder(s) of

---

171 M. MATTHÉ, 'Handhaving van de omgangsregeling met kinderen door middel van private sancties', *FJR* 2011/122, para. 3.
172 Rechtbank Leeuwaarden, 5 February 2009, LJN BH2027.
173 Hoge Raad, 9 July 2010, LJN BM4301.
174 Hof 's-Gravenhage, 23 February 2011, LJN BQ8296.

parental responsibilities. Research has not shown that this mechanism is used to enforce care arrangements.

4.7. SUMMARY

Around the start of this millennium there was much discussion on issues surrounding co-parenting, with joint parental responsibilities upon request and the automatic continuation of parental responsibilities after separation being adopted in quick succession in 1995 and 1998 and initiatives on regulating care arrangements and promoting residential co-parenting through legislation being proposed soon after.[175] When the Promotion of Continued Parenting and Proper Divorce Act (*Wet bevordering voortgezet ouderschap en zorgvuldige scheiding*) eventually came into force in 2009, it had been stripped of its more ambitious provisions such as a presumption that the parents should share the time spent with their child or children equally after separation and the introduction of administrative divorce. Instead the Act grants children the right to equal care by both parents after parental separation, which, as the *Hoge Raad* has ruled, does not entail a right to an equal division of time, and obliges the parents to make care arrangements for their child(ren) when they separate and to lay them down in a parenting plan.[176] While the right to equal care does not entail a right to residential co-parenting, it does seem to imply at least the joint exercise of parental responsibilities and encourages residential co-parenting.

The joint exercise of parental responsibilities after separation has become the norm. This can be easily explained by the fact that legal parents automatically gain parental responsibilities, and birthmothers, men married to or in a registered partnership with the birthmother, and women married to or in a registered partnership with the birthmother whose child was conceived with the help of an anonymous donor automatically become legal parents upon the child's birth. Unmarried partners can become legal parents (and thus gain parental responsibilities) through recognition or a court order. And even those who are not legal parents can gain parental responsibilities if two other persons do not already exercise these responsibilities.[177] Once a person holds parental responsibilities, losing them is not easy. In most cases a court order is needed.[178]

The holders of joint parental responsibilities should exercise them jointly, which in practice means that either holder can make daily life

175 See sections 4.1 and 4.2 of Chapter 4.
176 See section 4.2 of Chapter 4.
177 See section 4.3.2 of Chapter 4.
178 See section 4.3.4 of Chapter 4.

decisions about the child's upbringing and should regularly consult the other holder, especially when it comes to important decisions. The court can interfere when the holders of parental responsibilities cannot come to a decision together or when the well-being of the child is at risk.[179]

Children, especially those of 12 years of age or older, have the right to be heard, can in certain cases intervene in family law proceedings concerning them, and, in exceptional circumstances, can commence proceedings themselves.[180]

Finally, Dutch law contains various enforcement mechanisms for family law orders. However, in practice it is difficult for the courts to make use of these measures without (further) harming the child.[181]

---

179 See section 4.3.3 of Chapter 4.

180 See section 4.5 of Chapter 4.

181 See section 4.6 of Chapter 4.

CHAPTER 5
THE BELGIAN LEGAL SYSTEM

5.1. HISTORY OF THE MAIN LEGAL AND SOCIETAL DEVELOPMENTS

The Belgian rules on parentage, parental responsibilities and, much later, residential arrangements have been undergoing major changes from the late 1960s onwards. These changes are focused on placing the parents of both genders in an equal position and to stimulate joined care for their child, even in situations where the parents have never been or no longer constitute a couple.

Legal evolution followed and reflected the changes within society. Up until the 1970s the conservative, classic model was predominant: with the father working and the mother staying at home to care for the children and if the parents separated (which was relatively rare), the mother would usually be given sole parental authority (*hoederecht*) over the child or children and the father would be given contact every fortnight. From then onwards, however, many social changes occurred, such as families having less children, more women working outside the home, the growing number of people cohabiting outside of marriage, and the rise of fathers' rights movements, alongside with the growing insight into the psychology of 'good' parenting. These changes led to an evaluation of the laws surrounding parental responsibilities, thereby loosening the ties between marriage and parentage.[1]

The joint exercise of parental *authority* was first introduced in 1965, but only during marriage and with the father having the decisive authority in case of a dispute.[2] Not until 1974 did the spouses gain an equal right to concurrently exercise parental authority and to make decisions on their children's upbringing during marriage. Upon separation one of the parents would be granted sole parental authority over the child. This caused much frustration among divorced fathers as it was usually the mothers who would gain sole parental authority.[3]

---

1 D. MORTELMANS et al., *Scheiding in Vlaanderen*, Acco, 2011, p. 135.

2 F. SWENNEN, *Het personen- en familierecht*, Antwerp Intersentia, 2014, p. 401.

3 N. MASSAGER, *Droit familial de l'enfance. Filiation, autorité parentale, hébergement*, Bruylant, 2009, pp. 210-211.

The notion that parental authority was derived from marriage was replaced by parental authority being linked to (biological) parentage in 1987.[4] However, joint parental authority in the case of separated parents was still not possible. After divorce, one parent would get parental authority over the child or children and the other would gain a right of *contact*.[5]

At the beginning of the 1990s discussions started on revising the legislation concerning parental authority and the desire to introduce joint parental responsibilities (also post-parental separation) was heard. This resulted in multiple bills being submitted in 1992-93, which eventually led to the 1995 law reform.[6]

5.1.1. THE 1995 LAW REFORM

With the coming into force of the Act of 13 April 1995, the joint exercise of parental responsibilities became the legal norm, irrespective of the parents' (formal) relationship.[7] Disputes between the parents came under the jurisdiction of the courts. This Act did not address the child's residence, but focused instead on care. Article 374 of the Belgian Civil Code was changed to commence with the notion that 'when parents do not cohabit, they *continue* to exercise parental responsibilities jointly'.[8] However, the Article does give the courts the authority to deviate from this norm.

As an exception, the courts may decide to grant one of the parents sole, or partly sole, (exercise of) parental responsibilities if the parents cannot reach an agreement over the child's or children's residence or other important aspects of the child's or children's upbringing. If the court decides to order sole parental responsibilities, it must provide arguments as to why it is deviating from the norm, because there is theoretically no reason to depart from the norm of the joint exercise of parental responsibilities when both parents are present in the lives of the children and have the intention to do the best that they can.[9]

---

4 *Wet van 31 maart 1987 tot wijziging van een aantal bepalingen betreffende de afstamming*, BS (Belgisch Staatsblad), 27 May 1987.

5 F. SWENNEN, 2014, p. 401.

6 See the bill by Beaufays, 16 January 1992, Gedr. St. Kamer, B.Z. 1991-92, no. 34/1; the bill by Simons and Vogels, 13 February 1992, Gedr. St. Kamer, B.Z. 1991-92, nr. 165/1; the bill by Swennen and Landuyt, 9 March 1992, Gedr. St. Kamer, B.Z. 1991-92, no. 298/1; and the bill by Coveliers, 20 October 1993, Gedr. St. Kamer, 1993-94, no. 1187/1.

7 *Wet 13 april 1995 betreffende de gezamelijke uitoefening van het ouderlijk gezag*, BS, 24 May 1995, entered into force on 3 June 1995.

8 '*Lorsque les père et mère ne vivent pas ensemble, l'exercice de l'autorité parentale reste conjoint et la présomption prévue à l'article 373, alinéa 2, s'applique.*'

9 Court Brussels (appeal), 5 September 2007, 2006/JR/180.

An extensive justification of the decision on parental responsibilities is only necessary when granting sole parental responsibilities. If, alternatively, the court, in its decision, maintains the norm of joint parental responsibilities, the decision only needs to be tested against the best interests of the child. This test will usually be only *marginal* when *parents agree* on the exercise of parental responsibilities and have reached an agreement on a (provisional) care arrangement. If the *parents cannot agree* on certain aspects of the exercise of parental responsibilities, the court will first confirm the joint exercise of parental responsibilities and will then consider the issues over which there is not yet agreement.[10]

5.1.2. THE 2006 LAW REFORM

The joint exercise of parental responsibilities by separated parents has already been the legal norm in Belgium since 1995. However, the joint exercise of parental responsibilities, also known by the term shared care, is something which is not easily qualified, quantified or explained, especially in daily life. It is more than just the legal title of being a parent and more practical than parental authority. It implies parents working together to raise their child or children, but how this 'working together' is supposed to be shaped and how equal the division of the time a child spends with either parent should be is unspecified. How shared can the care be if the child lives with only one parent, who is the main carer in daily life?

Interest groups representing parents who were not the main carers of their children, usually consisting of fathers, such as the *Mouvement pour l'égalité parentale* and the *Belangenverdediging Gescheiden Mannen en hun Kinderen (BGMK)*, wanted to see shared care in a more practical, visible sense. These organisations wanted not just the undefined idea of care to be equally shared between the parents, but also the time a child spends with each parent, which is much easier to measure that the vague concept of care. In short, fathers' rights organisations wanted equally shared residence of their children in the form of a 50/50 residential co-parenting to become the legal norm.[11]

These wishes were met in 2004 and 2005, when several different bills on contact with children and parental responsibilities over children were submitted to the Chamber (*Kamer van Volksvertegenwoordigers*). The bills by Swennen, Wathelet and Onkelinx explicitly concerned the residential

---

10 R. UYTTENDAELE, in P. Senaeve, *Co-ouderschap en omgangsrecht. Commentaar op de Wet van 13 april 1995*, Maklu, 1995, pp. 159-162.

11 I. MARTENS, in P. Senaeve e.a., *Verblijfsco-ouderschap. Uitvoering en sanctionering van verblijfs- en omgangsregelingen. Adoptie door personen van hetzelfde geslacht*, Intersentia, 2007, p. 17.

arrangements concerning children. Swennen proposed that every time a dispute over the (potential) residential arrangement arose, the parents would be obliged to deliberate together and try to reach an agreement. If that failed, an investigation by the social services should be conducted to allow the judge to make an informed decision. Another proposition was that should a parent request equally divided residence, the court should grant this request, unless it can justify that such an arrangement is materially impossible. The dispute over the residence of the child should be decided first, before all other disputes in the case. And, finally, the courts should respect any residential arrangement the parents have reached by agreement.[12] Wathelet and Milquet saw residential co-parenting as one of the viable options after parental separation, but did not wish to give it a special or priority status.[13] Onkelinx proposed to make residential co-parenting into a priority model from which the court could only deviate if there were indications to the contrary.[14]

Eventually the first two propositions were dropped and the proposition by the Minister of Justice, Onkelinx, led to a law reform promoting residential co-parenting and establishing rules on the enforcement of residential arrangements.[15]

The new law introduced an obligation for the court to assess with *priority* whether *equally divided residence* would best serve the interests of the child (and those of the child's parents), in case one (or both) of the parents requests this arrangement. The introduction of this priority obligation was meant to make the outcomes of residence disputes more predictable (legal clarity) and to diminish the amount of residence disputes brought before the courts.[16] Additionally, it was meant to increase equality between the parents.[17]

5.2. BACKGROUND OF THE LAW CURRENTLY IN PLACE

The law which currently governs residential co-parenting in Belgium came about through a governmental proposition with the goal of encouraging the

---

12 *Wetsvoorstel betreffende de verblijfsregeling van minderjarige kinderen bij hun niet-samenlevende ouders*, Parl. St. Kamer, no. 51-0975/001, 30 March 2004.

13 *Wetsvoorstel tot wijziging van artikel 374 van het Burgerlijk Wetboek en tot invoeging in hetzelfde Wetboek van de artikelen 374bis tot 374quater, betreffende de wijze van huisvesting van het kind wiens ouders gescheiden leven*, Parl. St. Kamer, no. 51-1509/001, 14 December 2004.

14 *Wetsontwerp tot het bevoorrechten van een gelijkmatig verdeelde huisvesting van het kind van wie de ouders gescheiden zijn en tot regeling van de gedwongen tenuitvoerlegging inzake huisvesting van het kind*, Parl. St. Kamer, no. 51-1673/001.

15 Parl. St. Kamer, no. 51-1673/018.

16 Parl. St. Kamer, no. 51-1673/001, Memorie van toelichting, pp. 4-5.

17 *Ibid.*, pp. 5-6.

child's residence to be equally divided between the divorced parents and to provide regulations for the enforcement of residential arrangements.[18] After some amendments were made, the proposition was adopted by the Chamber (*Kamer van Volksvertegenwoordigers*) on 30 March 2006 and approved, without any amendments, by the Senate on 8 June 2006.[19]

The new law added certain provisions to Article 374 of the Belgian Civil Code on the courts' authority to decide residence disputes. These provisions only apply to the situation where the child's or children's parents do not cohabit, irrespective of their (previous) marital status.[20] This means that not only divorced parents fall within the scope of this Article, but also parents who have previously cohabited but have since split up and parents who have never cohabited in the first place.[21]

The point of departure is still that parents are the most suitable to make a decision about where their child should live, and therefore if the parents reach a residential agreement the court will respect this agreement and implement it in its order, unless the agreement is manifestly contrary to the child's best interests. However, if they fail to make that decision, the court now has to consider residential co-parenting as the first option, but *only* if one of the parents *asks* for this arrangement. If both parents request other options than equally divided residence, without, for example, asking for residential co-parenting as a subsidiary claim, *the court cannot make a decision establishing residential co-parenting against both parents' wishes*.[22]

The motivation behind the introduction of this priority assessment obligation was to send the courts a clear message that equally divided residence was preferred above arrangements that are not based on equality between parents and to prevent that residence would be appointed arbitrarily with one parent (usually the mother).[23]

When considering the original proposition for a law reform, several objections were raised against equally divided residence as a preferential model, many of which concerned the practicality of shared residence: if such a model was suitable for very young children, whether it would cost the parents more money, whether a priority model would ignore the myriad of different practical situations and what if some children simply fared better living with only one of their parents?[24] However, it was

18 Parl. St. Kamer 2004-05, no. 51-1673/001.

19 P. SENAEVE et al., *Verblijfsco-ouderschap. Uitvoering en sanctionering van verblijfs- en omgangsregelingen. Adoptie door personen van hetzelfde geslacht*, Intersentia, 2007, p. xvii.

20 '*Lorsque les parents ne vivent pas ensemble [...].*'

21 I. MARTENS, 2007, p. 7.

22 Article 374 of the Belgian Civil Code; '*A défaut d'accord, en cas d'autorité parentale conjointe, le tribunal examine prioritairement, à la demande d'un des parents au moins, la possibilité de fixer l'hébergement de l'enfant de manière égalitaire entre ses parents.*'

23 I. MARTENS, 2007, pp. 16-17.

24 Parl. St. Kamer, no. 51-1673/006, Amendement no. 21 (Wathelet), Verantwoording.

considered that in the end, the best interests of the child should prevail. Having a strong familial connection with both parents was in general seen to be in the best interests of the child, while long, confusing court cases were detrimental to the best interests of the child. Having a preferential model would create more clarity and make disputes over the child's residence more predictable and therefore less lengthy. Because equally divided residence would not be an obligatory residential arrangement, but the first option considered with room for deviation, the court could still give necessary consideration and weight to case-specific practical obstacles.[25]

Another objection was of a more theoretical nature; it was the fear that by setting up a priority residential model the government would intrude too much into the private lives of parents by prescribing a 'right' way to bring up their children. This argument was countered by the consideration that any residential arrangement that the court is asked to make in case of a dispute is already an intrusion into the private and family lives of parents, and that making one of the residential arrangements into a model to be assessed with priority does not change this situation for the better or for the worse.[26]

There has also been some discussion about the term 'equally divided residence', which implies a 50/50 division. It was suggested to change this term into 'as equally divided as possible' to make it less strict. Eventually the government retained the strict term to indicate that a preference for a 50/50 division was indeed intended.[27] This means that the Belgian model of equally divided residence is a narrower term than the term 'residential co-parenthood' as discussed in this book.

In addition to expanding on rules about the child's residence post-parental separation, the 2006 law reform was intended to improve the opportunities (for parents) to invoke enforcement measures in case of non-compliance with residence or contact arrangements. For this purpose, the new Article 387ter was added to the Belgian Civil Code. This Article gives the court the authority, in case of non-compliance with an earlier decision on residence or contact, to take enforcement measures (such as imposing a fine or ordering the forced execution of the original decision), to order an (extensive) investigation into the situation, to attempt to reconcile the parties, or to make a new order on parental responsibilities and/or residence.

While the 2006 law reform was mainly focused on introducing the preference for equally divided residence and issues concerning the

25 Parl. St. Kamer, no. 51-1673/014, pp. 6-8.

26 I. MARTENS, 2007, pp. 18-19.

27 Parl. St. Kamer, no. 51-1673/014, Verslag namens de subcommissie familierecht, 65.

enforcement of residential arrangements, an interesting procedural instrument was also proposed. It was an additional provision to Article 387bis of the Belgian Civil Code that would oblige a court making a decision about or having to do with parental responsibilities (including residence) to make a preliminary decision and then to revise this decision and make a final order at a later date, not exceeding one year.[28]

This part of the proposal was quickly disposed of, because it was considered that it was perfectly possible to evaluate whether the arrangements determined in the preliminary decision were working well and that no review was necessary. This does not mean that the court is unable to make a preliminary decision of its own accord, if it deems this to be necessary, and to determine a date (no longer than a year from the preliminary decision) on which this decision will be revised and the final decision will be taken. It merely has no obligation to do so in *every* case.[29]

In light of this research, it would have been very interesting to see the outcomes of the application of such an obligation, as this would demonstrate whether it is indeed possible for parents to oversee all the practical implications of both the separation and the new arrangements at the time of separation.

An important procedural innovation that ended up in the final version of the 2006 legal reform is that a case concerning parental responsibilities will remain pending from the moment it was first brought before a court until the child or children in question reach the age of majority or are emancipated.[30] This means that the procedure will be easier and cheaper as parties no longer have to file a new petition and can have easier and quicker access to the courts for, for example, enforcement orders in case of non-compliance (more about that in Chapter 6).[31]

5.3. JOINT PARENTAL RESPONSIBILITIES

In general, (legal) parents hold and exercise parental responsibilities over their minor child (that is, a child who has not yet reached the age of 18) until this child reaches the age of majority.[32] However, younger children are no longer subjected to parental responsibilities when they marry,[33]

---

28 Parl. St. Kamer, no. 51-1673/001, p. 28.
29 I. MARTENS, 2007, pp. 135-137.
30 Article 387bis of Book One of the Belgian Civil Code.
31 I. MARTENS, 2007, pp. 139-141.
32 Article 372 of the Belgian Civil Code.
33 Article 476 of the Belgian Civil Code. Instead, the spouse who has reached the age of majority becomes the financial representative of the other spouse, see DEKKERS, p. 170.

or are emancipated by a court order.[34] Only children over the age of 15 can be emancipated upon the parents' request, the request of the child's guardian or the request of the *procureur des Konings*.[35] If it turns out that after emancipation the minor is not able to care for himself or herself, the emancipation by court order can be retracted, and the parent or parents regain parental responsibilities over the minor. After such a retraction, a new emancipation order can no longer be made, although emancipation through marriage is still possible.[36]

5.3.1. PARENTAL RESPONSIBILITIES: MEANING AND CONTENT

The meaning and content of parental responsibilities are not explicitly and exhaustively provided within the Belgian Civil Code. However, legislation, case law and the literature provide plenty of examples as to what rights and duties may fall within the term.

According to Article 203 of the Belgian Civil Code, parents, meaning legal parents, are bound to provide, proportional to their means, for the housing, maintenance, health, supervision, upbringing, education and the development of their children. This seems to be mainly a financial provision, as all consulted case law associated with this article deals with financial disputes on child maintenance. Parents cannot make an agreement to the extent that one of them will limit or be discharged from all of his or her (financial) parental responsibilities vis-à-vis the child. They may however agree on their contribution, even with a so-called *nihilstelling* (one parent contributes nothing). The duty for legal parents to provide for their children is one of public order and therefore it is not up to the parents to divest themselves of this responsibility,[37] not even if the children treat their parents badly. It has been explicitly addressed in the case law of the *Cour de Cassation* that while children have a duty to respect their parents, the absence of this respect does not absolve their parents of their duty to provide for them.[38]

---

34 Article 477 of the Belgian Civil Code.

35 F. SWENNEN, *Het personen- en familierecht*, Intersentia, 2012, p. 479; A *procureur des Konings* is a state-appointed legal professional whose tasks are very similar to those of the *officier van justitie* in the Dutch legal system. These tasks are listed in Articles 137-156 of the *Gerechtelijk Wetboek* and include prosecution (in criminal cases), advice and intervention.

36 Articles 485-486 of the Belgian Civil Code; F. SWENNEN, *Het personen- en familierecht*, Intersentia, 2012, p. 189.

37 Cass. AR 8750, 27 September 1990, *RW* 1990-91, p. 1089.

38 Article 376 of the Belgian Civil Code.

While there is a great deal of case law dealing with the financial aspects of parental responsibilities, this case law has fleshed out the contents of parental responsibilities beyond only the financial aspects. In its decision of 8 October 2003, the Belgian *Cour de Cassation* explained that parental responsibilities exist first and foremost to provide a child with the specific protection he or she needs because of his or her physical and mental vulnerability and that it is in the best interests of the child to have his or her parents exercising these responsibilities.[39] To be able to provide this special protection, those who exercise parental responsibilities have the right and duty to make daily decisions over the child's life - such as the clothing the child wears, what the child is allowed to do in his or her free time, who he or she interacts with socially - as well as more important decisions on the child's education, health, religious upbringing, etc.[40]

Definitions of parental responsibilities have also been provided by various Belgian scholars. Swennen, in *Het personen- en familierecht*, states that: parental responsibilities encompass the competence to make decisions over the person of the child and, if necessary, to enforce these decisions. The goal of the exercise of parental responsibilities is to raise a child into an independent adult and this exercise is monitored by the government.[41] Pintens, in his national report for the CEFL, describes parental responsibilities as 'a collection of rights necessary for the parents to properly fulfil their duties relating to the person and property of their minor children'.[42] By gaining parental responsibility, parents gain authority over the child and the right to care for the child and to have contact with him or her. They may also represent the child in all civil actions and decide on fundamental options concerning the child's upbringing.[43]

5.3.2. ATTRIBUTION OF (JOINT) PARENTAL RESPONSIBILITIES

The main rule on the attribution of parental responsibilities is that the *legal* parents of the child automatically have parental responsibilities and that they should exercise them together even after separation.[44] This has been the case since the 1995 law reform, which introduced the Belgian

39 Cass. AR 134/2003, 8 October 2003, *Rev. Trim. Dr. Fam.* 2004, p. 185.
40 F. SWENNEN, 2014, pp. 403-406.
41 *Ibid.*, p. 401.
42 W. PINTENS in K. Boele-Woelki et al., *European Family Law in Action Volume III: Parental responsibilities*, Intersentia, 2005, p. 1.
43 *Ibid.*, pp. 20-21.
44 See Article 372 of the Belgian Civil Code for legal parents through affiliation and Articles 353-8 and 356-1 for legal parents through adoption.

concept of co-parenting,[45] although the link between legal parentage and parental responsibilities had already been established in 1987.[46] Parental responsibilities commence automatically from the moment a person's legal parentage with respect to the child has been established.[47]

This means that in order to know who has parental responsibilities over a child, it is necessary to know who can be a legal parent. A child can only have a maximum of two legal parents.[48] Below it is set out how parents can become legal parents (and thus acquire parental responsibilities over the child).

5.3.2.1. The mother

Maternity can be established in three different ways. By far the most common way is by recording the mother's name on the birth certificate immediately after the birth (mater semper certa est), which is prescribed by law.[49] Giving birth anonymously or even discretely is not allowed in Belgium.[50] There exists a legal presumption that the mother's name on the birth certificate is the name of the woman who has given birth to the child.[51]

If, for some reason, the birth certificate does not contain the mother's name, for example because the mother gave birth anonymously abroad, or if the birth certificate has been lost, then maternity can also be established by the voluntary recognition of a child by a woman or by a court order establishing maternity.[52] These two means of establishing maternity are only possible if there is not already a mother's name on the birth certificate and the latter also when the name on the birth certificate is incorrect. Recognition is voluntary, but might need the consent of the parent whose legal parentage has already been established, if there is one, and the consent of the child, if the child is older than 12 years. The court may substitute either type of consent with a court order.[53] Establishment by a court, on the other hand, is usually not voluntary.[54] Unfortunately, no statistical data are available on how often recognition by the mother actually takes place in Belgium.

---

45 Cass. C.09.0125.N, 3 June 2010.

46 By the *Wet van 31 maart 1987 tot wijziging van een aantal bepalingen betreffende de afstamming*, BS, 27 May 1987; N. Massager, *Droit familial de l'enfance. Filiation, autorité parentale, hébergement*, Bruylant, 2009, p. 222.

47 P. SENAEVE, *Compedium van het personen- en familierecht*, Acco, 2011, p. 377.

48 F. SWENNEN, 2014, pp. 309-310.

49 Article 312 of the Belgian Civil Code.

50 See www.kindengezin.be (last visited 30 April 2015).

51 G. VERSCHELDEN, *Handboek Belgisch Familierecht*, die Keure, 2010, p. 25.

52 Articles 313 and 314 of the Belgian Civil Code, respectively.

53 Article 313 of the Belgian Civil Code.

54 G. VERSCHELDEN, 2010, pp. 29-36.

Prior to 1987 the presumption that the woman who had given birth to the child was automatically the child's mother did not exist for unmarried women. Women had to legally recognize their illegitimate children to establish legal parentage. This legal practice was considered to be in violation of the right to family life and the prohibition of discrimination by the European Court of Human Rights because the interest of an illegitimate child in having such a maternal bond established at birth is no less than that of a legitimate child.[55]

5.3.2.2. *The father*

In Belgian law there exists a presumption of paternity in the case of marriage. This means that a child who is born within a marriage (or within 300 days after the dissolution or annulment of the marriage) is assumed to be the child of the (legal) mother's husband.[56] There are multiple possible exceptions to this presumption. The mother's husband does not become the child's legal father if the child was born more than 300 days after the husband's disappearance, after divorce proceedings have been started, or after the parents officially started living at different addresses; if, in the case of artificial insemination or another form of conception by another man, the husband did not consent to the conception; or if the father, mother, child, biological father, the female co-parent, relatives of the deceased husband or the previous husband of the mother successfully deny legal parentage in court.[57]

For a father who is not married to the legal mother of the child, irrespective of whether the two officially cohabit, there are two ways of becoming a legal parent and thus gaining parental responsibilities: recognition (*erkenning*) of the child or an order establishing parentage.[58] Just as in the case of the legal mother, recognition is a voluntary request by the father, while the establishment of parentage can also be imposed by the court against his will. For recognition it is important that the child does not already have a legal father or a legal female co-parent (*meemoeder*), he has not been charged with or convicted of the rape of the legal mother, he and the legal mother are not relatives within the prohibited degrees of consanguinity, and that the legal mother, if there is one, consents to the recognition of the child. If the mother will not give her consent, the dispute can be brought before the court and it may substitute the mother's consent with an order, unless it is proven that the man is not the biological

55 ECHR, 13 June 1979, App. no. 6833/74, para. 39.
56 Article 315 of the Belgian Civil Code.
57 Article 318(1) of the Belgian Civil Code. Also see G. VERSCHELDEN, 2010, pp. 41-42, 88-100.
58 Articles 319 and 322 of the Belgian Civil Code, respectively.

father of the child or if the court deems the recognition to be against the best interests of the child. Recognition can occur before the child is born. Then the father gains parental responsibilities upon his child's birth.[59] The mother, the child and even the father can start a procedure for an order establishing legal fatherhood. The court would then need to investigate the evidence and make a decision.[60]

5.3.2.3. *Mother's female partner*

Up until January 2015 the only way for the mother's female partner to gain parental responsibilities over the child was by means of adoption.[61] Being married to the mother did not create the same presumption of (legal) parentage that exists for the mother's husband. The mother's wife therefore did not automatically become the legal parent of the child born within her marriage to the legal mother.[62]

This changed when the 2014 Act on the establishment of the filiation of the female co-parent (*Wet houdende de vaststelling van de afstamming van de meemoeder*) came into force on 1 January 2015. This Act amended the Belgian Civil Code to give the mother's female partner (mostly) the same parentage rights as the mother's male partner would have in the same circumstances. Aside from a few other provisions, the Act ads Chapter 2/1 on the determination of the filiation of the female co-parent (*vaststelling van de afstamming van meemoederszijde*) to Title Seven of Book One of the Belgian Civil Code.

Article 325/1 of the Belgian Civil Code provides the point of departure, namely that as long as the child has no legal father, the legal parentage of the female co-parent may be established.[63]

If the child is born within the marriage (or not later than 300 days after the dissolution or annulment of the marriage) of the mother and her wife there exists a presumption that the wife is the child's legal parent and she becomes the legal parent upon the child's birth.[64] This presumption can be disputed before the family court by the mother, the child (after he or she has reached 12 years of age), a man seeking to establish his legal fatherhood, or a woman seeking to establish her legal co-parenthood.[65]

If the mother and her female partner are not married, the female partner can become the legal parent of the child by means of recognition.

---

59 Article 329bis of the Belgian Civil Code. See also G. VERSCHELDEN, 2010, pp. 45-51.
60 *Ibid.*, pp. 64-76.
61 Beleidsnota Justitie, Parl. St. Kamer, no. 53-2586/027, p. 18.
62 G. VERSCHELDEN, 2010, p. 38.
63 '*Lorsque la paternité n'est pas établie en vertu du chapitre 2, la comaternité peut être établie en vertu des dispositions du présent chapitre*'.
64 Article 325/2 of the Belgian Civil Code.
65 Article 325/3 of the Belgian Civil Code.

The woman wishing to recognise a child must fulfil the same conditions under Article 329bis of the Belgian Civil Code that a man wishing to recognise a child would have to fulfil: the consent of the mother (and the child if the child is 12 years or older) and not have been charged with or convicted of the rape of the legal mother. Her recognition request will be denied if she did not consent to the artificial insemination of the legal mother, if she and the legal mother are within the prohibited degrees of consanguinity that would make a marriage between them impossible, or if the recognition would be against the best interests of the child.[66] In the same way the presumption of the legal parentage of the legal mother's wife can be disputed, and the recognition can be contested by the legal mother, the child, or the man or woman who wishes to gain legal parentage over the child.[67]

Finally, the mother's female partner or ex-partner can request the family court to grant her legal parentage.[68] However, this is more a theoretic possibility than one that is likely to be used by the female partner, because she can legally recognize the child and if she does not have the mother's consent, she can ask the court to substitute a court order for consent. This provision is therefore more likely to be used by the mother or the child if the female (ex-)partner is unwilling to become the legal parent.

As has been explained earlier, legal parents are holders of parental responsibilities. Thus when the mother's female partner gains legal parentage, she automatically gains parental responsibilities over the child. This is of course unless legal parentage is established prior to the birth of the child. In that case the female co-parent gains parental responsibilities automatically upon the child's birth.

5.3.2.4. (Other) non-parents

A person over the age of 25 can, voluntarily, with the consent of the legal parent(s), become the child's guardian.[69] The guardian then takes over the responsibility of raising the child and managing the child's finances.[70] This is known as *pleegvoogdij*.[71] This is a contract between the parent(s)

---

66 Articles 325/4 and 325/5 of the Belgian Civil Code.

67 Article 325/7 of the Belgian Civil Code.

68 Articles 325/8-325/10 of the Belgian Civil Code.

69 Article 475bis of the Belgian Civil Code, '*Lorsqu'une personne âgée d'au moins 25 ans s'engage à entretenir un enfant mineur non émancipé, à l'élever et à le mettre en état de gagner sa vie, elle peut devenir son tuteur officieux, moyennant l'accord de ceux dont le consentement est requis pour l'adoption des mineurs.*'

70 Paragraph 1 of Article 405 of the Belgian Civil Code; '*Le tuteur prend soin de la personne du mineur. Il l'éduque en se conformant aux principes éventuellement adoptés par les parents, notamment […]*'.

71 Articles 475bis-475septies of the Belgian Civil Code. According to Swennen, this institution of *pleegvoogdij* is only rarely used in practice. See F. SWENNEN, 2014, p. 411.

and the prospective guardian, which needs to be approved by the family court (*familierechtbank*)[72] in order to be legally binding.[73] The guardian thus voluntarily takes on the exercise of the majority of parental responsibilities. If a prospective guardian is married, he or she will not only need the consent of the legal parent(s) of the child to become a guardian, but also the consent of his or her own spouse.[74] There are different ways in which guardianship can end. It ends automatically if the child or the guardian dies, the child reaches the age of majority (or becomes emancipated), or if the child is adopted.[75] Additionally, the family court (*familierechtbank*)[76] can terminate a guardianship at the request of the guardian, the legal parent(s) or the *procureur des Konings*.[77]

Various types of guardianship exist. There is the *gemeenrechtelijke voogdij* which is the most common and is appointed if the parents are deceased or are incapable of caring for the child(ren).[78] There is the *provoogdij*, when the court appoints a guardian after the parent(s)' parental responsibilities have been taken away, the *OCMW-voogdij*, in case no holders of parental responsibilities exist, for example when the child is a foundling, and the *NBMV-voogdij* over illegal or refugee minors without parents or guardians.[79]

Step-parents have no special rights to obtain parental responsibilities. For a step-parent to obtain rights over the child either the agreement of the legal parents appointing him or her as the child's guardian or a court order is needed and even then the step-parent only gains a fraction of the responsibilities a parent would have.[80]

Non-parents can also adopt children.[81] Belgian law recognizes 'normal adoption' (*gewone adoptie*), in which case a child retains his or her original filiation ties, and 'full' adoption (*volle adoptie*), in which case the original filiation ties are severed and new ones are created between the child and the adoptive parent(s). It is possible to have a 'partial full adoption' when, for example, the filiation link with one parent remains, while the filiation

72 Article 67 of the *Wet betreffende de invoering van een familie- en jeugdrechtbank*.
73 Article 475ter of the Belgian Civil Code; *'Cette convention ne produit ses effets qu'après avoir été entérinée par le tribunal de la jeunesse, à la requête du tuteur officieux.'*
74 Article 475bis of the Belgian Civil Code; *'Un époux ne peut devenir tuteur officieux qu'avec le consentement de son conjoint.'*
75 Article 475quinquies of the Belgian Civil Code.
76 Article 69 of the *Wet betreffende de invoering van een familie- en jeugdrechtbank*.
77 Article 475sexies of the Belgian Civil Code. A procureur des Konings is a state-appointed legal professional whose tasks are very similar to those of the officier van justitie in the Dutch legal system. These tasks are listed in Articles 137-156 of the Gerechtelijk Wetboek and include prosecution (in criminal cases), advice and intervention.
78 Articles 389-420 of the Belgian Civil Code.
79 See for an overview F. SWENNEN, 2014, pp. 410-411.
80 W. PINTENS, 2005, p. 390.
81 Title VIII of the Belgian Civil Code.

link with the other parent is replaced. This happens when, for example, a step-father adopts the child: the mother remains the legal mother of the child, but the step-father gains legal parentage instead of the man who had gained legal parentage through filiation.[82] By gaining legal parentage, the adoptive parent also gains parental responsibilities over the child.

5.3.2.5. *Overview*

As one can see in the table below and can be inferred from the information in this section, parental responsibilities are tied to legal parentage. Those who cannot become the legal parents, cannot fully gain parental responsibilities.

For persons who do not or cannot acquire legal parentage ex lege, there is the opportunity to request a court order, or, in case of the unmarried father or unmarried mother's female partner, to recognise the child with the consent of the legal mother.

Table 3

Persons eligible for PR	PR automatically granted	PR through legal agreement with mother	PR through court order
Mother	x*		
Mother's husband	x*		
Mother's wife	x*		
Unmarried father	x*		
Unmarried partner who is not the legal father			
Adoptive parents			Adoption order
Non-parents			

* Ex lege upon becoming the legal parent.

5.3.3. EXERCISING (JOINT) PARENTAL RESPONSIBILITIES

Both (legal) parents who are holders of parental responsibilities, and those who are not, have the capacity to make certain important decisions about the *civil status* of the child. If the child has more than one legal parent, they must make those decisions jointly or one parent must make the decision and the other must give his or her explicit consent. For these decisions, no

82 F. SWENNEN, 2014, pp. 378-379.

presumption of consent exists.[83] These decisions all relate to the person of the child. It concerns the right to agree to the child's adoption[84] or to allow the child to be placed in foster care (*pleegvoogdij*),[85] the right to request the emancipation of the child,[86] the right to consent to the child's marriage[87] or to request its annulment,[88] and the right to agree to the granting of Belgian nationality to the child.[89]

All (legal) parents additionally have the right to have contact with the child, which for parents who jointly exercise parental responsibilities means that if they cohabit, their child or children will reside with them and if they do not live together, then a residential arrangement concerning the child or children should be made.[90]

Parents who hold (joint) parental responsibilities have certain additional rights, mainly those of a financial nature. They are in charge of the administration of the child's property[91] and have the right to the profits from their belongings.[92]

Since the coming into force of the 1995 Act, as a general rule, both parents jointly exercise parental responsibilities and therefore all decisions about their child or children should be made by them jointly or by one of the parents with the consent of the other. However, it could be very complicated for third parties to know if a child still has both parents and if certain things, for example the joining of a sports club, have been approved by both of them. Therefore, a presumption of consent exists, meaning that it is assumed that the parent who makes the decision has the consent of the other parent.[93]

Important decisions that have seemingly been made by the parents jointly or in agreement, but then turn out to be based on an error can be reversed or remedied. The Court of Appeal of Liège allowed an appeal where the parents had agreed, at a lower court, upon a care arrangement, including the school choice for their three children, but during the appeal it became apparent that the agreement about the school choice was based on a misunderstanding and the mother did not actually agree on the established school choice. She successfully argued that the current school

---

83 F. SWENNEN, 2014, pp. 403-404.
84 Article 348-3 of the Belgian Civil Code.
85 Article 475bis of the Belgian Civil Code.
86 Article 477 of the Belgian Civil Code.
87 Article 148 of the Belgian Civil Code.
88 Article 191 of the Belgian Civil Code.
89 Articles 8 and 9 of the Wetboek van de Belgische Nationaliteit.
90 F. SWENNEN, 2014, p. 404.
91 Article 376 of the Belgian Civil Code.
92 Article 384 of the Belgian Civil Code.
93 See Articles 373 and 374 of the Belgian Civil Code.

choice was contrary to the interests of the children and the Court of Appeal ordered a change of school.[94]

Exceptions to the general rule that both parents should exercise parental responsibilities jointly and that they should make important decisions together, are, however, possible, both in the sense that the exercise of parental responsibilities can be attributed to only one of the parents, as well as that a certain component of parental responsibilities can be attributed to one parent only.[95] For example, the District Court of Brussels ruled that it is possible that one of the parents is granted the right to administer the child's property by a court order.[96]

Usually it is clear from the facts or precedent which decisions fall within the joint exercise of parental responsibilities. There has been extensive case law on decisions concerning the child's choice of school, health and finances. Recently it has also been decided that the right to choose the child's first name or to make a request to change it also primarily belongs to parents who jointly exercise parental responsibilities. This has been suggested in the *Rafifi* case. In this case the mother applied to the court to change her son's first name, but was denied, because the father had not petitioned for the name change together with the mother (as he did not agree with this name change) and the parents held joint parental responsibilities. According to the *Raad van State* these kinds of decisions should be made by both holders of parental responsibilities and a mother alone, as a legal representative of the child, cannot apply for a name change.[97]

The decision to move with the child abroad is also one that needs to be agreed upon by both holders of joint parental responsibilities. If the resident parent relocates with the child abroad without the other parent's consent, that would constitute child abduction and a parent suspecting the other parent of planning child abduction can request the court for an interim measure.[98]

5.3.3.1. *Court's procedural powers to restrict and regulate the exercise of parental responsibilities*

While parents are *expected* to exercise parental responsibilities jointly and reach consensus together, disputes do occur, and when that happens either parent can bring the dispute before the family court (*familierechtbank*). The court can then engage in one of the following: it can either authorize one of the parents to make certain decisions on his or her own, or it can decide

94 Court Liège (appeal), 26 August 2008, *JLMB*, 2009/3, pp. 128-132.
95 See Articles 373 and 374 of the Belgian Civil Code.
96 Court Brussels (first instance), 3 April 2007, *T. Fam.* 2007, vol. 96.
97 Raad van State, 18 September 2006, no. 162.503.
98 Court Ghent, 2 May 2005, *TJK*, 2006/3, pp. 246-251.

the disputed issue itself in the best interests of the child. In line with the court's ability to make an order authorizing a parent to act alone – without the consent of the other parent where this would normally be necessary – lies the opposite competence: to order that certain decisions concerning the child's upbringing can only be made with the explicit agreement of both parents (where this agreement would usually be assumed).[99]

Restricting a parent's parental responsibilities is sometimes a necessary measure to send a message to a parent failing in his or her duties and to remedy a practical problem without making use of the ultimum remedium of removing parental responsibilities from one of the parents. This happened in the 2007 Court of Appeal of Brussels case in which the court limited the father's rights in deciding on the children's school enrolment, philosophical and religious upbringing and health issues after he had failed to properly respond to requests from the children's school and had done little to improve communication with the mother.[100]

In disputes concerning the residence, health, upbringing, education, recreation or religious upbringing or the child or when there is no dispute, but the agreement the parents have reached is contrary to the best interests of the child, the court may decide to (partly or fully) attribute sole parental responsibilities to one of the (non-cohabiting) parents.[101]

In case a parent uses social benefits intended for the care of children for other purposes and raises a child in inappropriate circumstances (malnutrition, a lack of proper housing or hygiene), the juvenile court (*jeugdrechtbank*) may appoint a guardian to oversee these social benefits.[102]

When the child or children have committed a crime and have been penalised for this and the parents are clearly not concerned with their child(ren)'s delinquency, the juvenile court (*jeugdrechtbank*) may oblige the parent(s) to attend a parenting course (*ouderstage*) if it is likely that this will benefit the child.[103]

5.3.3.2. *Care arrangements*

Belgian law does not require separating parents to make parenting plans or other types of specified agreements on the care of their children after separation. However, on 7 January 2013 S. Becq, a member of the Belgian CD&V party, submitted a bill that would make parenting plans compulsory in the case of parental divorce and this was then followed by

---

99 Articles 373 and 374 of the Belgian Civil Code.

100 Court Brussels (appeal), 5 December 2007, Act. dr. fam., 2008, p. 13.

101 Paragraph 1 of Article 374 of the Belgian Civil Code.

102 Article 29 of the *Wet van 8 april 1965 betreffende de jeugdbescherming* (*Juvenile Protection Act*).

103 Article 29bis of the *Wet van 8 april 1965 betreffende de jeugdbescherming* (*Juvenile Protection Act*).

a new, revised, but very similar bill with the same name on 14 July 2014.[104] The bill is still pending and its future is as yet uncertain.

5.3.4. DISCHARGE OF (JOINT) PARENTAL RESPONSIBILITIES

Children are subject to parental responsibilities until they reach the age of majority. This means that parents automatically lose parental responsibilities when the child becomes 18 years of age or when he or she is emancipated, either by an emancipation order or because he or she marries.[105]

Parental responsibilities also come to an end upon the death of the child or the person exercising them.[106]

A discharge or loss of parental responsibilities in other situations requires a court order. This is either an adoption order, transferring parentage and parental responsibilities onto other person(s), or an order discharging a person or persons (fully or partially) from parental responsibilities in order to protect the child.

Those parents who have had a criminal penalty imposed for an act perpetrated against the child (or with the help of the child or his or her descendants); or who have endangered the health, security or morality of the child by maltreatment, abuse of authority, obvious bad behaviour or serious negligence; or who have married a person who has been discharged of their parental responsibilities, *can* be fully or partially discharged from their parental responsibilities by the court at the request of the public prosecutor (*openbaar ministerie*). The discharge can concern all children or only one or several.[107] While the court will usually ask the social services to conduct an investigation before deciding to discharge a parent or parents from parental responsibilities, it is not obliged to do so.[108] A discharge of parental responsibilities can be reversed and parental responsibilities can be regained by a court order, but only if this is in the best interests of the child.[109]

Finally, it is possible that a parent (partially) loses parental responsibilities because of a court order granting the other parent sole parental responsibilities. A parent who loses parental responsibilities in this manner,

---

104 *Wetsvoorstel tot wijziging van de wetgeving met het oog op de invoering van het ouderschapsplan bij* echtscheiding, Parl. St. Kamer, no. 53-2595/001 and Parl. St. Kamer, no. 54-0066/001.

105 Articles 388, 476 and 486 of the Belgian Civil Code respectively.

106 P. SENAEVE, p. 377; W. PINTENS, 2005, p. 55.

107 Article 32 of *Wet van 8 april 1965 betreffende de jeugdbescherming* (*Juvenile Protection Act).*

108 Hof van Cassatie, 20 May 2009, *RW*, 2010-11, no. 21, 22 January 2011, pp. 871-872.

109 Article 60 of *Wet van 8 april 1965 betreffende de jeugdbescherming*.

retains the right to have contact with the child and to information about the child's upbringing.[110]

5.4. CHILD'S RESIDENCE

According to Article 108 of the Belgian Civil Code, the child's official (or main) residence (*woonplaats*) is with (one of) the legal parent(s) or with his or her guardian. A person, including a child, can only have *one* official residence.[111] It is therefore not the case that children in a shared residence arrangement *legally* have two *official* residences. Nonetheless, in practice, the 2006 law reform encourages arrangements in which not only the care of the child or children is more or less equally shared between the parents, but also the time the child or children spend(s) with both parents.[112]

5.4.1. ASSIGNING OR CHOOSING RESIDENCE

Separated parents decide together with whom the child should have his or her residence. If they reach an agreement, the competent court will approve this agreement, unless the agreement is *manifestly contrary to the best interests of the child*.[113] The agreement could be on the full or partial residence arrangement (for example, only an arrangement on the division of holidays).[114] The point of departure is thus party autonomy: it is assumed that the parents are in the best position to judge what residential arrangement is best for their child or children and would be possible to execute in their daily lives. Additionally, if a residence arrangement is made by the parents, instead of being decided by the court, it is assumed that there is a greater possibility that they will abide by what they themselves have chosen and it is assumed that the child or children will experience the arrangement more positively, knowing that both parents have endorsed it.[115]

As seen above, the residential arrangement made by the parents will not be approved and incorporated in the decision if it is *manifestly* contrary

---

110 Paragraph 1 of Article 374 of the Belgian Civil Code.

111 F. SWENNEN, 2014, p. 158. In Flemish literature and translations of legal texts different words have confusingly been used to indicate residence: *woonplaats*, *huisvesting* and *verblijfplaats*. When this chapter mentions residence, the Flemish term *verblijfplaats* and the French term *l'hébergement* is meant, unless otherwise specified.

112 This is extensively explained in section 5.4.2 of Chapter 5.

113 Article 374 of the Belgian Civil Code.

114 H. VANBOCKRIJCK, in P. Senaeve et al., *Knelpunten echtscheiding, afstamming en verblijfsregelingen*, Intersentia, 2009, p. 193.

115 I. MARTENS, 2007, pp. 7-8.

to the best interests of the child. The words 'manifestly contrary' indicate that such a refusal to approve is not made lightly, that something more is needed than the fact that a different arrangement might be better for the child. The Explanatory Memorandum of the 2006 law indicates that the power of the court not to approve a residential arrangement agreed upon by the parents is even more restricted than it appears: residential arrangements agreed upon by the parents should only be tested *marginally* for clear counter-indications.[116]

This marginal test seems to be a departure from earlier case law as it appears that the 2006 law reform has made it more difficult for the courts to refuse to confirm arrangements made by the parents. In a 2004 District Court of Charleroi ruling the court refused to approve and incorporate a(n equal) shared residence arrangement, because it considered that the parents did not live apart in practice, but only wanted to establish a shared residence to be able to enjoy social and fiscal benefits. The incorporation was thus denied because it could result in financial fraud and not because it was (mainly) contrary to the best interests of the child.[117] It remains to be seen if such a situation will be dealt with similarly under the current law. Meanwhile, the Court of Appeal of Liège has ruled that for the court to be able to decide if a residential arrangement agreed upon by the parents is indeed contrary to the child's best interests, it needs to consider all the facts of the case, which may include having to hear the child.[118] This seems to be a more thorough investigation than the Explanatory Memorandum prescribes.

All this only applies if the parents manage to agree. If they cannot reach a compromise, then the competent court will have to make a decision. Even in disputes that concern (the exercise of) parental responsibilities, though not directly the child's residence, the court is in any case expected to make an order determining the child's official/main residence.[119] The court is also expected to first examine the possibility of (more or less) equally dividing the residence of the child between the parents *if at least one of the parents requests this*.[120]

---

116 Parl. St. Kamer, no. 51-1673/001, Memorie van toelichting, 11. '*Ce n'est que dans les cas où l'accord des parties lui paraîtra manifestement contraire à l'intérêt de l'enfant que le juge pourra s'y opposer. Il s'agit d'un contrôle marginal.*'

117 Court Charleroi, 14 May 2004, *Rev. Trim, dr. fam.* 2005, p. 238.

118 Court Liège (appeal), 29 May 2008, *JLMB*, 2009/3, pp. 127-128.

119 Article 374 of the Belgian Civil Code, '*Dans tous les cas, le juge détermine les modalités d'hébergement de l'enfant et le lieu où il est inscrit à titre principal dans les registres de la population.*'

120 Article 374 of the Belgian Civil Code, '*A défaut d'accord, en cas d'autorité parentale conjointe, le tribunal examine prioritairement, à la demande d'un des parents au moins, la possibilité de fixer l'hébergement de l'enfant de manière égalitaire entre ses parents.*'

A procedural side note: the competent court in these matters – meaning the court allowed to decide on matters of the child's residence – has for a long time been the juvenile court (*jeugdrechtbank*) in most cases. With the exception that if the proceedings concerned urgent, provisional measures, the *vrederechter* would have been the competent court, or if the decision on residence was made during summary divorce proceedings (*kort geding tijdens echtscheidingsprocedure)* the *voorzitter van de rechtbank* had been qualified to make the order.[121] However, on 30 July 2013 a law was passed with the intention to reform the judiciary system in order to create one family court for (most) family law proceedings.[122] This is to make access to court easier and more transparent. This law came into force on 1 September 2014 and established a new family court with a division into family chambers (*familiekamers*) and juvenile chambers (*jeugdkamers*).[123]

5.4.2. SHARED RESIDENCE

It is important to start with the explanation that Belgian law does *not* give the court the power to make a shared residence order whenever it deems this to be necessary. The court should consider equally divided residence as a first option, *but only if at least one of the parents requests this.*[124] This request can be secondary, meaning that both parents primarily request sole residence, but either or both also make a secondary request for shared parenting.[125] If both parents only request the child's residence to be solely with him or her, the court will theoretically have to choose to grant either request and it would seem that it does not have the authority to order shared residence instead. However, according to the testimonials of Belgian lawyers the courts have in fact done this by *partially* granting the request for sole residence, half of it, and thus in practice they have ordered residence that is equally divided between both parents. Unfortunately no (accessible) examples of such decisions have been found in the course of the research for this book.

In the same vein, the courts officially did not seem to possess the explicit power to impose, of their own accord, a residential arrangement that is neither a 50/50 division of time, nor sole residence and has not been

121 R. DEKKERS & A. WYLLEMAN, *Handboek Burgerlijk Recht Deel I: Personen en familierecht*, Intersentia, 2009, p. 78; 374 BCC, 223 & 1479 BCC, 1280 Ger. W.

122 *Wet betreffende de invoering van een familie- en jeugdrechtbank*, BS, 30 July 2013.

123 Wetsontwerp betreffende de invoering van een familie- en jeugdrechtbank, Belgische Senaat, Wetgevingsstuk nr. 5-1189/7, 12 June 2013.

124 Article 374 of the Belgian Civil Code, '*A défaut d'accord, en cas d'autorité parentale conjointe, le tribunal examine prioritairement, à la demande d'un des parents au moins, la possibilité de fixer l'hébergement de l'enfant de manière égalitaire entre ses parents.*'

125 I. MARTENS, 2007, pp. 22-23.

asked by either of the parents, but is, instead, a compromise.[126] However, in 2013 the *Cour de Cassation* approved a decision by the Court of Appeal of Ghent to impose a residential arrangement in which the children would reside every other week with the father, except for Wednesdays, which they would spend with the mother, even though neither parents had requested such an arrangement (the father had asked for equally divided residence and the mother requested sole residence with her). The court's deviation from a strictly equal division of time was prompted by the fact that on Wednesdays, the children only had school in the mornings, and while the father had to work, the mother had the Wednesdays off and therefore could accommodate the children after school.[127]

Additionally, the fact that the court has a duty to consider (equally) shared residence as the first option upon request does not mean that it cannot, after considering it, make a different decision which it sees as more suitable. When making a residential order, the court is required to explain the final decision (whatever that decision is) and to take into account the circumstances of the case and the interests of *both the child and the parents*.[128]

5.4.2.1. *Evaluation of the case law on equally divided residence*

Two recent case law evaluations, by Martens and Vanbockrijck, have examined the factors that can play a role in the court's decision as to whether or not to decide in favour of equally divided residence. In addition, some recent case law has been analysed by the author. These evaluations are presented below.

5.4.2.1.1. Evaluation by Martens

Martens, as part of her evaluation of divorce case law in the period between 2000 and 2006, has noted a set of factors that can play an important role in the decision to impose or deny equally divided residence.[129] According to her research a fundamental condition for a 50/50 residential arrangement being successful is the *ability of parents to communicate with each other*. Although this communication does not have to be very good, some communication is necessary to be able to discuss the upbringing of the child. In line with the requirement of communication is the necessity

126 H. VANBOCKRIJCK, 2009, p. 194.
127 Cass., C.12.0021.N, 4 January 2013.
128 Paragraph 2 of Article 374 of the Belgian Civil Code; A, possibly unnecessary, reminder in this context is that the duty to consider equally divided residence only exists if the parents in question exercise joint parental responsibilities.
129 At the time of writing the evaluation I. Martens was an assistant of G. Verschelden. She successfully defended her PhD research into maintenance obligations between former spouses at Ghent University in 2014.

of the *compatibility of each parent's ideas about the child's upbringing*, as two completely incompatible visions of upbringing could disturb the psychological balance of the child or children.

Martens found that in some cases, although this might seem paradoxical, the parents' hostile and exclusive attitude towards each other may be a reason for choosing a 50/50 residential order. While parental conflict is generally bad for the children, in some cases it is opportune to give one of the parents, who has been shut out of the child's life by the attitude and behaviour of the other parent, more influence on the child's life by means of shared residence.

A set of practical factors may also play a role in deciding whether or not a 50/50 residential arrangement is the suitable solution for any given case. The *distance between the parents' residences* can play and important role: a very long distance would make residential co-parenting practically unworkable. The *daily availability* of the parents or their network is also something that should be considered. While the fact that a parent leaves some of the caring for the child or children to his or her partner or family member(s) is not a necessary indicator against shared residence; however, a severe imbalance in the time both parents can spend on caring for the child or children is. The *opinion of the child* or children subjected to the residential arrangement may play a role in the court's decision as well as the *residence of other family members*, for example the child's siblings. And finally, and perhaps obviously, the fact that *one of the parents is incapable of or is completely uninterested in caring* for the child or children.[130]

Martens' case law study has been conducted over a period of time before the 2006 law reform and should therefore be used cautiously on the issue of 50/50 residential arrangements, especially if it is used as the (sole) representation of judicial standing.

5.4.2.1.2. Evaluation by Vanbockrijck

Vanbockrijck has evaluated the first 2 years of the application of the 2006 law reform, specifically the exercise and the sanctioning of residential and contact arrangements and has therefore continued where Martens left off.[131] In her piece evaluating two years of case law dealing with residential and contact arrangements, Vanbockrijck found many of the same factors as Martens to be decisive in judging whether a 50/50 residential arrangement was appropriate: the opinion of the child, the distance between the

130 I. MARTENS, 2007, pp. 26-31.

131 H. Vanbockrijck is a family law lawyer at *Maxius advocaten en bemiddelaars* and a postgraduate lecturer at *KU Leuven*.

parents, the ability of the parents to communicate with each other and the availability of each parent to care for the child.

In addition to these factors, she also found that the *age of the child* is an important criterion. Since a fixed residence can be important for a good development of very young children and a long separation from either parent can be detrimental to the bonding between parent and child, residence arrangements where the child stays alternating weeks with each parent are, for example, less suitable for (very) young children, although residential co-parenting has previously been ordered in cases with very young children.

Finally, she found that *if a residential arrangement already exists*, the courts take into account how well that arrangement is working. If it has been working well for some years, the courts are less inclined to change the existing arrangement (into a 50/50 arrangement).[132]

5.4.2.1.3. Recent case law

Later case law, gathered during the research for this book, supports the earlier findings of Martens and Vanbockrijck.[133] Here are some examples from recent cases:

In a 2012 District Court of Leuven case, the court considered three of the above-mentioned factors before deciding that there were no sufficient counter-indications for equally divided residence: the parents' ideas about the upbringing of the children, the children's age, and the ability of the parents to communicate with each other. While in an earlier decision the youngest child, who was 2½ at the time, was deemed too young for residential co-parenting, now that the child was 4 years old, he was considered old enough to function within such an arrangement. And although there were still problems with the parents' ability to communicate with each other, those problems were not severe enough to make residential co-parenting impossible.[134]

In a 2007 Court of Appeal of Mons judgement, the court considered the daily availability of both parents and decided that since the father did not seem to be willing to make any professional concessions to be more available for the children, the children should remain with the mother and the father's request for an equal division of residence had been justly denied.[135]

---

132 H. VANBOCKRIJCK, 2009, pp. 198-200.

133 For a description of the research method, see section 1.3 of Chapter 1.

134 Court of Leuven (first instance), 9 February 2012, *RABG*, 2012/12, pp. 806-812.

135 Court of Appeal of Mons, 12 June 2007, *JLMB*, 2009/3, pp. 116-120.

The distance between the parents, the age of the children and the residence of other family members, in this case the grandparents, played a role in the decision of the Court of Appeal of Brussels to deny an equal division of residence in a 2008 case in which the mother, after parental separation, took the children and, without any consultation with the father, moved with them to a different municipality. The court considered that due to the children's very young age and the great distance between the parents, residential co-parenting would not be in the best interests of the children and that they should have their residence with the father who had remained in the communal home and had the children's grandparents living nearby, who would assist him with the care for the children.[136]

The residence of other family members, this time siblings, was also considered in the 2009 appeal case dealing with a situation in which a residential arrangement had to be made for five children of a divorcing couple. The original proposition was to have a different residential arrangement for every child. Both the mother and the Court of Appeal were against such an arrangement as it was unnecessarily complicated and lacked the stability the children needed. The court added that in order to promote a sense of connectedness and a 'family feeling' the siblings should spend their time with each parent as much as possible together.[137]

The above shows that the court's power to impose equally divided residence is dependent on one parent's request and is limited by the interests of the child and parents and the practical circumstances of the case. However, when the 2006 law reform came into force, these nuances in the legislation went mostly unnoticed by the general public and the media, creating a mentality in which parents assumed that equally divided residence would legally be the default arrangement in the case of divorce (whether they wanted this or not).[138]

5.4.2.2. *Residential co-parenting in practice*

It is interesting to discover if this mentality combined with the ability (though limited) of the courts to impose equally divided residence on a parent against his or her wishes after the other parent's request has led to an overall increase in residential co-parenting in practice. A large-scale study conducted in 2010 among 1,870 divorced parents with children shows that of those divorced before the 1995 law reform only 6.8% of the parents had a residential co-parenting arrangement. Because at that time

---

136 Court of Appeal of Brussels, 5 February 2008, *RW*, 2009-10, no. 6, pp. 243-245.

137 Court of Appeal of Brussels, 12 May 2009, *Revue Générale de Droit Civil Belge*, 2010, pp. 286-293.

138 D. Mortelmans in an interview for the purpose of this research.

no rules existed on preferred care arrangements after separation, it is to be presumed that these were parents who had made and exercised shared residence on a completely voluntary basis. In the period after the 1995 reform, which had introduced the joint exercise of parental responsibilities after separation, but before the 2006 reform, the amount of residential co-parenting arrangements had increased to 21.1%. Even assuming that residential co-parenting was socially increasing in popularity over the years, a growth of over 14%, almost tripling the original figures, is very remarkable. In the period after the 2006 law reform, the proportion of parents in residential co-parenting arrangements increased even more, to 27.1%.[139]

These figures need some explanation as the increase in residential co-parenting did not necessarily increase as much as these numbers could make one believe. The children of the parents who separated before the 1995 law reform were in general older than the children of the parents separated after the reform (and definitely older than the children of parents who separated after 2006) at the time of the gathering of the information and the research also included 'children' over the age of 18. Figures show that children under the age of 12 are more likely to be raised in a residential co-parenting arrangement than those who are older (respectively: 36.1% of children under the age of 12 were being raised in a co-parenting arrangement, as opposed to 23.1% of children between the ages of 13 and 18, and 11.5% of children over the age of 18).[140] Therefore, while residential co-parenting in Belgium indeed did increase in the last two decades or so, the increase was less drastic than the figures may suggest. Nonetheless, shared residence was and still is on the rise and now with currently over a quarter of parents practising residential co-parenting, it has become a popular and important residential arrangement that can no longer be seen as marginal.

5.4.3. CHANGING RESIDENCE

Article 387bis of the Belgian Civil Code contains a provision giving the court which made the original decision on the residential arrangement to make a new decision if the parents or one of them brings the case before the court once again. If neither of the parents wants the involvement of the court they can, theoretically, change the arrangement in practice. However, this means that either parent may, at any time, go to the courts and complain that the other parent is not adhering to the official arrangement.

---

139 D. MORTELMANS et al., 2011, p. 137, table 6.1.

140 *Ibid.*, p. 138, table 6.2.

If the residential arrangement came about by agreement between the parents and was subsequently not implemented into an order by the court, it is legally not binding. This means that if the parents want to change the arrangement, they can do that without legal intervention and if a dispute arises they will have to start a (new) procedure and request a residential arrangement order.[141]

The fact that (one of) the parents requests the court to change an existing residential arrangement by no means entails that the court is obliged to do this. If at the time that the court has to make a judgement a residential arrangement has already been in place for some time and this arrangement has been exercised without any major problems, it is unlikely that it will be altered, even if the change would make the division of residence more equal. In such a situation the certainty of a stable and well-functioning arrangement (the so-called continuity standard) trumps the theoretical increase in equality, or in an opposite situation: a residential co-parenting arrangement that has worked well does not need to be changed only because conflicts had arisen between the parents.[142]

However, in situations where one of the parents wants to relocate with the child or has already done so, a change of residential arrangements is often inevitable. Unfortunately very little case law on changing residential arrangements and relocation has been published in Belgium and even less has been written about this topic in the legal literature.[143] Therefore anything that is said in this chapter needs to be approached with caution as it is based on very limited sources.

5.4.3.1. Relocation within Belgium

The few available cases on relocation within Belgium do not show that the courts employ a default reasoning in cases where one of the parents who are in a residential co-parenting arrangement or who apply for a residential co-parenting arrangement decides to move with the child. Instead the courts seem to consider the particularities of the case and the best interests of the child.

While in summary proceedings at the District Court of Nijvel it had been decided that although the mother had moved with the child from

141 H. VANBOCKRIJCK, 2009, pp. 151-152.

142 *Ibid.*, pp. 206-207.

143 This was the outcome of the case law evaluation underlying this book, and has been confirmed by the Belgian legal scholars F. Swennen, J. Verhellen and T. Kruger who have carried out research in the area of relocation. The reason for the lack of both case law on relocation and scientific interest in this topic is unclear. The case law that does exist concerns disputes that arise after a parent has already relocated with the child or children without the other parent's consent and therefore constitutes child abduction, an issue that is not discussed in this book.

Gembloux to Virton, a distance of 160 km, the already existing shared residence arrangement should be continued, because in this case the shared residence clearly served the best interests of the child.[144] By contrast, the same court ruled that a 50/50 residential arrangement could not be continued when the mother moved with the child from Chastre to Brussels, a distance of 47 km, and granted residence with the mother with whom the child had a closer relationship and whose relocation was justified.[145] The reason for these almost contradictory decisions is unclear and the facts are not described to the extent necessary so as to be able to draw a conclusion about the key factual differences between the cases.

A different court denied a father's request to change a classical residence arrangement (of one weekend each fortnight and shared holidays) into equally divided residence, because the distance of 33 km from the father's home to their school was seen as too long for the children to travel on days when they would stay with the father and it would have been too great a burden to submit them to this.[146]

It is also possible that instead of moving further away, a parent relocates closer to the other parent and requests a change of the residential arrangement based on that. This happened in the 2009 appeal case in which the father applied for equally divided residence and, being denied his request, moved from Denderleeuw to Buizingen, making the distance between his residence and the mother's residence much shorter. He subsequently appealed to the Court of Appeal of Brussels. The court considered that the reason that the lower court had denied the father's request for equally divided residence was that then he still lived in Denderleeuw. Now that the father had moved closer, the distance was no longer an obstacle for residential co-parenting. While the mother raised the father's busy job as a firefighter as an obstacle to equally divided residence, the court considered that in the debate on the organization of accommodation for children the question is not determined by which parent is most available to care for the child or children, because if that were the case, only unemployed parents would be able to accommodate their children. Now that the distance between the parents no longer constituted an obstacle, the court ordered in favour of equally divided residence and made a residence arrangement where the children would reside every other week with the father.[147]

---

144 Court of Nijvel, 19 September 2003, *Rev. trim. dr. fam.* 1/2005, p. 183.
145 Court of Nijvel, 5 September 2003, *Rev. Trim. dr. fam.* 1/2005, p. 179.
146 Court of Antwerp, 10 November 2006, *JR*, p. 5857.
147 Court of Brussels (appeal), 11 February 2009, *Rev. trim. dr. fam. 2/2011*, pp. 386-397.

5.4.3.2. Relocation outside Belgium

There is a serious lack of available Belgian case law that concerns a parent who requests the court's permission in a family law procedure, having been denied permission by the other parent while jointly exercising parental responsibilities with them, to relocate to another country with the child. Most of the case law seems to concern child abduction proceedings; cases in which a parent has already relocated with the child without asking or receiving permission from the other parent or after an order refusing relocation has been made. While child abduction exceeds the scope of this research, the lack of otherwise relevant case law warrants the mentioning of two similar child abduction cases specifically involving residential co-parenting. In two separate cases, one from 2009 and the other from 2005, the mother had abducted the children and taken them abroad, to Portugal and to Bulgaria respectively, and prevented contact with the father, after the court had made an order on residential co-parenting. In both cases the court awarded the father with sole parental responsibilities, because removing the children from their environment and creating parental conflict by doing so had the potential of harming the children and that the mother's lack of respect for the residential arrangement created the threat of her repeating the abduction in the future.[148]

5.5. CHILDREN'S PROCEDURAL RIGHTS

In family law proceedings, mainly divorce proceedings or proceedings concerning the parental responsibilities over the child or the child's residence, the most used and arguably most relevant child right is the right to be heard (by the court) and, tied to that, the right to be informed of the existence of that right.[149] The right to be heard is derived from Article 12 of the Convention on the Rights of the Child and until 2014 it was implemented in Belgian law in Article 56bis of the Youth Protection Act, which obliged the juvenile court to invite children of 12 years of age

---

148 Court of Brussels (juvenile court), 18 May 2009, *399/2008/17C*; Court of Brussels (first instance), 30 January 2005, *RTDF*, 2007, p. 215.

149 K. HERBOTS et al., 'Participatie van het kind in het gerechtelijk scheidingsproces: droombeeld of realiteit ?', *TJK*, 2012/01, p. 25.

or older to be heard in disputes concerning them,[150] and in Article 931 of the Judicial Code, which creates the possibility to hear a minor who has the necessary discernment in disputes that concern him or her.[151] The combination of these two provisions meant that in disputes on parental responsibilities, care arrangements or residential arrangements the juvenile court (*jeugdrechtbank*) must provide children of 12 years or older whom these disputes concern the opportunity to be heard, but the court (*any court*) also *can* provide this opportunity to children younger than this if it considers these children to be sufficiently mature to understand what is going on. If a child, irrespective of his or her age, has of his or her own volition requested the court to be heard, this request can only be denied if it is extensively reasoned that the child does not yet have the necessary understanding and is too immature to be heard.[152]

Senaeve urged that the Belgian legislation on the hearing of children needs to be revised and unified as the current law results in a discriminatory situation in which children whose parents bring a case before the juvenile court (*jeugrechtbank*) are treated differently from children whose parents bring their case before a different court. He proposed to change the laws in such way as not to invite all children concerned to be heard, but to hear the children who themselves indicate that they want to be heard and additionally to give the court the power to hear children in proceedings where it deems this to be necessary.[153] A revision has now taken place. In 2014, a chapter 'on the hearing of the minor' was added to the Judicial Code.[154] The new Article 1004/1, added by this chapter, grants all minors the right to be heard, and to decline to be heard, in matters concerning

---

150 *Loi relative à la protection de la jeunesse, à la prise en charge des mineurs ayant commis un fait qualifié infraction et à la réparation du dommage causé par ce fait: 'Le tribunal de la jeunesse doit convoquer la personne de douze ans au moins aux fins d'audition, dans les litiges qui opposent les personnes investies à son égard de l'autorité parentale, lorsque sont débattus des points qui concernent le gouvernement de sa personne, l'administration de ses biens, l'exercice du droit de visite, ou la désignation de la personne visée à l'article 34.'* This Article was abolished in 2014 by the coming into force of Article 244 of the *Wet betreffende de invoering van een familie- en jeugdrechtbank.*

151 Judicial Code: '*Néanmoins, dans toute procédure le concernant, le mineur capable de discernement peut, à sa demande ou sur décision du juge, sans préjudice des dispositions légales prévoyant son intervention volontaire et son consentement, être entendu, hors de la présence des parties, par le juge ou la personne désignée par ce dernier à cet effet, aux frais partagés des parties s'il y a lieu. La décision du juge n'est pas susceptible d'appel.*'

152 Article 931 of the Judicial Code: '*Lorsque le mineur en fait la demande soit au juge saisi soit au procureur du Roi, l'audition ne peut être écartée que par une décision spécialement motivée fondée sur le manque de discernement du mineur.*'

153 P. SENAEVE, 'Rechters die kinderen (moeten) horen', *Tijdschrift voor Familierecht*, 2011/1, p. 2.

154 Article 157 of the *Wet betreffende de invoering van een familie- en jeugdrechtbank.*

parental responsibilities, residence, or personal relationships.[155] Children of 12 years or older will be informed of their right to be heard by means of a standard letter.[156] Children younger than 12 years may be heard upon their own request, the request of the parties, the request of the public prosecutor, or when the court deems this to be necessary. The court may refuse the parties' request to hear the child, but not if the request is made by the child himself or herself or the public prosecutor.[157]

Hearing children can give judges more information about the case and help to locate problems. It is therefore interesting to know how judges themselves approach their authority to hear children. As part of a large-scale study into divorce, 3,474 experts involved with divorce were interviewed of whom 64 were judges.[158] Out of these 64 judges, 14 were interviewed in depth. This research has shown that in general judges prefer to speak to the children themselves, as opposed to via a court-appointed representative, and value the child's vision and opinion. While judges are reluctant to hear very young children, when they hear a child of 12 years or older, they sometimes also hear their younger sibling(s). The wishes of children above 14 years of age are likely to be substantially respected, while the opinion of young children is viewed with more scrutiny as younger children are more susceptible to the influence of (one of) the parents.[159]

A child who is being heard does not become a party to the dispute.[160] Even the children who write to the court themselves and ask to become a party in the proceedings can never gain the capability to act on their own in court. Children in court must be represented. In the normal course of affairs, parents with parental responsibilities are the ones who represent the child in legal proceedings. If there is a conflict of interests between

---

155 Article 158 of the *Wet betreffende de invoering van een familie- en jeugdrechtbank:* '*Tout mineur a le droit d'être entendu par un juge dans les matières qui le concernent relatives à l'autorité parentale, au droit d'hébergement ainsi qu'au droit aux relations personnelles. Il a le droit de refuser d'être entendu.*'

156 Article 158 of the *Wet betreffende de invoering van een familie- en jeugdrechtbank:* '*Le mineur qui a atteint l'âge de douze ans est informé par le juge, le cas échéant à l'adresse de chacun de ses parents, de son droit à être entendu conformément à l'article 1004/2. Un formulaire de réponse est joint à cette information.*'

157 Article 158 of the *Wet betreffende de invoering van een familie- en jeugdrechtbank:* '*Le mineur de moins de douze ans est entendu à sa demande, à la demande des parties, du ministère public ou d'office par le juge. Le juge peut, par décision motivée par les circonstances de la cause, refuser d'entendre le mineur de moins de douze ans, sauf lorsque la demande émane de ce dernier ou du ministère public.*'

158 Interdisciplinair Project voor de Optimalisatie van Scheidingstrajecten. This project was conducted between 2007 and 2011. More information can be accessed at: www.scheidingsonderzoek.ugent.be (last visited 30 April 2015).

159 K. HERBOTS et al., 2012, pp. 26-34.

160 Article 931 of the Judicial Code: '*L'audition du mineur ne lui confère pas la qualité de partie à la procedure.*' See also the new Article 1004/1, Article 158 of the *Wet betreffende de invoering van een familie- en jeugdrechtbank:* '*L'entretien avec le mineur ne lui confère pas la qualité de partie à la procédure.*'

one of the administrators of the child's property, the other administrator (parent) will represent the child. However, in a dispute between the parents over the child or if the conflict of interests is between both parents and the child, or between the holder of sole parental responsibilities and the child, the court has to appoint a legal professional as a guardian *ad hoc;* this is usually a lawyer.[161]

Not many cases exist in which a child has requested to be made a (represented) party to the proceedings, but it is not unheard of. In a 2010 Court of Leuven decision, for example, in which the parents could not agree on the residence arrangement and the choice of school for their daughter, she herself submitted a petition to become the intervening party (*vrijwillige tussenkomst*). The court granted her the status of an intervening party and appointed a legal representative.[162]

Finally, besides rights, children also have a certain duty under Belgian family law. This is the duty to respect their parents. This is a mutual duty, which parents also have towards their children.[163] What this duty entails precisely and how (or if) it can be enforced is uncertain. Case law has, however, made one thing clear: a lack of respect shown to parents by their children does not absolve the parents of their obligation to (financially) maintain their children.[164]

5.6. ENFORCEMENT OF ARRANGEMENTS IN CASE OF NON-COMPLIANCE

Court orders and legally binding arrangements differ from agreements which parents make with each other out of court in that they can be enforced if one of the parents does not abide by them. When parents (first) come before a court with a dispute connected to parental responsibilities or residence and they make a care agreement or a residential agreement, they can – but are not obliged to – ask the court to incorporate the arrangement into the court's eventual ruling. The incorporation will give the parents an executorial title, which they can use in the case of non-compliance to bring the case before the same judge to be considered with priority above all other affairs.[165] Evidently, in cases there was no consensus and the court had to make a decision on the residence of the child, a residence order

---

161 F. SWENNEN, 2014, p. 464.

162 Court of Leuven (first instance), 16 September 2010, *NJW*, 2011, no. 239, pp. 236-237.

163 Article 371 of the Belgian Civil Code: '*L'enfant et ses père et mère se doivent, à tout âge, mutuellement le respect.*'

164 Cass., 3 June 2010, *NJW*, 2011, p. 460.

165 I. MARTENS, 2007, p. 8; Paragraph 1 of Article 387ter of Book One of the Belgian Civil Code.

will have been made by the court, which will give the parents the same executorial title.

Connected with the above is the rule that any dispute concerning parental responsibilities (including residence) will remain pending until the child or children concerned reach the age of majority (or are emancipated), which makes it easier and cheaper for a parent to engage the court once again if the other parent is not heeding the arrangements they have made – and which have been implemented into a judicial decision – or that were ordered by the court.[166]

Once a parent has taken the step to bring the non-compliance of the other parent before the court, the court will first need to consider if an urgent interim measure is necessary. Not all forms of non-compliance need to be rectified immediately; many cases will require a thorough study of the facts until a suitable solution can be found. This was, for example, decided in a 2007 appeal case in which the court refused to make an interim enforcement order after the mother failed to return her son to the father who was the resident parent. Instead she enrolled the child in a school near her residence. The court considered that because the child was 14 and had now explicitly stated that he wished to live with his mother and that he did not experience the change of school as a problem in the initial proceedings, the court would have to consider his wishes and the whole situation, and acknowledge the fact that if it was truly the son's wish to live with his mother and this was not caused by pressure from the mother, a teenager that age might choose to stay away from the original residential parent despite the residence arrangement stating otherwise. To enforce an arrangement that an older child is explicitly against would, in this case, be contrary to the child's interests. In order to decide what would be best in these circumstances, the court needed to have time for a thorough evaluation of the facts and an interim enforcement order would have been ill-advised.[167]

If the issue is not urgent, in accordance with Article 387ter of the Belgian Civil Code the court can first try to reconcile the parties or point them towards the possibilities of mediation,[168] before it proceeds to enforcement, but if that fails or the parties are not interested in or are too hostile to try those options, the court can decide that it needs to examine the case in more depth. If the court is of the opinion that it needs more information, it

---

166 Article 387bis of the Belgian Civil Code.

167 Court of Ghent (appeal), 25 October 2007, 2007/EV/73.

168 Article 387bis of the Belgian Civil Code: '*Sans préjudice de l'article 1734 du Code judiciaire, le tribunal tente de concilier les parties*'; Article 387ter of the Belgian Civil Code. '*Sauf en cas d'urgence, [le juge] peut notamment: [...] – procéder à une tentative de conciliation, – suggérer aux parties de recourir à la médiation telle que prévue à l'article 387bis.*' The court has no power to force parties to participate in mediation.

can order the social services or experts to conduct an investigation of the facts.[169]

If it is clear to the court that the arrangements need to be enforced, it has the choice between *two enforcement mechanisms*: a fine or the enforced execution of the arrangement. The fine is meant to have a deterrent effect on the unwilling parent and can be executed by laying claim on (a part of) the welfare benefits or by seizing the belongings of a parent with limited means.[170] Enforced execution is a controversial enforcement mechanism and is seen as an ultimum remedium, because it is important that the child will not become the victim in that situation. Therefore it will not take the form of an official arriving at the door of the unwilling parent and taking the child by force to the other parent. More likely is facilitating the transfer of the child by a family member or another third party or to arrange mediation and contact at a counselling centre.[171]

Finally, the court can, instead of enforcing an existing arrangement, make a completely new decision and impose a different arrangement.[172] This means that the court could, for example, order residential co-parenting when a parent with whom the child has his or her main (and sole) residence is obstructing contact with the other parent, or it can even reverse the residence decision.

In making its decision to order (or not to order) an enforcement measure the court is not bound by any earlier enforcement decisions. This means that if in an earlier stage a court decided not to enforce an arrangement or order and the non-compliance remained, prompting the wronged party to start the proceedings anew, the court has the power to order an enforcement measure this time around.[173]

It is finally useful to note that outside of the private law dispute on the enforcement of the arrangement, a parent who refuses to adhere to a residence or contact arrangement commits the crime of the unlawful retention of a child (*niet-afgifte van een kind*) and is punishable under the Criminal Code.[174]

---

169 Article 387ter of the Belgian Civil Code: '*Sauf en cas d'urgence, [le juge] peut notamment […] procéder à de nouvelles mesures d'instruction telles qu'une enquête sociale ou une expertise.*'

170 H. VANBOCKRIJCK, 2009, pp. 160-167.

171 *Ibid.*, pp. 171-176.

172 Article 387bis of the Belgian Civil Code.

173 Cass., 25 February 2011, *RW*, 2012-13, no. 3, p. 1.

174 G. VERSCHELDEN, 2010, p. 25.

5.7. SUMMARY

The notion that parents should share the care for their child(ren) after separation has existed for many years in Belgian law. It was first made into a legal presumption in 1995 with the introduction of the ex lege continuation of the joint exercise of parental responsibilities after separation.[175] Eleven years later, Belgian law acknowledged and encouraged residential co-parenting by obliging the courts to seriously consider an arrangement in which the parents would equally (50/50) share the time the child(ren) spent with them if such an arrangement was requested by either parent.[176]

Another legal reform to increase equality was introduced in 2014. This time it was to improve the legal position of female co-parents and to provide them, as far as possible, with the same rights which fathers had.[177] While in the past female co-parents could only become legal parents of their children through the lengthy and complicated process of adoption, now both wives and husbands of legal mothers become legal parents ex lege, unless the presumption is disputed, and both male and female unmarried partners can legally recognize their child(ren) with the mother's consent or become legal parents by means of a court order. The limitation that a child may only have two legal parents at the same time remains. As legal parentage is directly linked to parental responsibilities in Belgian law this has consequences for the question of who gets to jointly exercise parental responsibilities.[178]

While, in theory, the holders of parental responsibilities should exercise them in close co-operation and all important decisions must have the consent of both holders of parental responsibilities, this consent is presumed to exist when it comes to dealings with third parties.[179] When the holders of parental responsibilities cannot agree on an important decision, they may ask the court to intervene. The court can then make an order deciding the matter in dispute, restricting one holder's parental responsibilities, or even in rare circumstances granting one of the parents sole parental responsibilities.[180]

While the joint exercise of parental responsibilities is the legal norm, equally shared time between both parents is not a legal presumption, it is simply an arrangement that the court should consider upon request and give grounds if it is rejected in favour of sole residence or another residential arrangement. There are many practical reasons why a 50/50

---

175 See section 5.1.1 of Chapter 5.
176 See section 5.1.2 of Chapter 5.
177 See section 5.3.2.3 of Chapter 5.
178 See section 5.3.2 of Chapter 5.
179 See section 5.3.3 of Chapter 5.
180 See sections 5.3.3.1 and 5.3.4 of Chapter 5.

division of residence might not be possible in certain circumstances. Besides, if the parents agree that sole residence with one of the parents is best for their child(ren), it is not up to the court to rule otherwise. The reverse is also true: where both parents agree on a residential co-parenting arrangement, the court has little reason to deviate from that unless the best interests of the child would be jeopardised by such an arrangement.[181]

As a part of safeguarding the best interests of the child, children possess the right to be heard in proceedings concerning their residence and care arrangements. Children of 12 years or older will receive a letter from the court informing them of their right to be heard. Younger children may be heard as well, but they do not automatically receive such a letter.[182]

Finally, there is the issue of enforcement. The practical difference between court orders on (the exercise of) parental responsibilities and residence and agreements between parents made out of court is that court orders can theoretically be enforced in case of non-compliance. However, in practice, enforcement is not easy, and before employing enforcement measures, the matter needs to be investigated thoroughly, to make sure that the enforcement does not end up disproportionately harming the child.[183]

---

181 See section 5.4.2 of Chapter 5.
182 See section 5.5 of Chapter 5.
183 See section 5.6 of Chapter 5.

CHAPTER 6
SOCIO-PSYCHOLOGICAL ASPECTS OF RESIDENTIAL CO-PARENTING

6.1. INTRODUCTION

This chapter compiles data on residential co-parenting from various empirical studies with a demographical, sociological, or psychological background. The goal is to present the law which is applicable to residential co-parenting and is discussed earlier in this book within its social framework. This is important because law in general, and family law specifically, does not operate in a vacuum. There exists an inevitable link between society and its law. The choice of parents or the court for a certain residential arrangement is not only influenced by legal considerations, but also – and perhaps primarily so – by the practical situation of the family, the general societal attitude towards different types of residential arrangements, the financial circumstances and the emotional relationship between all the parties involved.

It is impossible to address all of these factors in an in-depth, comprehensive manner within the confines of this book. Therefore, this chapter will be limited to answering two questions which have a direct influence on residential co-parenting legislation: does residential co-parenting occur in the three countries discussed, and if so, how predominant is it? And should residential co-parenting be stimulated or discouraged?

First, it must be examined whether residential co-parenting is an arrangement that is actually practised by separated parents and is not only an option that exists in theory. In order to do this, statistical information from the national systems is consulted and displayed to show the prevalence of residential co-parenting in each of the three countries whose legislation is presented in this book.

The second step is to investigate whether having legislation in place influences or has the potential to influence the choice of residential arrangement. Even if certain residential arrangements exist, the necessity of enacting legislation that regulates these arrangements should be questioned if evidence exists that the availability of legislation has no effect on the number of parents choosing a certain arrangement or courts ordering certain arrangements. Therefore, where this information is available, this chapter compares the numbers of parents who had residential co-parenting arrangements before special legislation thereon was enacted and the numbers of parents who have such arrangements afterwards. If the new legislation was intended to make residential co-parenting more accessible or a preferred model and the numbers of parents employing this residential arrangement have indeed increased, there is a valid reason to assume that legislation does influence residential co-parenting in practice.

The answers to the above are presented in section 6.3 of this chapter, with the help of statistical data from various empirical studies from the three countries which this book compares. Empirical studies from other countries are not included, because the focus of this section is to back up the legal framework of the three countries with the social framework in which the law is functioning. These studies are presented and explained in section 6.2.

If and once it is established that residential co-parenting is in fact employed by the parents and decided on by the courts in practice, as well as that it can be influenced by legislation, the second question should be answered.

In order to answer the second question - whether legislation should promote or discourage residential co-parenting - it is of importance to know what kind of influence would be the most desirable. Should legislation make residential co-parenting a default arrangement, should it promote it, should it discourage it, or even, should it prohibit this arrangement altogether?

This requires making a difficult value judgment first: the judgement whether residential co-parenting is a good or a bad arrangement and therefore whether it is desirable or not. When making this judgement, the best interests of the child criterion will be used in this context: an arrangement is considered beneficial or desirable if it is in the best interests of the child, an arrangement is considered detrimental or undesirable if it is contrary to the best interests of the child. While many other criteria exist by which the desirability of certain arrangements can be judged, the best interests of the child is a criterion against which nearly all legal decisions concerning children are tested. This criterion is international and prevalent and therefore has been chosen as the main assessment framework for the value of residential co-parenting within the scope of this book.

However, whether residential co-parenting is in the best interests of the child is not an easy question to answer. Many factors play a part in the influence of the residential arrangement on the well-being of the child. Additionally, some aspects of residential co-parenting can have a negative influence on the best interests of the child, while others have a positive influence (depending on the factual situation). Therefore, before any conclusions can be drawn, these aspects must be catalogued and weighed against each other. This is done in section 6.4 of this chapter. The aspects are taken from literature with both a legal and non-legal background, such as psychology and sociology. Because these aspects are much more strongly linked to psychology and factual situations (rather than law or demographics), the literature is not limited to sources originating from one of the three countries whose legal system is discussed in this book. Instead, international works that summarise the main empirical and psychological research findings on the subject of residential arrangements post parental separation are consulted.

6.2. SOCIOLOGICAL AND PSYCHOLOGICAL STUDIES

This section presents the available empirical studies on residential co-parenting (and related topics) of sufficient scale that have been conducted in England, the Netherlands and Belgium. Because the studies differ in their method and sample size, not every result can be relied upon to the same extent. Some findings, while interesting, cannot be assumed to apply to all separating parents in a country or even in a region. Therefore for all the empirical research findings used in this chapter an explanation of the research method, the source and the background is given below. This is done for each country separately, to give a clear overview.

6.2.1 ENGLAND

No large-scale English study on shared residence has so far been conducted. Instead there have been several smaller studies of different types over the course of the last decade or so. However, '[t]here are still large gaps in the knowledge base. Almost everything that is known about shared care is based on international research, mostly from North-America and Australia,' as Trinder points out in her review of the research evidence.[1]

Two recently completed UK studies that have a scale which is sufficient enough to be noteworthy are the one conducted by Gingerbread and the Nuffield Foundation in 2006-2007 and the one conducted by the Family Justice Review in 2011. Additionally, there is another study funded by the

1 More information about these organizations and their work can be found on their respective websites: www.gingerbread.org.uk and www.nuffieldfoundation.org (last visited 30 April 2015).

Nuffield Foundation into how county courts share the care of children between parents, which is currently still ongoing, but has yielded some interim findings.

6.2.1.1. Gingerbread and the Nuffield Foundation study

Both Gingerbread and the Nuffield Foundation are charitable organisations.[2] Gingerbread focuses on one-parent families, with research, resources, information and practical help. The Nuffield Foundation has a broader scope and has as its object the advancement of social well-being as a whole.

These two organisations put their resources together in order to assess the extent of contact problems between parents and children in separated families in Great Britain. This study did not therefore focus on residence, but on contact. However, because of the research method, data on residential co-parenting was also gathered.

To research the nature and extent of contact problems in the general population of separated families, a quantitative, nationwide, Omnibus survey of 559 separated parents with a child under the age of 16 was conducted. All parents were asked the same questions revolving around the issue of (possible) contact problems, but sometimes with different wording.[3] The survey was conducted in six waves, between July 2006 and March 2007 by the Office for National Statistics. It used random probability sampling stratified to best represent the general population. Respondents were asked about the contact arrangements and experiences of contact relating to one child only, even if they were the parents of more than one child. Unfortunately, because the study focused on *contact* and contact problems, *if the parents said that they shared the care of the child more or less equally, they were not asked further questions.*[4] This means that although this study gathered information on how prevalent equally shared care is in Great Britain, it did not gather any other information about these types of arrangements. This is unfortunate, especially if it is considered that among the questions not asked to the parents with shared care were questions about the manner in which the arrangement came about (i.e. by an agreement or through a court decision) and if the parents were satisfied with their current arrangement.

---

2 L. TRINDER, 'Shared residence: a review of recent research evidence', *Child and Family Law Quarterly*, 2010, Vol. 22, No. 4, p. 477.

3 V. PEACEY & J. HUNT, *Problematic contact after separation and divorce? A national survey of parents*, 2008, p. 5. Accessible online through the Gingerbread and the Nuffield Foundation websites: www.gingerbread.org.uk and www.nuffieldfoundation.org (last visited 30 April 2015).

4 *Ibid.*, p. 9.

6.2.1.2. *Family Justice Review*

In 2011 the final report of the Family Justice Review was published. This report deals with many different recommendations for the reform of the family justice system. This is because of concerns over its effectiveness and delays. The Family Justice Review began its work in March 2010 and is jointly sponsored by the Ministry of Justice, the Department for Education, and the Welsh Government.[5]

Three research projects were conducted by the Ministry of Justice specifically for the report: a study on the outcomes of public and private law family proceedings involving children,[6] a study analysing a sample of closed family cases in 2009,[7] and a study analysing legal aid administrative data from October 2004 to July 2010.[8] Additionally, after the Family Justice Review published its interim report, which drew on evidence from over 700 individuals and organisations, the panel took oral evidence and travelled both in England and Wales and to other countries to meet those involved in family justice and children and adults affected by it. The interim report received 628 replies, both from individuals as well as organisations, with respondents varying from parents to local authorities.[9]

While the Family Justice Review covered a very wide range of topics and provided a very extensive list of recommendations, one recommendation in particular is important for this book; it is the recommendation that 'no legislation should be introduced that creates or risks creating the perception that there is a parental right to substantially shared or equal time for both parents'.[10] This was decided 'drawing on international and other evidence', and was supported by charities, legal and judicial organisations and academics, while many individuals, many of whom were fathers, spoke out against this recommendation.[11]

6.2.1.3. *The Nuffield Foundation's study into county court decisions*

The Nuffield Foundation's study into county court decisions on shared care, conducted by Harding and Newnham, explores the relationship

5 Family Justice Review, *Final report*, 2011, p. 37. Accessible online through the UK government website: www.gov.uk/government/uploads/system/uploads/attachment_data/file/217343/family-justice-review-final-report.pdf (last visited 30 April 2015).

6 E. GIOVANNINI, *Outcomes of Family Justice Children's Proceedings – A Review of the Evidence*, 2011.

7 D. CASSIDY & S. DAVEY, *Family Justice and Children's Proceedings – Review of Public and Private Law Case Files in England and Wales*, 2011.

8 S. QUARTERMAIN, *Sustainability of Mediation and Legal Representation in Private Family Law Cases – Analysis of Legal Aid Administrative Datasets*, 2011.

9 Family Justice Review, 2011, pp. 37-38.

10 *Ibid.*, pp. 137-142.

11 *Ibid.*, p. 138.

between the formal labels given to court orders and the actual allocation of children's time between parents and perceptions of how those orders are applied, and how courts promote shared parenting in disputes between separated parents. The study has been designed in two phases. The first phase consists of a case file analysis of data from 193 cases, across five county courts. This phase has already been completed and a summary of the interim results has been made available. The second phase is at the time of writing still ongoing and will involve 60 interviews with stakeholders, including judges, barristers, solicitors and Cafcass on their perceptions of how Section 8 orders are applied.[12]

6.2.1.4. Other studies

Additional to the research conducted in England and Wales, English legal and sociological literature often makes use of research findings from other Commonwealth countries, such as Australia. Especially Australian research is often examined and studied, as it was one of the first countries to give the courts the ability to order shared residence and the first country to conduct research on the effect that this legislation had in practice.[13] These studies are occasionally mentioned and used in this chapter, where they provide relevant information on a side-subject or fill in a lacuna in the existing knowledge, but are not extensively explained and delved into.

6.2.2 THE NETHERLANDS

The sociological and demographic data on residential co-parenting in the Netherlands is derived mainly from the multi-disciplinary project 'Divided Parents, Shared Children' conducted by Utrecht University. This is an on-going socio-legal research project into residential arrangements after parental separation, of which this book is part.[14] While it focuses on residential co-parenting, many different types of residential arrangements are researched, as well as the child's well-being, the parent's well-being,

---

12 Family Justice Knowledge Hub, Research Bulletin 4, March 2014, p. 9. Accessible through the UK government website: www.gov.uk/government/publications/family-justice-research-bulletin-4-mar-2014. See also a short study overview on the Nuffield Foundation website www.nuffieldfoundation.org/how-do-county-courts-share-care-children-between-parents (both last visited 30 April 2015).

13 See for an in-depth review by Professor Trinder (University of Exeter) of various (mainly Australian) studies: L. TRINDER, 2010, pp. 475-498.

14 See for a description of the project and the researchers involved the Nieuwe families in Nederland website: nfn-onderzoek.nl (last visited 30 April 2015) or A. POORTMAN, 'Verblijfsarrangementen na scheiding: een sociologische analyse' in *Actuele ontwikkelingnen in het familierecht*, UCERF reeks volume 6, 2012, pp. 60-61.

the position of other family members, parenting plans and other related subjects. The data is gathered through various types of research: literature research, the gathering of court documents, interviews with parents and practitioners, and questionnaires.

Additionally, data gathered by the Research and Documentation Centre of the Dutch Ministry of Security and Justice (*Wetenschappelijk Onderzoek- en Documentatiecentrum, WODC*) as part of the 'parenting plan evaluation report' was consulted for this section.

6.2.2.1. *Study of 200 parenting plans*

In the preparation of this book, and as part of the 'Divided Parents, Shared Children' project, 200 parenting plans of separating couples were collected and analysed. To ensure that the results were both as recent and representative as possible, the following strategy was followed:

The parenting plans were gathered in two batches of 100, at two different (lower) courts: Rechtbank Utrecht and Rechtbank Arnhem in 2011 and 2012.[15] For the first batch, family law cases involving children were gathered from the court's archives in Utrecht, starting with the most recent and working back until 100 cases containing parenting plans were collected. This resulted in 100 cases with the decision date between 14 September 2011 and 23 November 2011. Only cases in which a final decision had been reached (and not cases with only a preliminary decision) were used. In order to guarantee that both sets of parenting plans were comparable the second batch, from the archives of the Rechtbank Arnhem, was not selected out of the most recently decided cases; instead, the case files were searched by date and they were archived (searching by the final decision date was not possible); to find cases that were decided around the same time the cases from the first batch had been decided. Because of the less than perfect search system the decision dates of the second batch are roughly divided over the same time period, but have a couple of outliers, which sets the final time period over which the decisions stretch at 29 July 2011 to 9 January 2012.

Both sets of 100 parenting plans and the cases in which they were included were analysed in depth and the resulting statistics were compared to each other. If the comparison had shown significant differences in the outcomes of the cases and the contents of the parenting plans, it would be considered probable that each court has its own way of dealing with such disputes and the gathered data could not have been considered as representative outside each court district. However, the comparison showed no significant differences between the two court districts.

15 Now renamed Rechtbank Midden-Nederland and Rechtbank Gelderland.

Therefore the data is presented together and can be considered to have value outside of the two court districts investigated, although there might still be differences with courts in other regions of the country, especially those with a demographic that strongly differs from that of the moderately urban Utrecht and Arnhem regions.

6.2.2.2. *Are the kids alright?*

As part of the Divided Parents, Shared Children project, a study on the risks and benefits of shared residence for children's well-being was conducted. This study examined, among other things, the validity of two common objections found in international literature against shared residence, namely that it creates instability for children and exposes them to ongoing parental conflict, and impact of residential arrangements on children's relationship with their parents.[16]

This study, documented in the PhD thesis 'Are the kids alright? A study into post-divorce residence arrangements and children's well-being', looks at three residential situations: the child living with the mother, the child living with the father, and the child living in a shared residence arrangement. The data analysed in this study was gathered through the New Families in the Netherlands Survey: a new large-scale online survey collected from a random sample of formerly married and cohabiting couples with minor children who officially divorced or ended their cohabitation in 2010 (therefore after the coming into force of the 2009 law reform). The sample was drawn by Statistics Netherlands from the Dutch Social Statistical Data Base and had 4,481 respondents.[17]

Instability was assessed by measuring the number of changes between the parents' homes and the distance between those homes.[18] Conflict was assessed by measuring the amount of tensions between parents and if any indicators of serious conflict had occurred since separation.[19] To measure the parent-child relationship, the parents were asked to rate the relationship in a scale from 1 to 10.[20]

6.2.2.3. *WODC parenting plan evaluation report*

When the 2009 law reform introduced and made obligatory the making of a parenting plan in cases of parental separation, the Ministry of Security

---

16 S. WESTPHAL, *Are the kids alright? Essays on postdivorce residence arrangements and children's well-being*, Utrecht, 2015, pp. 31-33.

17 *Ibid.*, p. 36.

18 *Ibid.*, p. 70.

19 *Ibid.*, p. 71.

20 *Ibid.*, p. 96.

and Justice indicated a desire to evaluate its functioning in practice three years after it came into force.[21] This evaluation was conducted and a report on the findings was published in 2013.[22] It drew its information from literature, existing data from the Dutch Social Statistical Data Base, expert meetings, interviews, and the study *Scholieren en Gezinnen.*[23] Especially data from this last study is relevant in the context of this chapter, because it contains information about the well-being of children of separated parents. Unfortunately, because the sample group was relatively small (450 children whose parents were separated) and only children between 12 and 16 years of age were involved, a clear distinction between children whose parents separated before and after the 2009 law reform could not be made, and because no distinction was made between children who experienced their parents' separation recently and those who had experienced it some years ago, the results of this study must be used with great caution.[24]

6.2.2.4. *The parenting plan and its effects on children*

A revised version of the study *Scholieren en Gezinnen*, mentioned above, focusing on the effects of the parenting plans on the well-being of the children involved was published in 2013.[25] While the study itself had already started in 2006, the new publication focused mainly on the results of the questionnaires that were gathered in 2013.[26] Children between the age of 12 and 16 were asked to fill in a questionnaire with questions on their family situation, their living arrangements, and their well-being.[27] Both children whose parents were still (living) together (1921) and children whose parents had separated (450) were questioned.[28] The children with separated parents were divided into three groups according to when their parents had separated: before 2004 (group 0 containing 153 children), between 2004 and 2008 (group 1 containing 169 children), and between 2009 and 2013 (group 2 containing 113 children).[29] It should be noted here that because the children questioned were roughly the same age, this subdivision brings with it the following implications: children in group 0 experienced the separation at a younger age than the children in groups 1

21 Handelingen I, Voortgezet ouderschap, 18 November 2008, EK 8 8-422.
22 M.J. VOERT & T. GEURTS, 'Evaluatie Ouderschapsplan. Een eerste verkenning', *WODC*, Cahier 2013-8.
23 *Ibid.*, pp. 19-23.
24 *Ibid.*, pp. 20-21, 41-43.
25 I. VAN DER VALK & E. SPRUIJT, 'Het ouderschap en de effecten voor de kinderen', *Jeugd & Gezin, Departement Pedagogische Wetenschappen, Universiteit Utrecht*, 10 October 2013.
26 *Ibid.*, p. 2.
27 *Ibid.*, pp. 3-8.
28 *Ibid.*, p. 3.
29 *Ibid.*, p. 4.

and 2 and children in group 1 had experienced parental separation at a younger age than children in group 2; for children in group 0 the separation had occurred a long time ago and they had had the time to adjust to the separation, while for children in group 2 the separation was still very recent. The children in the different groups not only experienced parental separation long ago or more recently, they also experienced it at different stages of maturity: children in group 0 were significantly younger when their parents separated than children in group 2.

6.2.3. BELGIUM: SCHEIDING IN VLAANDEREN

In 2009-2010, a large-scale study into divorce in Belgian Flanders had taken place under the name *Scheiding in Vlaanderen* (Divorce in Flanders). Between September 2009 and December 2010 information was gathered among persons who entered into their first marriage between 1971 and 2008. Some 12,110 people had responded to this multi-actor research.[30] The study is part of the research programme *Strategisch Basisonderzoek* by the *Instituut voor de aanmoediging van innovatie door Wetenschap en Technologie in Vlaanderen* (Institute for the promotion of innovation through Science and Technology in Flanders) and was conducted as a joint effort by five research organisations[31] and two advising partners[32].[33]

In this study a great deal of emphasis was placed on residential arrangements. Information on the residential arrangements of children after divorce was gathered among 1870 divorced parents and the children who were living with them. Those respondents who indicated that their child or children resided with both them and their ex-partner were asked more in-depth questions.[34]

---

30 S. VANASSCHE & K. MATTHIJS, 'Verblijfsco-ouderschap en de relaties tussen ouders en stiefouders', *Relaties en nieuwe gezinnen*, 2013, Vol. 3, No. 4, p. 2. More about the research and the research methods used may be found on the research website: www.scheidinginvlaanderen.be (last visited 30 April 2015).

31 Universiteit Antwerpen Centrum voor Longitudinaal en Levenslooponderzoek (CELLO), Health and demographic research (University of Ghent), Centrum voor Bevolkings- en Gezinsonderzoek (K.U. Leuven), Interface Demography (Vrije Universiteit Brussel) and Studiedienst van de Vlaamse Regering.

32 Antwerp University and K.U. Leuven.

33 See www.scheidinginvlaanderen.be, Wie zijn we? (last visited 30 April 2015).

34 D. MORTELMANS et al., *Scheiding in Vlaanderen*, Acco, 2011, pp. 136-137.

6.2.4. COMPARATIVE SYNTHESIS

As can be seen from the above paragraphs, in all three countries this book concerns studies into the residential arrangements of children after parental separation. The scope, the content, and the sample size of these studies differ strongly. The approach to residential co-parenting differs as well. Whereas some studies, like the Gingerbread and the Nuffield Foundation study, only collect the data on the prevalence of residential co-parenting and leave it at that, other studies, such as the Divided Parents, Shared Children project, attempt to investigate what effect residential co-parenting has on aspects of children's well-being.

It is clear, however, that there are still major lacunas in the existing knowledge. There are only a few studies that concern themselves with the question of what influences different residential arrangements have on the well-being of the children involved, and of those that do, very few gather this information from the children themselves. The information on the well-being of children is usually derived from what parents or practitioners have to say about the topic. It has also not been investigated what the reasoning is behind the parents' choice for the residential arrangement they have decided upon. What kind of considerations do parents have before deciding on a residential arrangement and does the legal framework or social pressure have any influence on that decision?

Additionally, most of these empirical studies are fairly recent and only capture one moment in the long process of post-separation settlement and adaptation. It would be much more interesting to see a long-term study that examines the changing circumstances of the people involved in different arrangements. In this way changes in the well-being of children (and parents) can be measured over time, as well as how (and if) the arrangements are adjusted to changing circumstances, such as changes in employment, children's education, and new partners. Currently this information is lacking in studies from all three countries.

6.3. FACTS AND FIGURES

England, the Netherlands and Belgium are three countries with a high divorce rate and a high number of children being born outside marriage.[35] This has as an outcome that many children grow up outside the legal confines of marriage. These children are raised in various residential arrangements. To make sure that the (national) legal systems accommodate arrangements that are in the best interests of children and that the law adjusts to changes within society, first an awareness needs to be achieved of what exactly is going on in real life when it comes to residential arrangements.

This section presents data on the prominence of residential co-parenting (and other residential arrangements) in the three countries on which this book is centred and any other statistical data on this topic. The information is gathered from the reports of the various studies explained and described in the previous section of this chapter.

6.3.1. ENGLAND

Harding and Newnham's interim findings in the study on how county courts share the care of children between parents show that a large part of cases in which a parent applies to the court to make a Section 8 order involves a father requesting a contact order (69 out of 193 cases). There were also many applications by mothers (38) and fathers (39) for sole residence orders. Only 11 out of 193 cases began with an application for a shared care order.[36] This means that in the sample, only about 5.6% of those resorting to the courts had the initial intention to enter into a shared residence arrangement.

These 193 county court cases resulted in the courts making the following orders:[37]

---

35 In 2011 117,558 divorces and 247,890 marriages took place in England and Wales. 57,219 divorced couples had one or more children below the age of 16. See data from the Office of National Statistics at www.ons.gov.uk (last visited 30 April 2015). In the Netherlands there were 1.9 divorces per 1,000 inhabitants against 4.4 marriages per 1,000 inhabitants, while in Belgium there were 3 divorces and 4 marriages per 1,000 inhabitants. See data from the Eurostat website at ec.europa.eu/eurostat (last visited 30 April 2015). 46.2%, 43.3% and 45.7% of all live births in England and Wales, the Netherlands, and Belgium respectively were outside marriage in 2009 (see Office of National Statistics for England and Wales and Eurostat for the Netherlands and Belgium). See for more figures the Eurostat website at ec.europa.eu/eurostat (last visited 30 April 2015).

36 Family Justice Knowledge Hub, Research Bulletin 4, March 2014, p. 10. (accessible through the UK government website: www.gov.uk/government/publications/family-justice-research-bulletin-4-mar-2014 (last visited 30 April 2015).

37 *Ibid.*

Table 4

Sole residence	22
Shared residence	17
Contact only	79
Sole residence and contact	60
No order as to contact or residence	15

This indicates that shared residence orders had been made in at least six cases in which the parents had not initially applied for such an order. As the chapter on English law has shown that the English courts are reluctant to go against the wishes of parents in family law matters, it would be interesting to see what caused the parents to agree on a different residential arrangement or the court to convince them to do so. This information will likely be included in the final report, once the study has been concluded. Due to the small sample size, however, the results of this study must be used with caution.

Because not all parents apply to the court for a Section 8 order, many instead decide on a residential arrangement for their children amongst themselves, and because, despite an existing order, the practical arrangement they find themselves in can very well differ from what was originally decided upon, it is important to look at what kind of residential arrangements parents in England actually decide upon.

According to the 2006-2007 Gingerbread and Nuffield Foundation study, 12% of the respondents reported that they share the care for their child or children with the other parent. Within the ramifications of the study, shared care is understood as both parents looking after the child for three or more days and nights a week, or for around half the year each overall.[38] These numbers, however, must not be taken at face value, without considering the following: there was an overall lower response rate by men, a lower response rate by non-resident parents who had never been married, and a particular reluctance by those parents who had no contact with their child or children to take part. Additionally, some of the respondents were reluctant to label themselves as non-resident parents.[39] This may mean that in practice shared care is less prevalent than the study results suggest. This is acknowledged by the authors themselves, who indicate that the actual percentage of shared care is more likely to be around 9%.[40]

---

38 V. PEACEY & J. HUNT, p. 19. Accessible online through the Gingerbread and the Nuffield Foundation websites: www.gingerbread.org.uk and www.nuffieldfoundation.org (last visited 30 April 2015).

39 *Ibid.*, p. 14.

40 *Ibid.*, p. 19.

Those parents who had indicated that they shared the care of their children were not asked all the questions which the other parents were asked. Still, the data gathered can shed some light on the profile of the average parent in a shared care arrangement. See the table below, the figures are in rounded-off percentages.[41]

Table 5

	Resident parent	Non-resident parent	Shared-care parent
Sex			
Male	9%	87%	28%
Female	91%	13%	72%
Marital status			
Single, never married	41%	27%	34%
Married, living with spouse	16%	29%	14%
Married, separated from spouse	14%	14%	25%
Divorced	29%	30%	26%
Age			
30 or under	22%	15%	14%
31-40	38%	40%	39%
41 or over	40%	26%	47%
Educational qualifications			
None, or low GCSE*	25%	38%	22%
Good GCSE	34%	25%	38%
A level or equivalent	20%	15%	16%
Above A level	21%	21%	24%
Employment status			
Working	64%	77%	75%
Not working	36%	23%	25%
Tenure type			
Own outright/with mortgage	43%	52%	53%
Social renter	42%	27%	36%
Private renter	15%	21%	11%

41 *Ibid.*, p. 16, table 2.2.

	Resident parent	Non-resident parent	Shared-care parent
Ethnic background			
White British/White other	91%	89%	85%
Any other background	9%	11%	15%

* GCSE stands for General Certificate of Secondary Education. It is an academic qualification awarded in secondary education in England, Wales and Northern Ireland.

Judging from the figures above, a parent in a shared care arrangement is most likely not married, is 31 years old or older, has at least good GCSEs, is employed, owns his/her own home and has a white ethnic background. However, the figures above show that parents in shared care arrangements do not have *significantly different* characteristics from other parents. The largest differences seem to occur between resident and non-resident parents, with shared care parents being somewhere in the middle.[42]

If the above figures are compared with the figures from the county court cases study, it is evident that the percentage (about 8.8%) of shared residence orders made by the county courts does in fact coincide with the adjusted estimated percentage (9%) and is not far removed from the exact percentage (12%) of parents who have reported that they share care for their child or children in the Gingerbread and Nuffield Foundation study. At first glance, this seems to indicate that the large majority of people who have a shared residence order made for them by the courts actually exercise residential co-parenting de facto and stick with the arrangement over time. However, because many residential arrangements are agreed upon outside the courts it is just as possible that many people who have a shared residence order have either never practised residential co-parenting or have since changed the de facto arrangement, but because there are more ex-partners who have made a residential co-parenting arrangement out of court and are still exercising it the figures are levelled.

6.3.2. THE NETHERLANDS

The study of 200 parenting plans (and the cases they are part of) conducted by this author showed that by far the most cases containing parenting plans are divorce cases (92%). 1% of the cases were legal separation orders (*scheiding van tafel en bed*), 3% were dissolutions of registered partnerships, and the remaining 4% were dissolutions of co-habitation contracts. No

[42] *Ibid.*, pp. 15-17.

cases were found where parental separation had occurred earlier and the parents brought a dispute before the court to alter or enforce an already existing parenting plan. This can be explained by the fact that making parenting plans is a very recent obligation and that starting another procedure is costly and time-consuming for the parents.

This study also shows that the choice for sole residence with one of the parents, with only limited contact with the other parent, is currently relatively rare (only 7.5% of the plans list residence only with the mother and 2% list residence only with the father). The most popular is the 'weekend plus' arrangement (found in 42.5% of the parenting plans studied). The 'weekend plus' arrangement is replacing the 'classic' weekend arrangement in which one parent (usually the father) has the child staying with him/her for one weekend in a fortnight. This new 'weekend plus' arrangement consists of a weekend in a fortnight and an additional night with the non-resident parent during the week the child otherwise spends with the resident parent or a weekend in a fortnight and multiple contact moments with the non-resident parent outside of this weekend. A surprisingly large proportion of the parenting plans analysed, 38%, contain a residential co-parenting arrangement where the child spends at least three nights on average each week with each parent. The remaining 10% of the parenting plans contain no residential arrangement. Various reasons were given for not including one, usually the reason being that the children were older and would decide themselves when they wanted to stay at which parent's home. Sometimes one of the parents was still searching for a residence and because the residential arrangement depended on where he or she was going to live, it could not yet be established.

Because the above figures only take into account what kind of residential arrangement is contained in each parenting plan analysed and many of the parenting plans are made for multiple children, they do not correctly represent the number of children involved in the different types of residential arrangements, nor do they show any of the children's characteristics. The table below shows how many children are involved in the various residential arrangements, what their age is, and what gender the children are in rounded-off percentages.

Table 6

Residential arrangement	Residence with mother	Residence with father	Residential co-parenting arrangement	Weekend (+) arrangement	No set arrangement
Child's age at time of court's decision					
0-4	0.80%	0%	8.31%	10.46%	0.54%
5-12	2.95%	0.27%	23.32%	22.52%	1.34%
13-15	1.88%	0.54%	5.63%	6.97%	3.49%
16-17	0.80%	0.54%	2.41%	1.07%	2.95%
18 and up	0.27%	1.07%	0.80%	0.27%	0.80%
Gender of the child					
Male	3.25%	0.81%	19.78%	19.97%	3.52%
Female	2.71%	1.63%	21.14%	23.04%	5.15%

As one can see from this table, parents of children of all ages choose residential co-parenting arrangements, even the parents of very young children. The age of the children who do not have a set arrangement is also spread out; this contradicts the original expectation that it would be only or mainly the parents of older children who would decide not to make a residential arrangement and leave it up to the children to decide where they wanted to live on a day-to-day basis.

The gender of the children does not seem to influence the choice of the residential arrangement, especially not in the sense that boys are more likely to live with the father and girls with the mother.

Another interesting outcome of the parenting plan analysis is that while 2.44% of the children live with the father and 40.92% live with both parents, 27% of the children have their father's residence registered as their main residence. This accounts for a little more than the children in a sole father residence plus half the children in a residential co-parenting arrangement. The parenting plans show that the choice for a main residence is predominately influenced by financial considerations, ergo, which parent is to receive child support and if one considers that men in general still tend to earn more money than women, this division of main residence makes sense from a practical point of view.

In the questionnaire that was part of the *Scholieren & Gezinnen* study children between the age of 12 and 16 whose parents were separated were asked to describe their residential arrangement. 286 children indicated that they lived only or mainly with the mother, 27 lived only or mainly with the father, and 116 had indicated that they lived in a residential co-parenting arrangement.[43]

In the 'Are the kids alright?' thesis one can read that approximately 29% of the 3,355 parents reported that their children alternate between their residence and that of the children's other parent.[44]

This brings the percentage of children who actually live in a residential co-parenting arrangement somewhere between 27 and 29 percent. This is lower than the outcome of the parenting plans study. Various explanations for this difference are possible. First of all, the parents in the parenting plans study had separated much more recently than the parents in the other two studies; therefore it is possible that residential co-parenting is becoming more popular. However, the figures from the *Scholieren & Gezinnen* study seem to dispute this hypothesis, because they show that actually the group of children whose parents have separated between 2004 and 2008 have a higher percentage of residential co-parenting arrangements (36.6%), than the children whose parents separated between 2009 and 2013 (27.4%).[45]

Another explanation is that there exists a natural discrepancy between the arrangement that parents make during their separation and the arrangement that they end up practically employing. The results would then indicate that while, theoretically, many parents aspire to have a residential co-parenting arrangement, in practice it sometimes does not work out.

6.3.3. BELGIUM

The *Scheiding in Vlaanderen* study has shown that roughly one fifth of the children live in a residential co-parenting arrangement, often with a 50/50 division of time. One in seven children lives in a classic weekend arrangement where he or she resides with one parent during the week and with the other at weekends or every other weekend. One in ten children has his/her main residence with the father, but the most common residential arrangement is still a main residence with the mother.[46]

In the table below, one can see how the time period in which parental separation took place affects the type of residential arrangements. The figures are in rounded-off percentages.[47]

---

43 I. VAN DER VALK & E. SPRUIJT, 2013, p. 6. Residential co-parenting meant in this study that the children spent at least three days a week on average with each parent.

44 S. WESTPHAL, 2015, p. 73, table 3.1.

45 *Ibid.*, p. 11.

46 D. MORTELMANS et al., 2011, p. 137.

47 *Ibid.*, p. 137, table 6.1.

Table 7

Child's living arrangement	161 children of parents divorced before June 1995	1,123 children of parents divorced June 1995-August 2006	488 children of parents divorced after 2006	Group as a whole
Full time with mother (100%)	50.9%	34.7%	29.3%	34.7%
Full time with father (100%)	9.2%	8.0%	8.9%	8.2%
Mainly with mother (66-99%)	8.7%	11.8%	15.0%	12.6%
Mainly with father (66-99%)	0.6%	1.5%	1.4%	1.4%
Residential co-parenting (33-66%)	6.8%	21.1%	27.7%	21.4 %
Week mother/ weekend father	13.7%	14.5%	9.2%	13.1%
Week father/ weekend mother	0.6%	0.6%	1.2%	0.8%
Bird's nest arrangement*	1.9%	0.7%	0.8%	0.8%
No residential arrangement	8.7%	7.0%	7.2%	7.2%

* This arrangement entails that children stay in one house and it is the parents who alternate their residence there.

The three time periods were not chosen arbitrarily; they signify the coming into force of two important law changes: the ex lege continuation of joint parental responsibilities after divorce and the obligation of the court to consider equally divided residence after separation as the first option if requested by a parent.[48] As can be seen above, where the parents divorced before the 1995 law reform, only 6.8% of them have a residential co-parenting arrangement. For parents who divorced in the period after the 1995 reform, but before the 2006 reform, the amount of residential co-parenting arrangements increased to 21.1%. Even assuming that residential co-parenting was socially increasing in popularity over the years, a growth of over 14%, almost tripling the original figures, is most remarkable, especially considering that the 1995 reform did not regulate residence arrangements, but only parental responsibilities. For the period after the

48 See sections 5.1 and 5.2 of Chapter 5 for an explanation of these two law reforms.

2006 law reform, the proportion of residential co-parenting arrangements further increased to 27.1%.[49] This would imply that legal changes have a strong effect on the eventual residential arrangement. This is either felt by the parents, who then decide to agree on an arrangement, the courts, when asked to make a residence order, or both.

However, these numbers must be seen in conjunction with the following findings on the age of the children in different residential arrangements. The figures are, once again, rounded off.[50]

Table 8

Child's living arrangement	454 children 0-12 years old	594 children 13-17 years old	775 children 18 years or older
Full time with mother (100%)	20.3%	31.1%	45.8%
Full time with father (100%)	2.0%	6.2%	13.3%
Mainly with mother (66-99%)	18.7%	15.0%	7.1%
Mainly with father (66-99%)	2.2%	1.5%	0.8%
Residential co-parenting (33-66%)	36.1%	23.1%	11.5%
Week mother/weekend father	15.9%	15.0%	9.9%
Week father/weekend mother	1.8%	0.5%	0.4%
Bird's nest arrangement*	0.9%	1.2%	0.5%
No residential arrangement	2.2%	6.4%	10.7%

* This arrangement entails that children stay in one house and it is the parents who alternate their residence there.

As can be seen above, residential arrangements seem to be influenced by the age of the child. Children under the age of 12 are more likely to be raised in a residential co-parenting arrangement than those who are older. Even very young children – 30% of children below 5 years of age – alternate their residence between the parents.[51] Children of the parents

49 Strictly speaking, a bird's nest arrangement is just a special type of residential co-parenting arrangement and thus should be included in the numbers. This would mean that before 1995 8.1% of the children lived in a residential co-parenting arrangement, after 1995, but before 2006 it was 21.8%, and after 2006 28.5%, bringing the total to 22.2% of the children living in a residential co-parenting arrangement.

50 D. MORTELMANS et al., 2011, p. 138, table 6.2.

51 D. MORTELMANS et al., 2011, p. 139.

who separated before the 1995 law reform would generally be older than the children of the parents who separated after the reform (and definitely older than the children of the parents who separated after 2006) at the time of gathering the information. Therefore, because the groups of children whose parents separated after the 1995 or after the 2006 law reform are likely to contain, on average, younger children than the group of children whose parents separated before the 1995 law reform, it is therefore likely that the increase in residential co-parenting after the law reforms was less drastic than the figures may suggest.

Additional to the data on the prevalence and growth or decrease of various residential arrangements, data was also gathered on the practical aspects of such arrangements and the specifications of the parents engaging therein. It was thus discovered that out of 896 children in the study who regularly alternated between their parents' homes, 2.1% did so only once or twice a month, 17.9% three times a month, 47.3% four times a month, 14% five to seven times a month, 8.9% eight times a month, 5% nine to twelve times a month, and 4.7% moved thirteen times or even more often.[52] The most popular days of the week for children to move from one home to the other were: Mondays, Friday nights, and Sunday nights.[53]

The research into the socio-economic profile of the parents of 1587 children showed that parents who have a residential co-parenting arrangement are in general highly educated and high earning.[54] See below the data gathered on the socio-economic background of mothers and fathers in various residential arrangements. The figures are in rounded-off percentages.[55]

52 *Ibid.*, p. 140, table 6.4. Percentages are rounded off.
53 *Ibid.*, p. 140, figure 6.1.
54 *Ibid.*, p. 141.
55 *Ibid.*, p. 142, table 6.5.

Table 9

Father	Residence with mother	Residence with father	Residential co-parenting	Week/ weekend residence	No residential arrangement
Level of education					
Low	24.6%	32.1%	11.9%	20.2%	30.7%
Medium	42.2%	42.5%	45.5%	48.5%	30.7%
High	33.2%	25.4%	42.6%	31.3%	38.7%
Income					
Low	9.0%	7.2%	6.3%	11.7%	13.6%
Medium	55.3%	51.2%	42.2%	46.9%	37.3%
High	35.7%	41.6%	51.6%	41.4%	49.2%
Employment status					
Working full time	87.0%	85.8%	88.0%	82.8%	85.5%
Working part time	2.8%	2.2%	6.0%	5.2%	4.8%
Not working	10.2%	11.9%	6.0%	11.9%	9.7%
Mother	**Residence with mother**	**Residence with father**	**Residential co-parenting**	**Week/ weekend residence**	**No residential arrangement**
Level of education					
Low	20.9%	22.5%	11.2%	11.9%	10.5%
Medium	44.4%	55.0%	39.6%	51.7%	40.3%
High	34.8%	22.5%	49.2%	36.4%	49.3%
Income					
Low	37.5%	55.3%	26.7%	42.5%	32.8%
Medium	44.3%	34.2%	22.8%	39.8%	40.6%
High	18.2%	10.5%	50.6%	17.7%	26.6%
Employment status					
Working full time	51.7%	43.6%	56.7%	50.4%	55.9%
Working part time	34.2%	38.5%	33.2%	36.5%	25.0%
Not working	14.1%	18.0%	10.2%	13.0%	19.1%

To elaborate more on the above results, it is evident from the table that both mothers and fathers in residential co-parenting arrangements are most likely to be highly or medium educated and high earning. Also, when it comes to the employment status of parents in a residential co-parenting arrangement, both fathers and mothers are most likely to be working full time. Fathers in general tend to work full time irrespective of the residential arrangement, while roughly a third of mothers work part time.

6.3.4. COMPARATIVE SYNTHESIS

One thing is abundantly clear form the figures displayed above: residential co-parenting is not merely a theoretical arrangement. In the countries considered, between 9% (England) and 27-38% (the Netherlands) of separating parents choose this residential arrangement. This provides a positive answer to the question whether residential co-parenting is an arrangement that is prevalent enough to necessitate further research.

The figures from the Belgian research additionally indicate that legislation on both parental responsibilities and residential arrangements does seem to have an influence on the number of residential co-parenting arrangements. While there are other factors capable of influencing the popularity of residential co-parenting arrangements, the influence of legal provisions should not be disregarded. This means that as, in Belgium at the very least, the law seems to influence the type of residential arrangements parents choose, it is important to make sure that this influence is the one which is intended.

The figures in this section, especially those from England and Belgium, have also revealed interesting information about the characteristics of the parents who choose residential co-parenting arrangements. Those parents are more likely to be medium to highly educated and financially stable. However, the difference between parents in residential co-parenting arrangements and parents in other types of arrangements are small, indicating that residential co-parenting is not necessarily employed only by a specific demographic. All kinds of parents share the residence of their children.

6.4. (OUTSIDE) FACTORS INFLUENCING THE WELL-BEING OF CHILDREN

The previous section indicates that residential co-parenting is not only a (moderately) popular residential arrangement, but also that the national legal framework has an influence on how popular it is. This begs the following question: if the law influences what residential arrangements parents choose for their child or children, what kind of influence should it exercise?

The answer is if one considers the international principle of the paramountcy of the child's best interests, then the law should promote that residential arrangement which is in the best interests of the child. However, which residential arrangement is in any given case in the best interests of the child depends on the circumstances of the case. This is no different for residential co-parenting.

The idea of a child being raised by and spending approximately an equal amount of time with both of his or her parents after parental separation seems positive for the child, who is not suddenly deprived of the care of either parent after parental separation, as well as for the promotion of the equality of parents. At face value this seems like a win-win situation for the parents and the child(ren). However, in the literature there is resistance against residential co-parenting as well as support for it. Even existing empirical research does not seem conclusive as reviewers of these studies have over the years presented varying conclusions.

> '[S]ome argued that the researched literature unequivocally supports joint custody [...]; others argued that variables such as parental conflict are more important than custodial arrangement in determining child outcomes [...] and that joint custody is likely to be inappropriate in high-conflict situations [...]. Still others presented mixed findings in which no single custody arrangement can be assumed to be preferable.'[56]

Because the author of this book lacks a background in sociological or psychological studies, no attempt has been made to gather socio-psychological data or to make value judgements about the various existing methodological studies. Instead, to establish the main arguments brought forward in psychological, sociological and legal literature in favour or against residential co-parenting arrangements, reviews have been consulted that summarise various outcomes of empirical studies and leading literature. For this purpose these reviews have not been limited to the three countries examined in this book. This is for two reasons. First, research that focuses on the various factors on which the well-being of children depends can much more easily be applied universally than legal research and statistical data. This kind of research looks at the intrinsic value of human interactions and is therefore not strictly bound to national systems. Second, in the three countries examined, an insufficient amount

---

56 R. BAUSERMAN, 'Child Adjustment in Joint-Custody Versus Sole-Custody Arrangements: A Meta-Analytic Review', *Journal of Family Psychology*, 2002, Vol. 16, No. 1, p. 92.

of such reviews, as well as empirical studies, have been conducted on which to base a comprehensive overview.

Three such overviews proved specifically useful. First, there is Bauserman's analysis of a great number of empirical studies into residential arrangements and a child's adjustment, which though highly regarded, is, having been published in 2002, unfortunately not up to date concerning the newer research.[57] Then there is Trinder's research review from 2010, with a strong focus on the Commonwealth and specifically Australia.[58] And, finally, the most recent (published in 2013) and possibly the most extensive overview from Sünderhauf.[59] The information from these overviews is supplemented with research from experts from the countries on which this book focuses, mainly Harris-Short from England and Westphal from the Netherlands.[60]

These reviews paint somewhat differing pictures. In her review Sünderhauf explains that there are three main reasons for resistance against residential co-parenting in the literature: the cultural tradition in favour of mother care (and therefore subsequently against father care or joint care), not proven or falsely interpreted psychological concepts of stability, a fear of loss and identity building, and the subconscious resistance of lawyers and psychologists against shared care.[61] Needless to say, these reasons are not seen as justifiable by the reviewer. However, she does evaluate certain factors that *could* have a negative influence on residential co-parenting arrangements in particular cases, namely: the wish of the parents to be part of such an arrangement, the communication and co-operation between parents, the (high) amount of parental conflict, the burdening effect of switching between households, the need for stability, and the geographical proximity of the parents. She then goes on to dismiss most of these factors on the basis of empirical evidence.

However, not all reviewers are that dismissive of reasons against residential co-parenting. Harris-Short, for example, sees the increase of 50/50 shared care and especially the increase of residential orders to that extent as an undesirable development.[62] Like Sünderhauf, Harris-Short discusses factors that have an influence on the desirability of

---

57 R. BAUSERMAN, 2002.

58 L. TRINDER, 'Shared residence: a review of recent research evidence', *Child and Family Law Quarterly*, 2010, Vol. 22, No. 4.

59 H. SÜNDERHAUF, 'Vorurteile gegen das Wechselmodell: Was stimmt, was nicht? – Argumente in der Rechtsprechung und Erkenntnisse aus der psychologischen Forschung (Teil I)', *FamRB-Beratungspraxis*, 9/2013.

60 S. HARRIS-SHORT, 'Resisting the march towards 50/50 shared residence: rights, welfare and equality in post-separation families', *Journal of Social Welfare & Family Law*, 2010, Vol. 32, No. 3, and S. WESTPHAL, 2015.

61 H. SÜNDERHAUF, (Teil I), 2013, pp. 291-292.

62 S. HARRIS-SHORT, 2010, pp. 257-274.

residential co-parenting. However, unlike Sünderhauf, she presents them as prerequisites in order for a residential co-parenting arrangement to work. These prerequisites are: geographical proximity, a high level of co-operation between the parents, mutual respect between parents, flexibility, and a high degree of responsiveness to the needs of the child.[63]

Westphal's empirical research indicates that residential co-parenting arrangements contribute to children's well-being after separation, that children in residential co-parenting arrangements not only experience higher levels of psychological well-being than children in sole residence arrangements, but also possessed better relationships with their family members.[64] However, she cautions that: 'it is important to keep in mind that shared residence should not be regarded as a universal solution in custody decisions', because there are strong discrepancies in outcomes within the shared residence group when it comes to parental conflict and it is also possible that 'the positive association between shared residence and child well-being might be partly the result of parents' self-selection into shared residence' and thus might disappear if unwilling parents are forced into such arrangement.[65]

These various factors have been encountered before in this book, namely in the chapters discussing national law, or more specifically, case law. They were used by the courts in their decisions to rule in favour or against a residential co-parenting arrangement.

This indicates that the question whether residential co-parenting arrangements should be encouraged by the legislature might not be simply answered with a yes or no. Instead, it appears that the answer might depend on these different factors and how they apply in any specific case.

This section therefore sets out four of the most important factors that have been put forward in the literature and case law as being of influence, either positively or negatively, on the well-being of children in residential co-parenting arrangements: the level of conflict (including the willingness to communicate and co-operate) between parents, the geographical distance between parents, the age of the child or children involved, and the willingness of (both) parents to have a residential co-parenting arrangement.

---

63 S. HARRIS-SHORT, 2010, pp. 265.
64 S. WESTPHAL, 201, p. 159.
65 *Ibid.*, p. 157.

6.4.1. LEVEL OF CONFLICT BETWEEN PARENTS

That parental conflict is detrimental for the child's well-being has been established and affirmed in many different studies.[66] Unfortunately, parental separation usually causes conflict between the ex-partners. This is not something the legislature is able to 'fix' by making laws, but there might be a way to lessen the impact of parental conflict on the well-being of children.

There exists a hypothesis that residential co-parenting is undesirable in cases of high levels of parental conflict, because it exacerbates the conflict and places the children in the middle of it. Accordingly, previous chapters show that parental conflict is seen by the courts as one of deterring factors and *can* lead to a court denying a parent's request for an equal division of time.[67] This is based on the assumption that good communication between parents is necessary for well-functioning residential co-parenting. However, the courts generally do not consider a lack of communication or communication difficulties as an *insurmountable* obstacle to residential co-parenting, especially if it is brought forward as the only argument against residential co-parenting.[68] Paradoxically, in some cases parental conflict is used as a reason to rule *in favour* of residential co-parenting, in order to ensure that one of the parents does not prevent contact between the child and the other parent.[69]

While the courts seem to embrace the hypothesis that residential co-parenting in cases of a high level of conflict between the parents is undesirable because it would have an adverse effect on the well-being of the children, the empirical evidence shows a distinctly different picture.

Empirical research has shown that not only can residential co-parenting work just as well, if not better than sole residence and can bring positive benefits to both children and parents,[70] it can also *diminish* parental conflict. In a residential co-parenting arrangement there tends to be fewer conflicts than in sole residence arrangements, parental conflicts are resolved more quickly, and children in residential co-parenting arrangements do not experience parental conflict any differently, meaning more acute or more detrimental to their well-being, than children in sole residence

---

66 See for a summary of what various socio-psychological studies have to say about the effect of parental conflict on the well-being of children: A. MOONEY et al., *Impact of Family Breakdown on Children's Well-Being*, Evidence Review, Research Report DCSF-RR113, Thomas Coram Research Unit, Institute of Education, University of London, June 2009, p. 10.

67 See for examples of this in Dutch case law section 4.4.2 of Chapter 4 and in Belgian law section 5.4.2.1 of Chapter 5.

68 See sections 3.4.2 of Chapter 3 and 5.4.2.1 of Chapter 5.

69 *Ibid.*

70 S. HARRIS-SHORT, 2010, p. 264.

arrangements.[71] However, Trinder notes that studies from Australia show that while parents who share care communicate more often and are more likely to share the decision-making than parents in other arrangements, only fathers report lower levels of conflict in shared care compared to other arrangements.[72] Matters are also complicated by the fact that the greater majority of empirical studies rely on the parents to report on the conflicts they experience, as well as the general well-being of their children. These studies rarely, or in most cases do not at all, document the conflicts and their influence on the children through the child's own perspective.

The Dutch study by Westphal tested whether children who lived with the mother, children who lived with the father, and children who lived in a residential co-parenting arrangement were affected the most by parental conflict.[73] The outcome was that parents in residential co-parenting arrangements reported lower post-separation levels of conflict than in the other two arrangements.[74] Additionally, children in residential co-parenting arrangements experienced less emotional problems than children living in sole residence arrangements.[75] No evidence was found that conflict affected children differently depending on the residential arrangements.[76]

The above evidence therefore suggests that there is no necessity for the courts to deny residential co-parenting on the sole basis of a high level of conflict or hostility between the parents. It can even be questioned if parental conflict must be considered as a factor at all when deciding on the residential arrangement.

6.4.2. GEOGRAPHICAL DISTANCE BETWEEN THE PARENTS' HOMES

A practical problem that occurs when parents separate is that they no longer live in the same house. This is self-evident, but it brings along a myriad of issues, one of which being the distance between the two residences. If the parents are to continue shared care of their children, especially in the form of residential co-parenting, both homes need to have the necessary space for the children to comfortably live in, the children

---

71 H. SÜNDERHAUF, 'Vorurteile gegen das Wechselmodell: Was stimmt, was nicht? - Argumente in der Rechtsprechung und Erkenntnisse aus der psychologischen Forschung (Teil II)', *FamRB-Beratungspraxis*, 10/2013, p. 328; and R. BAUSERMAN, 2002, p. 95.

72 L. TRINDER, 2010, p. 481.

73 S. WESTPHAL, 2015, pp. 61-85.

74 *Ibid.*, p. 76.

75 *Ibid.*, p. 75.

76 *Ibid.*, p. 81.

will need to travel between the parents' homes, and if the children are of school age, they will need to be able to go to school from both their parents' houses. Does this mean that if the parents live further apart than a certain distance, then residential co-parenting, as far as the children are concerned, is detrimental, impossible, or should be denied by the courts?

From what has been shown in the chapters on national law, case law does not seem to support this vision. While the courts of the three countries studied do consider the (great) distance between the parents as a factor in their decisions on residential arrangements, similarly as with existing conflict between the parents, the courts do not consider the sole existence of a geographical distance between the parents' homes as a prohibitive factor for residential co-parenting. Instead, the decision as to whether the distance between the parents forms an obstacle to residential co-parenting, is seen as dependant on other facts of the case, such as the possibility for the child to attend school while still living with both parents,[77] communication between the parents,[78] and the residence of other family members.[79]

Not only the distance between the homes matters here; the strain of constantly moving between two residences on the children involved should be considered as well. For some children, an alternating residence can be more of a strain than for others, and therefore in cases involving children who are more susceptible to stress from changing daily circumstances, for example because of a chronic or terminal illness, the courts may deny a residential arrangement even if they would have ruled in favour in a case with the same facts, but which involved different children.[80]

The same study by Westphal that tested the effect of parental conflict on children in different residential arrangements also tested the effect of 'instability' by measuring the number of changes between parents' homes within a month and the distance between parents' homes.[81] The outcome was that while children in residential co-parenting arrangements on average change residences more frequently than children in sole residence arrangements, the distance between the homes is on average shorter for children in residential arrangements and while the distance between the

---

77 See sections 4.4.3 of Chapter 4, 3.4.2 of Chapter 3 and 5.4.2 of Chapter 5.

78 See section 4.4.3 of Chapter 4 for examples of how residential co-parenting between parents who lived very far away was not objected to by the courts because there was very good communication between the parents. See section 3.4.2 of Chapter 3 for examples where residential co-parenting was ordered despite a great geographical distance between the parents because there was poor communication between the parents and there existed a fear that without such an order one parent would preclude communication between the other parent and the child.

79 See section 5.4.2.1 of Chapter 5.

80 See section 4.4.2 of Chapter 4.

81 S. WESTPHAL, 2015, pp. 61-85.

parents' homes is shown to increase the children's emotional difficulties, the number of changes between parents' homes does not.[82]

This signifies that the courts are indeed right in considering the distance between the parents when deciding on the arrangements for the children, but should take into account that a long distance between the parents is not only harmful for the well-being of children in residential co-parenting arrangements, but to the same extent for children in other arrangements as well.

A difficulty lies in the fact that 'distance' in itself is a vague criterion. First of all, empirical studies of residential arrangements that take account of distance as a factor influencing the well-being of the child only speak of a 'long' distance between the parents being detrimental for the children involved, yet there is no indication of when the distance is considered to be long. After how many kilometres between the parents' residences can a decline in a child's well-being be measured? Is such a measurement even possible? And should the measurement indeed be in kilometres, or should it be in the time it takes a child to travel from one house to the other? What about the mode of transportation? Is distance less of a barrier if the child can travel himself or herself instead of being transferred or accompanied by the parents? When considering what distance can be seen as a burden for the child, does this depend on the child's age? All these questions have not yet been properly addressed in the empirical research. What we do know is that some smaller studies have found that among parents with a residential co-parenting arrangement the distance between their homes in the majority of cases lies somewhere between 0 and 19 km.[83]

Aside from the question of distance, what about the idea that the changing of residence itself amounts to a 'burden' for children? Trinder explains that 'shared care can work as both a pleasure and a burden' and while such an arrangement works for some children, others may find it oppressive.[84] Sünderhauf's review of existing empirical research is cautiously positive about children's experience with alternating residences. She clarifies that young children, under the age of 5, experience the changes without any problems at all. Older children, while admitting that it is an *effort*, do not experience it as a *burden*.[85]

An important thing to consider in discussions about distance and residence alterations is that while a residential co-parenting arrangement *usually* involves more residence alterations than sole residence, this is not always the case. Certain sole residence arrangements with overnight

---

82 *Ibid.*, pp. 76, 82-83.
83 H. SÜNDERHAUF, (Teil II), 2013, pp. 333-334.
84 L. TRINDER, 2010, p. 486.
85 H. SÜNDERHAUF, (Teil II), 2013, p. 330.

contact with the non-resident parent may in fact involve more residence alterations than some residential co-parenting arrangements. For example, a currently popular weekend-plus arrangement is a fortnight arrangement that has the child spending one weekend of one week and one day of the other week with the non-resident parent. In such an arrangement the child would be changing residence four times in 14 days, while a residential co-parenting arrangement in which a child spends every other week with each parent would only require two alterations. Because only a small percentage of children live exclusively with one parent, without visits and overnight stays with the other parent, most children of separated parents, independent of whether they are strictly speaking in a sole residence arrangement or residential co-parenting, have to deal with alternating between residences.

6.4.3. AGE OF THE CHILDREN INVOLVED

Children in different stages of their lives need different things from their parents and their environment. Very young children need almost constant care and attention, while teenagers need more freedom and to have their wishes and opinions taken into account. A residential co-parenting arrangement can give rise to different problems depending on the age of the children involved. For example, children under the age of four will need constant supervision and it would be difficult for a parent who works full time to provide this, while children above that age will have to go to school and will need to be escorted there and picked up later while they are still young.

Some courts do take the age of the child into consideration when deciding on the suitability of residential co-parenting.[86] Yet as section 6.3 of this chapter has shown, residential co-parenting is not limited to children of a specific age; in fact, children of all ages grow up in such arrangements.

The question is should the age of the child matter? The literature has remained sitting on the fence here. While Swedish and Australian experts have voiced strong concerns about raising very young children in a residential co-parenting arrangement, arguing that it 'disrupts the child's need to develop a secure attachment to a primary carer',[87] other studies show that children in residential co-parenting arrangements are better adjusted than children in sole residence, irrespective of their ages,[88] or that very young children actually fare better in residential co-parenting

86 See section 5.4.2 of Chapter 5.
87 S. HARRIS-SHORT, 2010, p. 264.
88 R. BAUSERMAN, 2002, p. 98.

arrangements than older children.[89] Trinder describes one Australian study in which some subdivision according to the children's age had been made. It did not find any different behavioural outcomes among children aged four to five that depended on the various residential arrangements. Instead these children's well-being was influenced by parental conflict and parental warmth. Children under the age of 4 who were being raised in a residential co-parenting arrangement, on the other hand, exhibited more developmental and behavioural problems than children in other residential arrangements.[90]

It is clear that more research is necessary before conclusions can be drawn on what kinds of residential arrangements are most suitable for children in specific age categories or what kinds of risks are paired with specific residential arrangements for children of various ages. Before this is made clear through empirical research, it is impossible to say with any certainty that residential co-parenting is inadvisable for children of a certain age, or in reverse, that it is highly recommended for children in certain age groups.

6.4.4. WILLINGNESS OF (BOTH) PARENTS TO HAVE A RESIDENTIAL CO-PARENTING ARRANGEMENT

In most countries where residential co-parenting arrangements are possible, the courts cannot force parents to accept such an arrangement against their wishes. This is the case in the three countries examined in this book. However, the fact that the court cannot force both parents into an unwanted residential arrangement does not mean that it cannot force *one* of the parents to accept such an arrangement at the request of the other parent. Also, the fact that the court cannot rule in favour of residential co-parenting against both parents' wishes under current law does not mean that the law cannot be changed to give the court this authority.

Considering this, it is important to know whether the fact that residential co-parenting appears to be generally better for children stems from the fact that it is entered into mostly on a voluntary basis and the beneficial effects of residential co-parenting would disappear once this voluntary aspect is removed.

There are some indications supporting this hypothesis. Westphal's study has found that the fact that parents in residential co-parenting arrangements have a lower level of conflict than parents in sole residence arrangements is connected to the fact that these parents also had a lower

89 H. SÜNDERHAUF, (Teil II), 2013, p. 330.
90 L. TRINDER, 2010, pp. 491-492.

level of conflict previous to their separation. In other words: parents who had fewer conflicts than others when they were still together chose for a residential co-parenting arrangement and continued to have fewer conflicts than others.[91]

A related outcome was found in the *Scheiding in Vlaanderen* study. Before the 1995 law reform that introduced the continuation of joint parental responsibilities and resulted in an increase in residential co-parenting, parents in residential co-parenting arrangements experienced a significantly lower level of parental conflict than parents in other residential arrangements. This difference in the level of parental conflict between the different residential arrangements was not found among parents who separated after 1995.[92] This change possibly indicates that where before 1995 only those parents who entered into a residential arrangement voluntarily and in agreement were able to continue parenting in relative harmony, while after 1995 some parents who were more hostile towards each other still felt compelled (by society or the courts) to enter into a residential co-parenting arrangement, but were not able to conduct it as harmoniously as parents who entered into such an arrangement completely voluntarily.

However, there is also evidence against this hypothesis. Sünderhauf points out that empirical evidence exists that children growing up in a residential co-parenting arrangement are mentally better adjusted than children in a sole residence arrangement *irrespective* of whether their parents originally wanted to have a residential co-parenting arrangement or not.[93]

It is therefore uncertain whether the beneficial effects on the child's well-being would be diminished or disappear altogether if residential co-parenting could be ordered by the courts against both parents' wishes or even if residential co-parenting would become the preferential model.

6.4.5. COMPARATIVE SYNTHESIS

This section shows that the question whether residential co-parenting is a desirable arrangement that should be legally promoted is a difficult one to answer. With the literature demonstrating ingrained resentment and prejudice against residential co-parenting and empirical research being either lacking or contradictory, it is difficult to draw a clear conclusion.

---

91 S. WESTPHAL, 2015, p. 76.

92 A. SODERMANS et al., 'Characteristics of joint physical custody families in Flanders', *Demographic Research*, 2013, Volume 28, p. 833.

93 H. SÜNDERHAUF, (Teil I), 2013, p. 292.

The various factors that influence the feasibility of residential co-parenting in any given case seem to be the key to understanding the workings and influences of residential arrangements on the welfare of children. When these factors are examined separately they show two things: the courts are not always using the right factors or in the correct way and none of the factors discussed appears to influence the outcome of residential co-parenting in a particularly negative way. The evidence seems to suggest that, in general, residential co-parenting is better for the children involved than sole residence, but that there are factors that can make this distinction disappear. Thus residential co-parenting in any given case would either have a positive influence on the well-being of the child or it would be the same as sole residence.

6.5. SUMMARY

At the beginning of this chapter two questions were posed: does residential co-parenting occur in the three countries discussed, and if so, how predominant is it (and do or can legal changes influence the parents' choice of residential arrangements)? And should residential co-parenting be stimulated or discouraged?

These questions were then answered using national and international empirical studies and demographic figures. One thing that is glaringly evident from the empirical evidence presented in this chapter is that when it comes to residential co-parenting, or even residential arrangements in general, there are still many lacunas in the knowledge on almost all facets of these arrangements. There are no studies that map the long-term effects on the parties involved in residential co-parenting. The studies that research the well-being of children in different arrangements do so mainly through answers provided by the children's parents, which has the potential to make such answers subjective. Many key issues have not yet been (sufficiently) researched, such as the influence of new legislation on the parents' decision-making concerning residential arrangements, how residential arrangements are adjusted to changing circumstances, and the influence of the child's age on the desirability of residential parenting.

Still, enough knowledge is available to make at least a good start in answering the questions which are central to this chapter. Statistical data show that residential co-parenting is indeed an important residential arrangement in all three countries studied, with a prevalence rate between 9% and 27-38%. Research from Belgium also shows that the introduction of new legislation in favour of joint exercise of parental responsibilities and residential co-parenting is associated with the growth of residential co-parenting in practice, which would strongly suggest that such legislation does influence parents' (and the courts') decisions when it comes to choosing a particular residential arrangement.

The last question – what influence does residential co-parenting have on children's well-being and whether it should therefore be encouraged or discouraged – is impossible to answer with certainty given the current status of the empirical research on residential arrangements. Not only is there a lack of vital information and the studies themselves often contradict each other, there are also many (outside) factors that influence the residential co-parenting arrangement and the child's well-being. The most important factors are the following: the level of parental conflict, the geographical distance between the parents' homes, the age of the child involved, and the willingness of the parents to enter into a residential co-parenting arrangement in the first place. These factors can either negatively or positively influence the functioning of the arrangement. The more we can discover about this influence, the easier it will be to predict, based on the facts of any specific case, if a residential co-parenting arrangement would be in the best interests of the child or children involved.

CHAPTER 7
COMPARATIVE SYNTHESIS

7.1. INTRODUCTION

The legal systems discussed in Chapters 3, 4 and 5 have been selected for various reasons. All three contain provisions on the joint exercise of parental responsibilities after separation and allow residential co-parenting arrangements. All three have gone through family law reform that started roughly in the 1990s and over the course of the following three decades rapidly changed post-separation parenting.

While the three countries have encountered similar societal changes over the last three decades - more women working full time, fathers demanding more equality when it comes to parenting after separation, same-sex families - the way the law has reacted to these issues has not been the same. Each legal system has its own way of solving the problems which arise and it may be possible to learn from each other, or at least to look at complicated issues from different perspectives to further understand these issues. This is the main purpose of this chapter, and by extension, of this thesis.

The following sections give an overview of the similarities between the three legal systems and highlight the most interesting differences between them.

7.2. HISTORY AND BACKGROUND OF THE LAW

When looking at the legal background of the three legal systems presented in this book, on the face of it the most notable distinction can be drawn between the English legal system on the one hand, and the Dutch and Belgian legal systems on the other. This is because the English legal system belongs to the common law family, while the other two systems are part of the civil law tradition. In practice, however, this distinction is not as all defining as it may seem. While case law indeed carries more weight in the English legal system than the Dutch, and definitely the Belgian systems, the main provisions concerning parentage and parental responsibilities in all three systems are contained in written law (the Civil Code for the Dutch and Belgian systems, and the Children Act 1989 for the English system respectively) and have only been explained or developed more through case law.

However, residential co-parenting arrangements have mainly been developed through case law in England by means of shared residence orders, while in the Netherlands the issue has been discussed extensively by Parliament in the light of the preparation for the 2009 law reform and in Belgium a provision on (50/50) residential co-parenting has even made it into the Civil Code. One could therefore say that the reform of residential arrangements, specifically residential co-parenting arrangements, has been predominately developed by the courts in England and by the legislature in the Netherlands and Belgium.

When looking more closely at the law reform in the three countries, it is evident that even though the outcomes of the reform are similar, the process of the reform was not. Where in England the Children Act 1989 has laid down the foundations for the joint exercise of parental responsibilities and residential co-parenting with its entry into force, it took a long evolution through the case law before these arrangements developed into the form they are in today. This process was organic and followed the needs and wishes of the parents themselves through their petitions to the courts.[1]

The process can be said to have been somewhat reversed in the Netherlands. There joint parental responsibilities after separation were first introduced through the *Hoge Raad* and were then laid down in the Civil Code through the 1995 law reform allowing for joint parental responsibilities upon a joint request. The criterion of the joint request was discarded three years later with the 1998 reform that made joint parental responsibilities continue automatically after separation. Then finally the 2009 reform introduced the right of the child to equal care by both parents (read: the joint and equal exercise of parental responsibilities) and the obligation to make a parenting plan upon separation.[2]

Belgium solved the issue of the continuation of joint parental responsibilities post-parental separation by reforming the Civil Code in 1995 in such a way as to link parental responsibilities to legal parentage Therefore legal parents became the holders of parental responsibilities and remained as such, irrespective of their relationship with each other. In 2006 an obligation for the courts was introduced to consider a 50/50 residential co-parenting arrangement if either (or both) of the parents requested such an arrangement.[3]

---

1 See section 3.1 of Chapter 3.
2 See section 4.1 of Chapter 4.
3 See section 5.1 of Chapter 5.

These three different paths led to a similar outcome in all three legal systems: that when parents separate, they continue to jointly exercise parental responsibilities and if they wish to, they may do that in the form of residential co-parenting. This is opposed to the situation before when only one of the parents would be granted parental responsibilities upon separation and legalising or enforcing a practical residential co-parenting arrangement was impossible.

7.3. JOINT PARENTAL RESPONSIBILITIES

7.3.1. PARENTAL RESPONSIBILITIES: MEANING AND CONTENT

None of the three legal systems has a clear and extensive definition of what parental responsibilities entail. Minimum, and often vague, descriptions are provided, supplemented by a few examples of rights or duties that fall within parental responsibilities. The definition if further filled in by the case law and legal literature. It can be said that a general consensus exists that parental responsibilities encompass the rights and duties relating to the person and property of the child which are necessary for the upbringing, care and protection of this child, including the right to make decisions about the child. This power to make decisions about the child is not unlimited. It can be limited by law (criminal or private), a court order, or by the rights of another holder of parental responsibilities or the child himself or herself.

7.3.2. ATTRIBUTION OF (JOINT) PARENTAL RESPONSIBILITIES

The first thing that needs to be established with regard to the attribution of parental responsibilities is that the point of departure is different in each legal system examined. In English law the attribution of parental responsibilities, while liked to legal parentage, is regulated and separately from it with less stringent rules on acquisition. In Belgian law parental responsibilities are inextricably intertwined with legal parentage, so much so that persons who are not legal parents cannot, strictly speaking, hold parental responsibilities. Although guardianship is possible, it is treated as an issue which is separate from parental responsibilities and it confers less rights on the guardian. The Dutch legal system can be placed somewhere in between these opposite points of departure. While parental responsibilities are linked to legal parentage in the sense that legal parents automatically become holders of parental responsibilities, it is possible for a person who is not a legal parent to attain parental responsibilities.

Another major difference between the three legal systems, or more precisely between the English system on the one hand, and the Dutch and Belgian systems on the other, is that in the Dutch and the Belgian systems no more than two persons can hold parental responsibilities over the same child. The English system does not have this limitation. While it is rare for more than two persons to exercise parental responsibilities over a child in England, it can solve unnecessary problems when two women are raising a child, but the known donor is also involved in the child's upbringing, or when the parents have been separated for some time, both still hold parental responsibilities, but a step-parent is in practice much more involved in the care of the child than one of the parents.

There are three possible means of gaining parental responsibilities, although not every possibility is open to every type of parent or in every legal system: ex lege, with the birthmother's consent by means of registration at the civil registry, and by court order. England and the Netherlands have all three possibilities in place, while in Belgium only the ex lege method is recognized, with parents only gaining parental responsibilities (ex lege) when they become legal parents.

There are many similarities between the three legal systems in terms of who obtains or can obtain parental responsibilities in what way. First of all, (birth) mothers in all three legal systems gain parental responsibilities ex lege upon the child's birth, as do fathers married to the birthmother.

Dutch and English unmarried fathers will either need the mother's consent or a court order to become holders of parental responsibilities. In Belgium legal parents gain parental responsibilities ex lege. However, an unmarried father will need either the mother's consent or a court order to become the legal parent.

English and Belgian law have recently made the legal position of the female partner of the birthmother equal to that of the father in matters surrounding parental responsibilities: women married to the birthmother gain parental responsibilities over a child born within the marriage ex lege, while unmarried partners need either the mother's consent or a court order.[4] The Dutch legal system does the same for the female partners of birthmothers if the child was conceived with the help of an anonymous donor, but treats wives of birthmothers whose child was conceived

---

4 For Belgium: they need this to gain legal parentage and then gain parental responsibilities ex lege. See section 5.3.2.3 of Chapter 5. Also in English law the partner needs to consent to the artificial insemination treatment.

with the help of a known donor differently, as they do not gain parental responsibilities (or legal parentage) ex lege.

Non-parents will need a court order to gain parental responsibilities together with the holder of parental responsibilities in all three legal jurisdictions.[5] This could be an adoption order, an order establishing guardianship, or an order granting a step-parent parental responsibilities. The guardianship or parental responsibilities order may confer less rights on the holder than the a parent with parental responsibilities would hold.

A difference between the Belgian system, on the one hand, and the English and Dutch systems on the other, is that the Belgian system does not have the institution of a registered partnership in the sense of a separate formalised relationship that has influence on the children of the partners. The two systems that do, give registered/civil partners the same rights as husbands or wives.

7.3.3. EXERCISING (JOINT) PARENTAL RESPONSIBILITIES

As has been stated in section 7.2 of this chapter, joint parental responsibilities now automatically continue after parental separation in all three legal systems. This means that even if the parents separate, they will still have to work together for the sake of the child(ren) in order to properly exercise their parental responsibilities. However, the starting point in English law is manifestly different from the Dutch and Belgian approach. In English law, each holder of parental responsibilities can and should exercise them on his or her own, unless there is a specific prohibition. While case law has established that for certain important decisions, such as medical treatment and the school choice, the consent of the other holder(s) of parental responsibilities is necessary, the holders are, in principle, autonomous. In the Dutch and Belgian systems the holders of parental responsibilities can exercise them on their own, especially in matters of daily care. The point of departure is joint exercise. Important matters need to be discussed and agreed upon by both holders of parental responsibilities. This is where the problems usually tend to arise and when the courts are petitioned to make a decision on which the parents themselves cannot agree.

Some of these 'important matters' are specifically addressed in legal provisions or frequently emerge in the case law in all three legal systems. These include the right to give the child up for adoption or to place him

5 In the Netherlands those who wish to gain parental responsibilities to exercise them jointly with someone who is already a holder of parental responsibilities will need that person's consent to petition the court for an order. See section 4.3.2.4 of Chapter 4.

or her in care, to give consent to the child's marriage, to name the child or change the child's name or surname, to choose the child's school, to remove the child from the jurisdiction and to make decisions about medical treatment, religious upbringing, or finance.

In order to adequately deal with the requests to intervene in parental disputes and to protect the best interests of the child the courts in the three countries have been given the power to restrict and regulate the exercise of parental responsibilities. Whether that is done by specifically named orders, as it is in the English system, or through a more general power to decide disputes, as it is in the Dutch and Belgian systems, the outcome is the same: the court can decide disputes between parents and restrict or redistribute aspects of parental responsibilities when needed. The court can make an order deciding a specific issue, such as the school choice, granting a certain aspect of parental responsibilities, for example the right to manage the child's property, to be exercised exclusively by one of the holders of parental responsibilities, or it can preclude a holder of parental responsibilities from an act that would usually fall within the realm of parental responsibilities, like the right to take the child on a holiday abroad.

Outside of serious disputes that require court intervention, the parents are expected to be able to exercise joint parental responsibilities over their child(ren) in co-operation, even when they are no longer in a relationship with each other. In order to make this process run smoother, some parents draw up a care arrangement when they separate. They are not always free in this choice. In the Dutch legal system making a parenting plan upon separation has been made compulsory and refusing to do so may result in delays in being granted a divorce order, a dissolution of the registered partnership, or a requested order.[6] While there is no obligation in English law to draw up an extensive document detailing the parents' plans on how they intend to regulate the exercise of their joint parental responsibilities over the child after their separation, parents who file for divorce, a civil partnership dissolution, a (judicial) separation or the nullity of a marriage should include in their petition a statement of the arrangements for children. These statements of the arrangements for children are not as extensive as Dutch parenting plans tend to be and a large portion of separating parents do not manage to agree on arrangements.[7] Belgian law does not require separating parents to make care arrangements upon separation, although there has been a proposal to that extend, which was discarded.[8]

It is difficult to say which legal system has the better approach in this. There seems to exist a general assumption among legislative bodies

[6] See section 4.3.3.2 of Chapter 4.
[7] See section 3.3.3.2 of Chapter 3.
[8] See section 5.3.3.4 of Chapter 5.

that making (extensive) care arrangements at the time of separation will improve subsequent co-operation between the parents and will therefore improve the situation of the child(ren). However, no empirical research is currently available on whether this assumption is accurate. One might just as easily imagine that forcing parents to make arrangements at a time when conflict and uncertainly about the future are at their peak might lead to increased conflict instead of better communication, and laying down arrangements in an official document might cause the parents to become inflexible when dealing with changes of circumstances.

7.3.4. DISCHARGE OF (JOINT) PARENTAL RESPONSIBILITIES

Now that the legal reform has made joint parental responsibilities automatically continue after separation, separation is no longer a reason for a parent to lose his or her parental responsibilities. This does not mean that a parent can never lose parental responsibilities, but it has become more difficult for a parent to either voluntarily give up parental responsibilities or to have parental responsibilities taken from him or her. Especially the English legal system is very strict when it comes to the discharge of parental responsibilities: a parent who had gained parental responsibilities ex lege cannot give them up or lose them, except if the child is given up for adoption or reaches the age of majority. Parents who had gained parental responsibilities through registration with the agreement of the mother or by a court order can still lose it, but the reason for this must be weighty and a court order is needed.[9] The Dutch and Belgian systems do allow the discharge of parental responsibilities by a court order even when the parent has gained them ex lege, but such an order is not made lightly either.[10]

This difference between the legal systems can be explained by the fact that in the English system more than two persons can hold parental responsibilities over the same child. This means that for example in order to grant parental responsibilities to a step-parent who is factually raising the child together with a parent who has parental responsibilities, parental responsibilities do not need to be first stripped form another estranged holder, something that would be necessary in the Dutch or Belgian legal system.

Parental responsibilities naturally come to an end as the child reaches the age of majority or is emancipated.

9 See section 3.3.4 of Chapter 3.
10 See sections 4.3.4 of Chapter 4 and 5.3.4 of Chapter 5.

7.4. CHILD'S RESIDENCE

When parents separate and reach an agreement about the child(ren)'s residence without dispute the courts of any of the three countries analysed will not intervene in this decision unless this residence arrangements would somehow clearly be contrary to the child's best interests.

If the parents cannot agree and the court is asked to make a decision on the child(ren)'s residence, however, the approach to this decision-making process is different in all three legal systems, especially when the decision is about whether or not to make an order in favour of residential co-parenting.

Belgian law is the only legal system of the three that has any legislation in place concerning residential co-parenting. It describes residential co-parenting as an equal, meaning 50/50, arrangement, and obliges the courts to seriously consider this arrangement if one or both parents have requested it.[11] While Dutch law gives children the right to equal care by both parents, it does not actually mention residential arrangements and equal care is understood to mean the joint exercise of parental responsibilities and not residential co-parenting.[12] English legislation does not address residential co-parenting; shared residence orders have developed through the case law.[13]

When looking at case law that deals with the question of whether or not residential co-parenting arrangements should be ordered, certain factors that the courts consider tend to come up frequently: the (geographical) distance between the parents' homes, how well the parents are able to communicate and co-operate, the age of the child and more. This case law has evolved over time. The courts are now less likely than they were previously to deny residential co-parenting if only one of these factors shows a counter-indication. For example, the sole fact that the parents do not get along is unlikely to be considered as a decisive reason against a residential co-parenting arrangement. Despite this, Dutch and Belgian courts still mainly focus on the practical viability of a (mostly) equal division of residence, a viability in the sense that it is both 'doable' and in the best interests of the child. The English case law, however, seems to be shifting more towards the notion of formal equality: shared residence orders are granted even in cases where there exists no intention of equally dividing the residence, instead the shared residence order is used as some sort of formal acknowledgement of the equal position of the parents.

---

11 See section 5.4.2 of Chapter 5.

12 See section 4.4.2 of Chapter 4.

13 See section 3.4.2 of Chapter 5.

All this applies to cases in which parents are separating and need to establish a residential arrangement for their child(ren), because the previous arrangement, living together in one house, is no longer possible due to the separation. There are also cases in which one or both parents seek to change a residential arrangement that is no longer viable due to changed circumstances. Changing an existing residential arrangement is something the courts in all three countries are reluctant to do as it is considered that continuity in living arrangements is in the best interests of the child. This continuity is seen as more important than, for example, an increase in equality between the parents due to a more equal division of residence.

When one of the parents wants to relocate with the child this is not only likely to disrupt the residential co-parenting arrangement which is in place, but also to severely disrupt the child(ren)'s life. Therefore the courts, when presented with this question, are reluctant to allow a relocation in the case of residential co-parenting, unless there exists an important reason for the relocation. No true consensus seems to exist within any of the legal systems examined as to when relocation should be allowed and when not, and decisions are made on a case by case basis. The courts do, however, seem to be much more unlikely to allow relocation abroad than relocation within the country. This is not surprising, as relocation abroad is likely to have a serious impact on contact with the parent remaining in the country more severely.

7.5. CHILDREN'S PROCEDURAL RIGHTS

In all three legal systems children enjoy some procedural rights in procedures that concern them. Generally speaking, it concerns three rights: the right to be heard, the right to become involved in the proceedings, and the right to initiate proceedings.

The main as well as the most employed procedural right is the right to be heard, derived from Article 12 of the Convention on the Rights of the Child, which all three countries discussed in this book have ratified and implemented into their legislation. All courts should hear children of any age in proceedings concerning them, but the courts in the Netherlands and Belgium also inform children of 12 years or older of their right to be heard (and their right to decline that opportunity). This is done by a standardised letter.

What weight is given to the thoughts and wishes of the child will depend on the child's age, maturity, and other circumstances, such as whether the judge suspects that the child has been strongly influenced by one of the parents (against the other parent).

It is rare for the courts to involve children in proceedings as a party to those proceedings. This is only done if there is a conflict between the parent(s)'s interests and the interests of the child. In such cases a special representative is often appointed to represent the child's interests (this is the *bijzondere curator* in the Netherlands, and a guardian *ad hoc* in England and Belgium).

The final right is the right of the child to commence proceedings on his or her own by petitioning the court. This right does not seem to exist in the Belgian legal system, because in Belgium a child can never act in court without a guardian.[14] In England and the Netherlands the cases in which a child petitions the court for a (family law) order are rare, but not unheard of.[15]

7.6. ENFORCEMENT OF ARRANGEMENTS IN CASE OF NON-COMPLIANCE

The law (including the case law) on the enforcement of care and residence arrangements in the three countries discussed exhibits strong similarities. This is perhaps unsurprising, because there are only so many enforcement measures that are possible and the problems with these measures are fairly universal.

Decisions, orders and all arrangements that have been specifically included therein are theoretically enforceable. All three legal systems give the courts the power to order one of the following enforcement measures in case of non-compliance: a monetary penalty, an unpaid work requirement or incarceration following a criminal conviction, the removal of the child (in order to hand him or her over to the other parent), a change or reversal of parental responsibilities or residence.

The first three enforcement measures are problematic and will most likely be detrimental to the well-being of the child and therefore should be avoided (especially the criminal conviction of a parent is only used as an ultimum remedium). A change or reversal of parental responsibilities or residence is used, but this measure can be practically impossible or undesirable, for example if the other parent cannot properly accommodate the child the reversal of residence is not really an option.

Sometimes enforcement is undesirable because it is not the parent who frustrates compliance with an order, but the (older) child. If the child refuses

14 See section 5.5 of Chapter 5

15 See for examples sections 3.5 of Chapter 3 and 4.5 of Chapter 4.

to visit or stay with one of the parents and the court's main consideration should be the best interests of the child, enforcing an arrangement that clearly goes against the child's wishes would cause the child distress and would therefore be paradoxical.

Because of all these difficulties care or residence arrangements are sometimes unenforced despite the availability of multiple enforcement measures. The courts in all three countries struggle with this and none have found a solution as yet, if indeed a solution even exists.

7.7. SUMMARY

Overall the three legal systems have many similarities and often the same outcomes are achieved, though not always by the same means. In other words: where the (procedural) law in theory may differ, the practical outcome is often similar.

However, there are still some important differences to take into account. The law (including the case law) of the three countries differs when it comes to the attribution of parental responsibilities, the obligation to make care arrangements upon separation and the approach to residential co-parenting. Which legal system's approach is the superior approach and could be used as an example for other countries depends on what outcome is desired. If a choice has to be made between two or more desirable effects, which should be chosen? What is more important, parental equality or the best interests of the child? Should certain types of arrangements be stimulated to the potential detriment of party autonomy? Should a legal system promote legal certainty or flexibility? In the next, and final, chapter of this book the findings from this and other chapters are discussed in the light of these choices and the main questions presented in the introduction are answered.

CHAPTER 8
CONCLUSIONS AND RECOMMENDATIONS

The goal of this book and the PhD research it is based upon was to find out if (residential) co-parenting after separation is in the best interests of children and if this is the case whether (residential) co-parenting can and should be stimulated through legal action, and if (residential) co-parenting is detrimental to the best interests of children, whether it can and should be discouraged through legal action.

One side of the coin is the legal situation: the international, European and national legal framework, the other is the social context in which it has to function. Chapter 2 showed that international and European instruments in their current form only encourage the retention of joint parental responsibilities post-separation and do not contain provisions that would either encourage or discourage (residential) co-parenting. This does not mean that international, and especially European, law should be disregarded in the discussion of (residential) co-parenting. Over the years the amount of instruments with a (possible) influence on family law has grown and the provisions have become more substantial with greater encroachment upon the national systems. Instruments such as the ECHR have the potential to become more involved in issues surrounding (residential) co-parenting in the future and the CRC has already influenced the way in which national courts deal with the child's right to be heard.

Turning to the national laws of the three countries it is clear that there are many similarities and overlaps. It is no longer contested that joint parental responsibilities should continue after the parents separate, nor that same-sex parents should have the same rights as different-sex parents do, or that children should have the right to be heard in proceedings concerning them. These things have become the legal norm. The national courts struggle with the same kind of petitions from parents and with similar difficulties of enforcement.

Perhaps because there are so many similarities between the three countries socially and legally, it is even more interesting to encounter differences as it means that the same, or similar, problems can have multiple solutions and perhaps some solutions are better (for the child(ren) involved) than others.

The first major difference concerns the attribution of (joint) parental responsibilities. The fact that English law does not link parental responsibilities to legal parentage and does not impose a limit on how many persons may hold parental responsibilities over the same child avoids the difficulties that may arise in complicated situations where multiple people are (practically) involved in the care and upbringing of a child and the most suited person to exercise parental responsibilities may not be (one of) the legal parent(s). With modern society redefining what a family or a parent is, and the emphasis shifting from biological to social parents, it might be time to consider whether the Dutch and Belgian way of dealing with parentage and parental responsibilities is not outdated and whether the English system might hold possible alternatives.

The second difference concerns the obligation (or the lack of such an obligation) to make care arrangements for the children when parents separate. The Dutch and the Belgian legal systems are opposites when it comes to this issue with the Dutch system containing an obligation to make a parenting plan and the Belgian system not requiring any care arrangements at all, with the English system somewhere in between with the requirement to make minimal care arrangements, a requirement that is often not observed or enforced. It is hard to say whether the obligation to make care arrangements is beneficial or detrimental to the well-being of children. While there is no clear empirical evidence, one could argue either way: on the one hand, if parents are obliged to make a care arrangement they are forced to think about the children, to focus on what is really important, instead of their anger towards each other and having a care arrangement based on agreement might prevent arguments and problems in the future. On the other hand, forcing parents to make important decision at a moment when their communication and will to co-operate is likely to be at an all-time low might cause conflicts to flare up even more and turn them further against each other when they are expected to make compromises. Also having a set of arrangements in place may make parents less flexible in adjusting to changed circumstances.

The third and final main difference is in how the three legal systems deal with residential co-parenting. As the English courts seem to move away from the necessity of the residence order to reflect the factual arrangement and instead placing more emphasis on the legal equality of the parents, the Belgian law encourages residential co-parenting in general and prescribes that it is preferable for this residential arrangement to constitute a 50/50 division of time. And then there is the Dutch situation which remains legally and conceptually ambiguous. Which of the three approaches is preferential depends on whether residential co-parenting is a residential arrangement in which the children's best interests are better safeguarded than in other types of residential arrangements and on whether the law, in fact, is able to influence what residential arrangements parents apply in practice.

Legal differences and similarities only paint half a picture, to know what legislation is needed, one must be aware of the practical situation and issues. Is residential co-parenting more than just a theoretical arrangement and does the law have and influence on the residential choices that parents make?

Section 6.3 of Chapter 6 has shown that not only is residential co-parenting an arrangement that is widely employed in the three countries by parents from all walks of life, it is also an arrangement that has significantly increased in popularity over the last 20-30 years. The fact that the percentage of parents and children in residential co-parenting arrangements is significantly higher in the countries that actively promote (residential) co-parenting (Belgium and the Netherlands) than in the country that does not (England) seems to indicate that the law indeed has an influence on the residential arrangements the parents practice. One might question if this is not a chicken or the egg situation: did the legal reform stimulate the increase in residential co-parenting or did the rise in popularity of residential co-parenting prompt the law reform? It is likely to be a bit of both, but the legal influence should not be disregarded as Belgian empirical research does show that after the coming into force of each co-parenting-friendly law reform there was a rise in the percentage of co-parenting arrangements.[1]

If the law therefore can and does influence parents' and courts' decision-making process in decisions on residential arrangements, what kind of influence should it exercise? Thus we are back to the question that has prompted the research on which this book is based.

Section 6.4 of Chapter 6 indicates that this question is not easily answered. Empirical research on residence arrangements is full of blind spots and in the areas where it does provide information, the information is often incomplete or is based on very small samples. However, one thing seems to be clear: practical factors that are not necessarily part and parcel of the (type of) residential arrangement influence the well-being of children much more than the type of residential arrangement itself. These factors, however, are inextricably linked to the residential arrangements and can make a certain type of residential arrangement beneficial or detrimental to the child's best interests.

---

1 See section 6.3.3 of Chapter 6.

The four factors that have been most relied upon in residential disputes and that have attracted the largest amount of empirical research have been discussed in sections 6.4.1-6.4.4 of Chapter 6. These are the level of conflict between parents, the geographical distance between the parents' homes, the age of the children involved, and the willingness of (both) parents to have a residential co-parenting arrangement.

Parental conflict is a major (detrimental) influence on the child's well-being and the courts in their decisions have often considered conflict in residential co-parenting arrangements to have a more negative impact on children than conflict in sole residence arrangements. Section 6.4.1 of Chapter 6 indicates that this assumption is not necessarily supported by empirical research. The also prevalent assumption that residential co-parenting is detrimental to very young children is not supported by empirical evidence either, simply because little to no empirical studies are available that have researched this question.[2]

Practical considerations such as the distance between homes, both geographical and travel-time related, the number of alternations between homes in a month, the ability of particular children to deal with alternating between homes, the available facilities at both homes, and the practical ability and willingness of both parents to provide care, on the other hand, are important when considering whether residential co-parenting is the right arrangement for a certain family.[3]

While it is true that based on the findings in the previous chapters and the conclusions drawn in this chapter, it seems that *in general* children who are brought up in residential co-parenting arrangements are doing better than children brought up in sole residence arrangements. However, *in practice*, the type of residence arrangement in and of itself has very little influence on the child's well-being, as opposed to the factual circumstances and other considerations. These circumstances and considerations have the effect that, depending on the factual situation, a residential co-parenting arrangement could be the best option, could be practically impossible, or could be undesirable. Therefore the author of this book would advise caution and would suggest against making residential co-parenting a preferential or compulsory legal model, unless the parents and/or the courts are given sufficient opportunities to deviate from this model in cases where residential co-parenting is practically unfeasible or undesirable due to circumstances which are specific to the family in question.

Instead, empirical research into the influence of various factors of post-separation residence on the well-being of children should be promoted in order to facilitate parents and courts to make well-informed decisions.

---

[2] See section 6.4.3 of Chapter 6.

[3] See sections 6.4.2 and 6.4.4 of Chapter 6.

The government has a role to play here, but also other actors, such as universities and national and international statistics bureaus, which are in a position to promote or carry out this type of research. Perhaps even a European Union-funded, Europe-wide research could be set up.

Many questions have not yet been answered. Empirical research that does exist draws heavily on the reports of parents about their children's well-being instead of questioning or observing the children themselves. No large-scale longitudinal studies are available that follow the development and adjustment of children in different residential arrangements over the course of time. These kinds of studies are crucial to fully understand the correlation between residential arrangements and the well-being of children, especially to see if the effects of residential arrangements change depending on the child's age. More research and more information will also diminish the prejudices against residential arrangements that are outdated and are not supported by empirical research.

Meanwhile, legal practitioners in general, and the courts specifically, have an important role to play when it comes to decisions on residence. Mediators and lawyers who assist parents in making residential arrangements upon separation should be able to provide them with information, derived from empirical research, that will facilitate them in making an unbiased choice for the residential arrangement that is best for their children. They should actively seek out and be aware of (recent) empirical evidence in this area. The fact that this evidence is sparse does not mean that it is completely unavailable. This book is an example of this.

Courts should evaluate whether their considerations in residence disputes are still valid: which assumptions that have guided judicial decisions in the past are actually (still) supported by empirical research? Which practical factors and circumstances should a judge be made aware of before making a decision? The author would like to see the courts consult (recent) empirical and psychological studies and exchange information among themselves on what kinds of problems they encounter and how they have been able to find a solution. A uniform checklist of all significant factors that a judge needs to find out and consider before making a residential decision based on this (empirical and inter-court) information would be highly beneficial for transparency and legal certainty in decisions on residential co-parenting. Such a checklist should then be employed by all national courts in the same or at least a similar way. The factors that have been discussed in this book may be used as a starting point for this purpose.

This is not an easy task and would require the government, the legislature, legal practitioners, academics, parents and children to work together. This study may prove useful in taking the first steps in this endeavour.

REFERENCES

LITERATURE

- J. ACKERMANS-WIJN, 'De nieuwe aanbevelingen van het LOVF met betrekking tot het ouderschapsplan', *EB* 2012/74.
- M. ANTOKOLSKAIA, 'Shared Residence from a Comparative Perspective: A Solomon's Judgment New-Style?' in *Private Law, national – global – comparative. Festgeschrift für Ingeborg Schwenzer zum 60. Geburtstag*, Stämpfli Verlag AG, 2011.
- M. ANTOKOLSKAIA, 'Solomo's oordeel nieuwe stijl: verblijfsco-ouderschap in België en Nederland. Over de rol van de wetenschap, invloed van de politiek, en nattevingerwerk in het wetgevingsproces', *TPR*, 2010, pp. 1179-1243.
- R. BAUSERMAN, 'Child Adjustment in Joint-Custody Versus Sole-Custody Arrangements: A Meta-Analytic Review', *Journal of Family Psychology*, 2002, Vol. 16, No. 1.
- K. BOELE-WOELKI et al., *Principles of European Family Law Regarding Parental Responsibilities*, Intersentia, 2007.
- D. CASSIDY & S. DAVEY, *Family Justice and Children's Proceedings – Review of Public and Private Law Case Files in England and Wales*, 2011.
- R. DEKKERS & A. WYLLEMAN, *Handboek Burgerlijk Recht Deel I: Personen en familierecht*, Intersentia, 2009.
- S. DETRICK, *A commentary on the United Nations Convention on the Rights of the Child*, 1999.
- J. EEKELAAR, 'Parental Responsibility: State of Nature or Nature of the State?', *Journal of Social Welfare and Family Law*, Vol. 13, 1991.
- B. FEATHERSTONE, 'Fathers Matter: A Research Review', *Children and Society*, Vol. 18, 2004, pp. 312-319.
- B. FEATHERSTONE, 'Taking Fathers Seriously', *British Journal of Social Work*, Vol. 33, 2003, pp. 239-254.
- J. FORTIN, *Children's Rights and the Developing Law*, Cambridge University Press, 2009.
- R. GEORGE, 'Practitioners' views on children's welfare in relocation disputes: comparing approaches in England and New Zealand', *Child and Family Law Quarterly*, Vol. 23, No. 2, 2011.
- E. GIOVANNINI, *Outcomes of Family Justice Children's Proceedings – A Review of the Evidence*, 2011.
- P. HARRIS & R. GEORGE, 'Parental responsibility and shared residence orders: parliamentary intentions and judicial interpretations', *Child and Family Law Quarterly*, Vol. 22, No. 2, 2010.
- S. HARRIS-SHORT & J. MILES, *Family Law: texts, cases, and materials*, Oxford University Press, 2011.
- S. HARRIS-SHORT, 'Resisting the march towards 50/50 shared residence: rights, welfare and equality in post-separation families', *Journal of Social Welfare & Family Law*, Vol. 32, No. 3, 2010.

- K. HERBOTS et al., 'Participatie van het kind in het gerechtelijk scheidingsproces: droombeeld of realiteit?', *TJK*, 2012/01.
- J. HERRING, *Family Law*, Pearson Education Limited, 2011.
- J. HERRING, *Family Law: issues, debates, policy*, Willan Publishing, 2001.
- C.G. JEPPESEN DE BOER, *Joint parental authority: a comparative legal study on the continuation of joint parental authority after divorce and the breakup of a relationship in Dutch and Danish law and the CEFL principles*, Doctoral thesis, Intersentia 2008.
- S. JOSEPH et al., *The international covenant on civil and political rights: cases, materials, and commentary*, 2004.
- U. KILKELLY, *The Child and the European Convention on Human Rights*, Ashgate, 1999.
- T. KNIJN & P. SELTEN, 'Transformations of fatherhood: the Netherlands' in B. Hobson, *Making men into Fathers. Men, Masculinities and Social Politics of Fatherhood*, Cambridge University Press, 2002.
- Law Commission, *Family Law Review of Child Law: Guardianship and Custody*, Law Com No. 172, London: HMSO 1988.
- N. LOWE & G. DOUGLAS, *Bromley's Family Law*, Oxford University Press, 2007.
- N. LOWE, *A study into the rights and legal status of children being brought up in various forms of marital or non-marital partnerships and cohabitation*, 21 September 2009, CJ-FA (2008) 5.
- J. MAIR & E. ÖRÜCÜ (eds.), *Juxtaposing Legal Systems and the Principles of European Family Law on Parental Responsibilities*, Intersentia, 2010.
- I. MARTENS, in P. Senaeve et al., *Verblijfsco-ouderschap. Uitvoering en sanctionering van verblijfs- en omgangsregelingen. Adoptie door personen van hetzelfde geslacht*, Intersentia, 2007.
- N. MASSAGER, *Droit familial de l'enfance. Filiation, autorité parentale, hébergement*, Bruylant, 2009.
- J. MASSON et al., *Cretney's Principles of Family Law*, Thomson, Sweet and Maxwell, 2008.
- M. MATTHÉ, 'Handhaving van de omgangsregeling met kinderen door middel van private sancties', *FJR* 2011/122.
- E. MINK, 'De procespositie van de minderjarige in de civiele procedure', *FJR*, 2012/41.
- D. MORTELMANS et al., *Scheiding in Vlaanderen*, Acco, 2011.
- P. NEWIS, *Firm Foundations: Shared care in separate families: building on what works*, Gingerbread, 2011.
- N. NIKOLINA, 'The Influence of International Law on the Issue of Co-Parenting: Emerging Trends in International and European Instruments', *Utrecht Law Review*, Vol. 8(1), 2012, pp. 122-144.
- V. PEACEY & J. HUNT, *I'm not saying it was easy…: Contact problems in separated families*, Report, Gingerbread 2009.
- W. PINTENS in K. Boele-Woelki et al., *European Family Law in Action Volume III: Parental responsibilities*, Intersentia, 2005.
- L. PUNSELIE, 'De positie van de minderjarige in het civiele proces', *Actuele ontwikkelingen in het familierecht. UCERF reeks*, 2010.
- S. QUARTERMAIN, *Sustainability of Mediation and Legal Representation in Private Family Law Cases – Analysis of Legal Aid Administrative Datasets*, 2011.
- F. SCHONEWILLE, 'De Wet bevordering voortgezet ouderschap en zorgvuldige scheiding is een feit: exit klassieke omgangsregeling!', *WPNR* 2009, 6800.

- W. SCHRAMA & M. VONK, 'On the move: staat voortgezet gelijkwaardig ouderschap aan verhuizing in de weg?', *FJR* 2009, 82.
- P. SENAEVE, *Compedium van het personen- en familierecht*, Acco, 2011.
- P. SENAEVE, 'Rechters die kinderen (moeten) horen', *Tijdschrift voor Familierecht*, 2011/1.
- P. SENAEVE et al., *Verblijfsco-ouderschap. Uitvoering en sanctionering van verblijfs- en omgangsregelingen. Adoptie door personen van hetzelfde geslacht*, Intersentia, 2007.
- C. SMART, 'Children and the Transformation of Family Law', in J. Dewar & S Parker eds., *Family Law: processes, practices, pressures; Proceedings of the Tenth World Conference of the International Society of Family Law, July 2000, Brisbane, Australia*, Hart Publishing, 2003.
- A. SODERMANS et al., 'Characteristics of joint physical custody families in Flanders', *Demographic Research*, 2013, Volume 28.
- E. SPRUIJT & V. DUINDAM, 'Was there an increase in caring fatherhood in the 1990s? Two Dutch longitudinal studies', *Social behaviour and personality*, 30(7), 2002.
- E. SPRUIJT & H. KORMOS, *Handboek scheiden en de kinderen: voor de beroepskracht die met scheidingskinderen te maken heeft*, 2010.
- H. SÜNDERHAUF, 'Vorurteile gegen das Wechselmodell: Was stimmt, was nicht? - Argumente in der Rechtsprechung und Erkenntnisse aus der psychologischen Forschung (Teil I)', *FamRB-Beratungspraxis*, 9/2013.
- T. SVERDRUP, 'Equal parenthood: recent reforms in child custody cases' in *The International Survey of Family Law*, 2011.
- F. SWENNEN, *Het personen- en familierecht*, Intersentia, 2012.
- F. SWENNEN, *Het personen- en familierecht*, Intersentia, 2014.
- J. TOBIN, 'Beyond the Supermarket Shelf: Using a Rights Based Approach to Address Children's Health Needs', *International Journal of Children's Rights*, 2006.
- M. TOMASSEN-VAN DER LANS, *Het verplichte ouderschapsplan: regeling en werking*, Doctoral thesis, Boom Juridische Uitgevers, 2015.
- L. TRINDER, 'Shared residence: a review of recent research evidence', *Child and Family Law Quarterly*, 2010, Vol. 22, No. 4.
- University of Oxford Department of Social Policy and Intervention, *Family Policy Briefing 7. Caring for children after parental separation: would legislation for shared parenting time help children?*, Oxford 2011.
- R. UYTTENDAELE, in P. Senaeve, *Co-ouderschap en omgangsrecht. Commentaar op de Wet van 13 april 1995*, Maklu, 1995.
- I. VAN DER VALK & E. SPRUIJT, 'Het ouderschap en de effecten voor de kinderen', *Jeugd & Gezin, Departement Pedagogische Wetenschappen, Universiteit Utrecht*, 10 October 2013.
- H. VANBOCKRIJCK, in P. Senaeve et al., *Knelpunten echtscheiding, afstamming en verblijfsregelingen*, Intersentia, 2009.
- S. VANASSCHE & K. MATTHIJS, 'Verblijfsco-ouderschap en de relaties tussen ouders en stiefouders', *Relaties en nieuwe gezinnen*, 2013, Vol. 3, No. 4.
- G. VERSCHELDEN, *Handboek Belgisch Familierecht*, die Keure, 2010.
- M. VOERT & T. GEURTS, 'Evaluatie Ouderschapsplan. Een eerste verkenning', *WODC*, Cahier 2013-8.
- M. VONK, *Children and their parents. A comparative study of the legal position of children with regard to their intentional and biological parents in English and Dutch law*, Doctoral thesis, Intersentia, 2007.

- S. WESTPHAL, *Are the kids alright? Essays on postdivorce residence arrangements and children's well-being*, Utrecht, 2015.
- R. WHITE et al., *A guide to the Children Act 1989*, Butterworths, 1990.

LEGISLATION

INTERNATIONAL AND EUROPEAN INSTRUMENTS

- *1950 European Convention for the Protection of Human Rights and Fundamental Freedoms*, 213 United Nations Treaty Series 221.
- *1966 International Covenant on Civil and Political Rights*, 999 United Nations Treaty Series 171.
- *1984 Recommendation No. R (84) 4 on Parental Responsibilities.*
- *1989 Convention on the Rights of the Child*, 1577 United Nations Treaty Series 3.
- *1996 European Convention on the Exercise of Children's Rights*, European Treaty Series 160.
- *1996 Hague Convention on jurisdiction, applicable law, recognition, enforcement and co-operation in respect of parental responsibilities and measures for the protection of children*, 19 October 1996.
- *2000 Charter of Fundamental Rights of the European Union*, 2000/C 364/01.
- *2003 Council Regulation (EC) No. 2201/2003 concerning jurisdiction and the recognition and enforcement of judgments in matrimonial matters and the matters of parental responsibility, repealing Regulation (EC) No. 1347/2000*, Official Journal L 338, 23 December 2003.
- *2003 Convention on Contact Concerning Children*, European Treaty Series 192.
- *2003 Council Regulation concerning jurisdiction and the recognition and enforcement of judgments in matrimonial matters and the matters of parental responsibility, repealing Regulation (EC) No 1347/2000 (Brussels II bis Regulation)*, Official Journal L 338, 23 December 2003, pp. 1-29.
- *2007 Treaty of Lisbon amending the Treaty on European Union and the Treaty establishing the European Community*, Official Journal 2007/C 306/01.
- Council of Europe Committee of Experts on Family Law, *Draft Recommendation on the rights and legal status of children and parental responsibilities*, 27 May 2010, CJ-FA-GT3 (2010) 2 rev. 2.
- Council of Europe Committee of experts on Family Law, *Report on principles concerning the establishment and legal consequences of parentage – 'The White Paper'*, 23 October 2006, CJ-FA (2006) 4 e.
- Council of Europe European Committee on Legal Co-operation, *'White Paper' on principles concerning the establishment and legal consequences of parentage*, 15 January 2002 (adopted 11-14 May 2004), CJ-FA (2001) 16 rev.
- Human Rights Committee, *General Comment 17 (Thirty-fifth session, 1989)*, 7 April 1989.
- Human Rights Committee, *General Comment 19 (Thirty-ninth session, 1990)*, 27 July 1990.

ENGLISH

- *Adoption and Children Act 2002.*
- *An Act to reform the law relating to children; to provide for local authority services for children in need and others; to amend the law with respect to children's homes, community homes, voluntary homes and voluntary organisations; to make provision with respect to fostering, child minding and day care for young children and adoption; and for connected purposes* (*Children Act 1989*).
- *Education Act 1996.*
- *Human Fertilisation and Embryology Act 2008.*
- *Marriage Act 1949.*

DUTCH

- Dutch Civil Code/Burgerlijk Wetboek.
- *Wet van 19 februari 2000, houdende regels inzake het recht op aanpassing van de arbeidsduur (Wet aanpassing arbeidsduur), Stb.* 114.
- *Wet van 25 november 2013 tot wijziging van Boek 1 van het Burgerlijk Wetboek in verband met het juridisch ouderschap van de vrouwelijke partner van de moeder anders dan door adoptie, Stb.* 480.
- *Wet tot nadere regeling van het gezag over en van de omgang met minderjarige kinderen, Stb.* 240.
- *Wet tot wijziging van onder meer, Boek 1 van het Burgerlijk Wetboek in verband met invoering van gezamenlijk gezag voor een ouder en zijn partner en van gezamenlijk voogdij, Stb.* 507.

BELGIAN

- Belgian Civil Code/Burgerlijk Wetboek.
- *Wet betreffende de invoering van een familie- en jeugdrechtbank*, BS, 30 July 2013.
- *Wet van 8 april 1965 betreffende de jeugdbescherming.*
- *Wet van 31 maart 1987 tot wijziging van een aantal bepalingen betreffende de afstamming*, BS, 27 May 1987.
- *Wet 13 april 1995 betreffende de gezamelijke uitoefening van het ouderlijk gezag*, BS, 24 May 1995.

CASE LAW

ECtHR

- *Dąbrowska v. Poland*, Appl. No. 34568/08, 2 February 2010.
- *Hokkanen v. Finland*, Appl. No. 19823/92, 23 September 1994.
- *Hoppe v. Germany*, Appl. No. 28422/95, 5 December 2002.
- *Johansen v. Norway*, Appl. No. 17383/90, 7 August 1996.
- *Keegan v. Ireland*, Appl. No. 16969/90, 26 May 1994.
- *Kroon v. the Netherlands*, Appl. No. 18535/91, 27 October 1994.
- *Lebbink v. the Netherlands*, Appl. No. 45582/99, 1 June 2004.
- *Marckx v. Belgium*, Appl. No. 6833/74, 13 June 1979.
- *McMichael v. the United Kingdom*, Appl. No. 16424/90, 24 February 1995.
- *P.K. v. Poland*, Appl. No. 43123/10, 10 June 2014.
- *Salgueiro Da Silva Mouta v. Portugal*, Appl. No. 33290/96, 21 December 1999.
- *Zaunegger v. Germany*, Appl. No. 22028/04, 3 December 2009.

ICCPR

- Communication No. 201/1985, *Hendriks v. the Netherlands*, Views adopted on 27 July 1988.
- Communication No. 417/1990, *Santacana v. Spain*, Views adopted on 15 July 1994.
- Communication No. 514/1992, *Fei v. Colombia*, Views adopted on 4 April 1995.
- Communication No. 945/2000, *L.P. v. Czech Republic*, Views adopted on 4 August 2005.

ENGLISH COURTS

- *A v A (Children) (Shared Residence)*, [2004] EWHC 142 (Fam).
- *A v L (Contact)*, [1998] 1 FLR 361.
- *A v N*, [1997] 1 FLR 533.
- *B v B (M v M) (Transfer of Custody: Appeal)*, [1987] 2 FLR 146.
- *Clayton v Clayton*, [2007] 1 FLR 11.
- *Dawson v Wearmouth*, [1999] 1 FLR 1167.
- *D v D (Shared Residence Order)*, [2001] 1 FLR 495.
- *Downing v. Downing (Downing Interfering)*, [1976] Fam 288.
- *Gillick v West Norfolk and Wisbech Area Health Authority*, [1986] 1 AC 112 (HL).
- *Holmes Moorhouse v Richmond-Upon-Thames LBC*, [2009] 1 FLR 904.
- *L v L (Minors) (separate representation)*, [1994] 1 FLR 156.
- *P v D*, [2014] EWHC 2355 (Fam).
- *P v W*, [1984] Fam 32.
- *Re A (Children) (Shared Residence)*, [2003] 3 FCR 656.
- *Re A (Shared Residence)*, [2001] EWCA Civ 1795.
- *Re A (Temporary Removal from Jurisdiction)*, [2004] EWCA Civ 1587.
- *Re B (A Child)*, [2009] UKSC 5.
- *Re B (Leave to Remove: Impact of Refusal)*, [2005] 1 FLR 239.

- *Re B (Leave to Remove)*, [2006] EWHC 1783 (Fam).
- *Re B (Prohibited Steps Order)*, [2008] 1 FLR 613.
- *Re B (T) (A Minor) (Residence Order)*, [1995] 2 FCR 240.
- *Re C (A Child) (Immunisation: Parental Rights)*, [2003] EWHC 1376 (Fam).
- *Re C (Residence Order)*, [2007] 1 FLR 211.
- *Re D (Residence: Imposition of Conditions)*, [1996] 2 FCR 820.
- *Re D (Children) (Shared Residence Orders)*, [2001] 1 FCR 147.
- *Re DW (A Child) (Termination of Parental Responsibility)*, [2013] EWHC 854 (Fam).
- *Re F (Children) (Shared Residence Order)*, [2003] EWCA Civ 592.
- *Re F (Shared Residence Order)*, [2003] EWCA Civ 592.
- *Re G (A Minor) (Parental responsibility: Education)*, [1994] 2 FLR 964.
- *Re H (Shared Residence: Parental Responsibility*, [1995] 2 FLR 883 (CA).
- *Re J (Specific Issue Orders: Child's Religious Upbringing and Circumcision)*, [2000] 1 FCR 307.
- *Re L (Care: Threshold Criteria)*, [2007] 1 FLR 2050.
- *Re L (Internal Relocation: Shared Residence Order)*, [2009] 1 FLR 1157.
- *Re L-W (Children) (Enforcement and Committal: Contact)*, [2010] EWCA Civ 1253.
- *Re M (Family Proceedings: Affidavits)*, [1995] 2 FLR 100.
- *Re M (Intractable Contact Dispute: Court's Positive Duty)*, [2006] 1 FLR 627.
- *Re PC (change of Surname)*, [1997] 2 FLR 730.
- *Re R (A Child) (Residence Order: Treatment of Child's Wishes)*, [2009] 2 FRC 572.
- *Re R (Children) (Residence: Shared Care: Children's Views)*, [2005] EWCA Civ 542.
- *Re S (Contact: Application by Sibling)*, [1998] 2 FLR 897.
- *Re T (Abduction: Child's Objections to Return)*, [2000] 2 FLR 193.
- *Re W (A child)*, [2009] EWCA Civ 370.
- *Re W (A Minor) (Medical Treatment: Court's Jurisdiction)*, [1993] Fam 64.
- *Re Y (Leave to Remove from Jurisdiction)*, [2004] 2 FLR 330.
- *Riley v Riley*, [1986] 2 FLR 429.

DUTCH COURTS

- Hof Amsterdam, 4 May 2010, LJN BM3895.
- Hof Amsterdam, 3 January 2012, LJN BV8225.
- Hof Arnhem, 10 January 2013, LJN BZ1896.
- Hof 's-Gravenhage, 18 October 2006, LJN AZ209.
- Hof 's-Gravenhage, 20 January 2010, LJN BL2337.
- Hof 's-Gravenhage, 23 June 2010, LJN BN3877.
- Hof 's-Gravenhage, 21 July 2010, LJN BN5758.
- Hof 's-Gravenhage, 9 February 2011, LJN BP6275.
- Hof 's-Gravenhage, 23 February 2011, LJN BQ8296.
- Hof 's-Gravenhage, 11 May 2011, LJN BR3529.
- Hof 's-Gravenhage, 29 February 2012, LJN BW7358.
- Hof 's-Hertogenbosch, 26 November 2002, LJN AF2655.
- Hof 's-Hertogenbosch, 21 February 2012, LJN BV6414.
- Hof Leeuwaarden, 4 November 2010, LJN BO3724.
- Hoge Raad, 4 May 1984, LJN AG4807, *NJ* 1985, 510.
- Hoge Raad, 21 March 1986, LJN AC9283, *NJ* 1986, 585.
- Hoge Raad, 21 March 1986, LJN AC9284, *NJ* 1986, 586.

- Hoge Raad, 10 September 1999, LJN ZC2963, *NJ* 2000, 20.
- Hoge Raad, 15 December 2000, LJN AA9042, *NJ* 2001.
- Hoge Raad, 21 May 2010, LJN BL7407.
- Hoge Raad, 9 July 2010, LJN BM4301.
- Rechtbank Alkmaar, 20 June 2005, LJN AT9598.
- Rechtbank Alkmaar, 16 February 2011, LJN BQ1141.
- Rechtbank Arnhem, 21 November 2011, Case No. 222527/FARK 11-12655.
- Rechtbank Arnhem, 10 October 2012, LJN BY7647.
- Rechtbank Breda, 4 December 2012, LJN BY7479.
- Rechtbank Dordrecht, 19 September 2012, LJN BX9134.
- Rechtbank Groningen, 6 April 2010, LJN BM 3955.
- Rechtbank Groningen, 12 October 2010, LJN BO2900.
- Rechtbank Groningen, 9 August 2011, LJN BS8007.
- Rechtbank Haarlem, 15 April 2005, LJN AT4422.
- Rechtbank Haarlem, 10 November 2010, LJN BO6046.
- Rechtbank 's-Gravenhage, 13 January 2010, LJN BL1926.
- Rechtbank 's-Gravenhage, 13 January 2010, LJN BL1932.
- Rechtbank 's-Gravenhage, 13 January 2010, LJN BL2081.
- Rechtbank 's-Gravenhage, 1 april 2010, LJN BM3090.
- Rechtbank 's-Gravenhage, 28 July 2010, LJN BN3236.
- Rechtbank 's-Hertogenbosch 9 June 2005, LJN AT7299.
- Rechtbank Leeuwaarden, 5 February 2009, LJN BH2027.
- Rechtbank Maastricht, 27 October 2010, LJN BO1950.
- Rechtbank Utrecht, 9 September 2009, Case No. 270441/FARK 09-3982.
- Rechtbank Utrecht, 29 December 2010, Case No. 292780/FA RK 10-5355.
- Rechtbank Zwolle, 19 August 2004, LJN AQ7125.
- Rechtbank Zwolle, 20 June 2011, LJN BQ9836.

BELGIAN COURTS

- Cass. AR 8750, 27 September 1990, *RW* 1990-91.
- Cass. AR 134/2003, 8 October 2003, *Rev. Trim. Dr. Fam.* 2004.
- Cass. 20 May 2009, *RW*, 2010-11, nr. 21, 22 January 2011.
- Cass. 3 June 2010, *NJW*, 2011.
- Cass. 25 February 2011, *RW*, 2012-13, nr. 3.
- Cass. C.09.0125.N, 3 June 2010.
- Cass. C.12.0021.N, 4 January 2013.
- Court Antwerp, 10 November 2006, *JR*, p. 5857.
- Court Brussels (first instance), 30 January 2005, *RTDF*, 2007.
- Court Brussels (first instance), 3 April 2007, *T. Fam.* 2007.
- Court Brussels (appeal), 5 September 2007, 2006/JR/180.
- Court Brussels (appeal), 5 December 2007, Act. dr. fam., 2008.
- Court Brussels (appeal), 5 February 2008, *RW*, 2009-10, nr. 6, pp. 243-245.
- Court Brussels (appeal), 11 February 2009, *Rev. trim. dr. fam. 2/2011*, pp. 386-397.
- Court Brussels (appeal), 12 May 2009, *Revue Générale de Droit Civil Belge*, 2010, pp. 286-293.
- Court Brussels (juvenile court), 18 May 2009, *399/2008/17C.*
- Court Charleroi, 14 May 2004, *Rev. Trim, dr. fam.* 2005.
- Court Ghent, 2 May 2005, *TJK*, 2006/3.

- Court Ghent (appeal), 25 October 2007, 2007/EV/73.
- Court Leuven (first instance), 16 September 2010, *NJW*, 2011, nr. 239, pp. 236-237.
- Court Leuven (first instance), 9 February 2012, *RABG*, 2012/12, pp. 806-812.
- Court Liège (appeal), 29 May 2008, *JLMB*, 2009/3.
- Court Liège (appeal), 26 August 2008, *JLMB*, 2009/3.
- Court Mons (appeal), 12 June 2007, *JLMB*, 2009/3, pp. 116-120.
- Court Nijvel, 5 September 2003, *Rev. Trim. dr. fam.* 1/2005.
- Court Nijvel, 19 September 2003, *Rev. trim. dr. fam.* 1/2005.
- Raad van State, 18 September 2006, nr. 162.503.

DIGITAL SOURCES

- conventions.coe.int
- ec.europa.eu/eurostat
- nfn-onderzoek.nl
- treaties.un.org
- twohomes.org
- www2.ohchr.org
- www.alternativefamilylaw.co.uk
- www.cabinetoffice.gov.uk
- www.cbs.nl
- www.direct.gov.uk
- www.fatherhoodinstitute.org
- www.fathers-4-justice.org
- www.fnf.org.uk
- www.gingerbread.org.uk
- www.hfea.gov.uk
- www.homeoffice.gov.uk
- www.kindengezin.be
- www.nwo.nl
- www.ons.gov.uk
- www.parliament.uk
- www.rechtspraak.nl
- www.scheidingsonderzoek.ugent.be

SAMENVATTING

Inleiding

De positie en structuur van de familie binnen de Nederlandse samenleving is sterk veranderd in de afgelopen vijftig jaar. Zowel het concept van ouderschap als het concept van familie is drastisch geëvolueerd. Ook het recht onderging meerdere malen een hervorming teneinde alle maatschappelijke veranderingen te kunnen waarborgen.

Een scheidingspercentage van 1 op 3, een groeiende vraag naar gelijke behandeling van de ouders en het toenemende besef dat kinderen intrinsieke rechten bezitten die gewaarborgd dienen te worden, vereisten een heroverweging van de manier waarop de uitoefening van gezag en de verblijfsarrangementen geregeld was.

Als een nieuwe vorm van opvoeding na scheiding is vervolgens het verblijfsco-ouderschap opgekomen: een verblijfsregeling waarbij de kinderen (min of meer) evenveel tijd doorbrengen bij iedere ouder. Deze regeling waarborgt de gelijke positie van de ouders en zorgt ervoor dat de feitelijke situatie van het kind relatief gelijk blijft na de scheiding in die zin dat hij of zij door beide ouders verzorgd wordt en beide ouders evenveel ziet. Er wordt echter ook kritiek geuit in relatie tot verblijfsco-ouderschap: deze regeling zou kinderen in hoge mate blootstellen aan conflictsituaties en instabiliteit die gepaard gaat met het wisselen van huishoudens.

Het standpunt van de Nederlandse wetgever is dat kinderen na het uiteengaan van hun ouders recht hebben op verzorging door hen beiden. Dit is vastgelegd in de Wet bevordering voortgezet ouderschap en zorgvuldige scheiding van 2009. Het is echter niet duidelijk wat precies onder deze gelijkwaardige verzorging wordt verstaan. Volgens de Hoge Raad creëert deze wet in ieder geval geen voorkeurspositie voor verblijfsco-ouderschap.

Niet alleen in Nederland is er veel discussie over verblijfsco-ouderschap en wint de regeling aan populariteit. Deze trend is wereldwijd, in ieder geval in de westerse landen, waarneembaar. Er is echt een groot gebrek aan kennis als het gaat om co-ouderschap in het algemeen en deze verblijfsregeling in het bijzonder. Dit proefschrift brengt meer duidelijkheid en beantwoordt de volgende vragen: Hoe is (verblijfs)co-ouderschap juridisch geregeld in Engeland (en Wales), Nederland en België en wat kunnen deze landen van elkaar leren in dat opzicht? Hoe wijdverspreid is verblijfsco-ouderschap in de drie landen? Dient verblijfsco-ouderschap juridisch aangemoedigd of ontmoedigd te worden?

Internationaal kader

Internationaal gezien kan er een verschuiving worden waargenomen van een ouder-georiënteerde verdeling van gezag naar een kind-georiënteerde gezamenlijke uitoefening van de ouderlijke verantwoordelijkheden. Waar internationaal en Europees recht in het verleden terughoudend was om zich met nationale regelgeving op het gebeid van familierecht te bemoeien, introduceert internationale wetgeving steeds meer nieuwe specifieke en substantiële regels op dit vlak. Deze nieuwe regels stimuleren de gezamenlijke uitoefening van de ouderlijke verantwoordelijkheden na scheiding. Hoewel geen van de internationale en Europese instrumenten verblijfsco-ouderschap verbiedt, zou het te voorbarig zijn om te stellen dat internationaal en Europees recht deze verblijfsregeling actief stimuleert. Voor het overgrote deel zwijgt internationaal en Europees recht over het verblijf van het kind.

Engeland en Wales

De Children Act 1989 en de daaruit voortkomende jurisprudentie heeft de huidige Engelse wetgeving inzake kinderen vormgegeven. Het heeft ouderlijke verantwoordelijkheden geïntroduceerd en biedt rechters de mogelijkheid 'Section 8 orders' uit te vaardigen.

In de praktijk geeft - zeer beperkt - onderzoek aan dat verblijfsco-ouderschap nog steeds vrij zeldzaam is in Engeland (en Wales) en in minder dan 10% van alle afspraken na een scheiding voorkomt. Pogingen om een wettelijk vermoeden te scheppen ten behoeve van verblijfsco-ouderschap zijn dan ook tot dusver verre van succesvol geweest.

De meeste ouders hebben binnen het Engelse systeem gezamenlijke ouderlijke verantwoordelijkheden en verliezen deze niet bij een scheiding. Elke drager van ouderlijke verantwoordelijkheden mag deze alleen uitoefenen en er bestaat geen hiërarchie tussen individuele dragers van ouderlijke verantwoordelijkheden. In geval van bepaalde belangrijke beslissingen over het leven van het kind is deze vrijheid echter beperkt door de jurisprudentie en dienen de dragers van ouderlijke verantwoordelijkheden met elkaar te overleggen en consensus bereiken. De rechtbank kan in zo'n geval knopen doorhakken.

Als ouders uit elkaar gaan zouden ze afspraken moeten maken over waar en met wie het kind gaat wonen. Als ze niet tot een overeenkomst kunnen komen, kunnen ze de rechtbank vragen om een verblijfsregeling vast te stellen. De rechter mag voorwaarden stellen aan een verblijfsregeling. Hij mag ook een verblijfsco-ouderschapsregeling vaststellen ten gunste van beide ouders. Dit type regeling is in de loop der jaren steeds minder uitzonderlijk geworden en wordt ook toegekend op verzoek van de ouders als er geen werkelijk gelijkwaardige verdeling van verblijf plaatsvindt.

Hoewel het wijzigen van een verblijfsregeling mogelijk is, zijn rechters terughoudend om dit te doen, tenzij een belangrijke verandering van omstandigheden dit noodzakelijk maakt. Indien een verblijfsregeling van kracht is, moet een ouder die van verblijf wil wisselen de andere drager(s) van ouderlijke verantwoordelijkheden of de rechter om toestemming vragen. Verandering van verblijf binnen het Verenigd Koninkrijk is meestal toegestaan, tenzij de omstandigheden uitzonderlijk zijn. Bij verhuizing naar het buitenland wordt besloten op basis van de feiten van de betreffende zaak en het welzijn van het kind.

De waarneembare wensen en gevoelens van een kind dat volwassen genoeg is om de procesvoering te begrijpen, is een van de factoren die de rechter mee moet afwegen wanneer er besloten moet worden om een 'Section 8 order' vast te stellen, aan te passen of nietig te verklaren. Bovendien mogen kinderen in sommige gevallen een beroep doen op de rechter en kunnen de mogelijkheid krijgen een om om een 'Section 8 order' the vragen, een verandering of nietigverklaring hiervan te verzoeken of om tussenbeide te komen in de procesvoering van hun ouders.

Tot slot heeft de rechter verschillende uitvoerende instrumenten tot zijn beschikking als er niet in overeenstemming met een regeling wordt gehandeld. Hieronder vallen bijvoorbeeld boetes of celstraf voor de overtreder. Echter, uitvoering kan bemoeilijkt worden doordat het schadelijk kan zijn voor het kind voor wie de oorspronkelijke regeling was vastgesteld.

Nederland

Aan het begin van dit millennium was er veel discussie over kwesties omtrent co-ouderschap, met het achtereenvolgens in werking treden van gezamenlijke ouderlijke verantwoordelijkheden op aanvraag in 1995, de automatische continuatie van ouderlijke verantwoordelijkheden na scheiding in 1998, en met de initiatieven voor het reguleren van zorgafspraken en voor promotie van verblijfsco-ouderschap door wetgeving die kort hierna werden voorgesteld. Toen de Wet bevordering voortgezet ouderschap en zorgvuldige scheiding uiteindelijk van kracht werd in 2009, was deze ontdaan van de meest ambitieuze voorzieningen, zoals een aanname dat ouders de tijd met hun kind of kinderen gelijkmatig dienen te verdelen na scheiding en de introductie van een administratieve scheiding. In plaats daarvan geeft de wet kinderen het recht op gelijke verzorging door beide ouders na ouderlijke scheiding – wat zoals de Hoge Raad oordeelde niet een gelijke verdeling van tijd inhoudt – en de ouders verplicht om zorgafspraken te maken voor hun kinderen als ze scheiden en om deze vast te leggen in een ouderschapsplan. Hoewel het recht op gelijke zorg niet een recht op verblijfsco-ouderschap inhoudt, lijkt het op zijn minst te duiden op de gezamenlijke uitoefening van ouderlijke verantwoordelijkheden en moedigt het verblijfsco-ouderschap aan.

Het uitgangspunt is dat de dragers van gezamenlijke ouderlijke verantwoordelijkheden deze gezamenlijk moeten uitvoeren, wat inhoudt dat beide dragers dagelijkse beslissingen kunnen nemen over de opvoeding van het kind en dat zij regelmatig moeten overleggen met elkaar, zeker als het gaat om belangrijke beslissingen. De rechter kan tussenbeide komen als de dragers van gezamenlijke ouderlijke verantwoordelijkheden niet samen tot een beslissing kunnen komen, of als het welzijn van het kind in gevaar is.

Kinderen, zeker van 12 jaar en ouder, hebben het recht om gehoord te worden, kunnen in sommige gevallen tussenbeide komen in procesvoering op het gebied van familierecht dat hen aangaat, en kunnen in exceptionele gevallen deze procesvoering zelf starten, vertegenwoordigd door een bijzondere curator.

Tot slot heeft het Nederlands recht verschillende mechanismen om regelingen op het gebied van familierecht op te leggen. Het is echter moeilijk voor rechters om deze maatregelen te toe te passen zonder het welzijn van het kind in gevaar te brengen.

België

Het standpunt dat ouders voor hun kind(eren) moeten zorgen na scheiding bestaat al vele jaren in de Belgische wetgeving. Het werd voor het eerst een wettelijk vermoeden in 1995 met de introductie van de *ex lege* voortzetting van gezamenlijke uitoefening van ouderlijke verantwoordelijkheden na scheiding. Elf jaar later heeft de Belgische wetgever verblijfsco-ouderschap erkend en aangemoedigd door rechters te verplichten om serieus afspraken te overwegen waarin de ouders gelijkmatig (50/50) de tijd met hun kind(eren) kunnen delen als zo'n afspraak is aangevraagd door een van de ouders.

Hoewel de dragers van gezamenlijke ouderlijke verantwoordelijkheden, in theorie, deze dienen uit te voeren in goede samenwerking en alle belangrijke beslissingen de toestemming van beide dragers van ouderlijke verantwoordelijkheden nodig hebben, wordt aangenomen dat deze toestemming aanwezig is als het gaat om derden te goeder trouw.

Als de dragers van gezamenlijke ouderlijke verantwoordelijkheden niet tot overeenstemming kunnen komen bij belangrijke beslissingen, mogen zij de rechter vragen tussenbeide te komen. De rechter kan dan een regeling vaststellen, om de kwestie te beslissen, om de ouderlijke verantwoordelijkheden van een van de dragers te beperken, of om in zeldzame gevallen een van de ouders de volledige ouderlijke verantwoordelijkheid te geven.

Hoewel gezamenlijke uitoefening van ouderlijke verantwoordelijkheden de norm is, is dit niet een wettelijk vermoeden. Het is simpelweg een afspraak die de rechter op aanvraag dient te overwegen. Er zijn veel reden waarom een 50/50 verdeling van verblijf niet mogelijk is in bepaalde omstandigheden. Daarnaast is het niet aan de rechter om anders te beslissen als de ouders overeenkomen dat een enkel verblijf het beste is voor hun kind(eren). Het omgekeerde is ook het geval: als beide ouders een verblijfsco-ouderschap overeenkomen, heeft de rechter weinig reden om daar van af te wijken, tenzij zo'n afspraak het welzijn van het kind in gevaar brengt.

Als onderdeel van het waken over het welzijn van het kind, hebben kinderen het recht om gehoord te worden in procesvoeringen betreffende afspraken over hun verblijf en zorg. Kinderen van 12 jaar en ouder ontvangen van de rechtbank een brief om hen te informeren over hun recht om gehoord te worden. Jongere kinderen mogen wellicht ook gehoord worden, maar ontvangen niet automatisch een brief om hen hierover te informeren.

Tot slot is er het probleem van handhaving. Het praktische verschil tussen door de rechter vastgestelde regelingen inzake (de uitvoering van) ouderlijke verantwoordelijkheden en verblijf, en afspraken tussen ouders die buiten de rechtbank om gemaakt zijn, is dat door de rechter vastgestelde regelingen kunnen worden afgedwongen indien de ouders zich hier niet aan houden. In de praktijk is handhaving echter niet gemakkelijk en voordat er maatregelen getroffen kunnen worden ter handhaving dient grondig te worden onderzocht of deze niet onevenredig veel schade kunnen toebrengen aan het kind.

Sociaalpsychologische aspecten van verblijfsco-ouderschap

Als het op verblijfsco-ouderschap aankomt of op afspraken over verblijf in het algemeen, zijn er nog veel hiaten in de kennis over bijna alle facetten van deze afspraken. Er zijn geen onderzoeken die de gevolgen op de lange termijn voor alle bij verblijfsco-ouderschap betrokken partijen in kaart brengen. De onderzoeken die het welzijn van kinderen onder verschillende afspraken bestuderen, doen dit voornamelijk door het bestuderen van de antwoorden gegeven door ouders van deze kinderen, hetgeen de kans groot maakt dat deze antwoorden subjectief zijn. Veel van de belangrijkste zaken zijn nog niet (voldoende) onderzocht, zoals de invloed van nieuwe wetgeving op de besluitvorming van ouders over verblijfsafspraken, hoe verblijfsafspraken (kunnen) worden bijgesteld bij veranderende omstandigheden, en de invloed van de leeftijd van het kind op de wenselijkheid van verblijfsco-ouderschap.

Toch is er genoeg kennis aanwezig om ten minste een goede start te maken met het beantwoorden van de vragen die centraal staan in dit proefschrift. Statistische data laten zien dat verblijfsco-ouderschap inderdaad een belangrijke verblijfsafspraak is in alle drie de onderzochte landen, met een prevalentie tussen 9% en 27%-38%. Onderzoek uit België laat tevens zien dat de introductie van nieuwe wetgeving ten gunste van gezamenlijke uitoefening van ouderlijke verantwoordelijkheden en verblijfsco-ouderschap geassocieerd kan worden met de groei van verblijfsco-ouderschap in de praktijk, wat suggereert dat zulke wetgeving de beslissingen van de ouders (en de rechtbank) beïnvloedt bij de keuze van een specifieke verblijfsafspraak.

De laatste vraag – welke invloed heeft verblijfsco-ouderschap op het welzijn van het kind en moet het aangemoedigd of ontmoedigd worden – is onmogelijk met zekerheid te beantwoorden, gezien de huidige staat van het empirisch onderzoek naar verblijfsafspraken. Niet alleen is er een gebrek aan belangrijke informatie en spreken de bestaande onderzoeken elkaar vaak tegen, ook zijn er veel factoren (van buitenaf) die de verblijfsco-ouderschapsafspraak en het welzijn van het kind beïnvloeden. De meest belangrijke factoren zijn: de omvang van ouderlijke conflicten, de geografische afstand tussen de woningen van de ouders, de leeftijd van het betrokken kind en de bereidheid van beide ouders om überhaupt een verblijfsco-ouderschapsregeling aan te gaan. Deze factoren kunnen het naleven van de afspraak positief of negatief beïnvloeden. Hoe meer we over deze invloeden te weten komen, des te makkelijker zal te voorspellen zijn of, op basis van de feiten in een specifieke zaak, een verblijfsco-ouderschapsregeling het beste is voor het welzijn van het betrokken kind of de betrokken kinderen.

Wel laten nieuwe empirische onderzoeken zien dat in het algemeen kinderen in verblijfsco-ouderschappen minder psychologische problemen ondervinden dan kinderen in moeder- of vaderverblijven. En hoewel conflictsituaties het psychologisch welzijn van kinderen verlagen, is er geen bewijs gevonden dat conflictsituaties in verblijfsco-ouderschap een sterkere negatieve invloed hebben op het welzijn van kinderen dan conflictsituaties binnen moeder- of vaderverblijven.

Rechtsvergelijkende synthese

Over het algemeen hebben de drie rechtssystemen veel overeenkomsten en worden er dikwijls soortgelijke resultaten bereikt, echter niet met dezelfde methoden. Er zijn echter nog steeds een aantal belangrijke verschillen om rekening mee te houden. De wetgeving (inclusief jurisprudentie) van de drie landen verschilt als het aankomt op toekenning van ouderlijke verantwoordelijkheden, de verplichting tot het maken van zorgafspraken bij scheiding en de benadering van verblijfsco-ouderschap. Welk juridisch systeem de beste benadering heeft en als voorbeeld kan dienen voor andere landen, hangt af van het gewenste resultaat.

Zo lijkt de partijautonomie (van de ouders) het best gewaarborgd te worden binnen het Engelse rechtssysteem dat toekenning van ouderlijke verantwoordelijkheden mogelijk maakt voor meer dan twee personen, zo min mogelijk regels heeft omtrent de uitoefening ervan en waarin de rechtbank een verblijfsco-ouderschapsregeling zal vaststellen op gezamenlijk verzoek van beide ouders, ook al is er geen feitelijk verblijfsco-ouderschap.

De Nederlandse en Belgische systemen daarentegen geven meer restricties aan wat de ouders gerechtigd zijn om te doen. Beide landen beperken de ouderlijke verantwoordelijkheid tot twee juridische ouders en geven de rechter meer mogelijkheden om tegen de wensen van de ouders in te gaan indien dat in het belang van het kind is. Zo moeten de ouders in Nederland een ouderschapsplan opstellen alvorens zij kunnen scheiden of een beschikking aanvragen en kan de rechter in zowel Nederland als België een door de ouders voorgestelde zorg- of verblijfsregeling weigeren.

Ook is er in het Belgische systeem duidelijk een voorkeur voor 50/50 verdeling van verblijf opgenomen, waar in de andere twee rechtssystemen geen sprake van is.

Conclusie

Niet alleen is verblijfsco-ouderschap een verblijfsarrangement dat in alle drie de landen veel voorkomt, het is een verblijfsarrangement dat sterk aan populariteit wint, voornamelijk in de twee landen die deze regeling aanmoedigen: Nederland en België. Is deze aanmoediging terecht? Dit is moeilijk met zekerheid te zeggen.

Hoewel het beschikbare empirisch onderzoek aangeeft dat in het algemeen kinderen die in een verblijfsco-ouderschap opgroeien minder psychologische en andersoortige problemen ondervinden, kunnen specifieke factoren een feitelijke situatie ongeschikt maken voor een dergelijke regeling. Met name moet er gedacht worden aan de afstand tussen de woningen, hoe vaak de kinderen van verblijf moeten wisselen, de beschikbaarheid en de wil van beide ouders om voor de kinderen te zorgen, en hoe goed de kinderen zelf kunnen omgaan met een verblijfsco-ouderschap.

Om deze reden pleit de auteur ervoor om verblijfsco-ouderschap niet een juridisch preferentiële regeling te maken, maar het aan de rechtbank over te laten om per zaak te beoordelen wat het beste is voor de betrokken kinderen. Om de rechter in staat te stellen een dergelijke beoordeling te maken, is het noodzakelijk dat er meer empirisch onderzoek komt naar de invloed van verschillende feitelijke factoren (zoals de leeftijd van het kind) op het welzijn van het kind in het kader van verschillende verblijfsregelingen.

Informatie op alle vlakken is zeer belangrijk: de ouders dienen door de juristen goed ingelicht te worden over de voor- en nadelen van de verschillende verblijfsregelingen en de rechtbanken dienen hun afwegingen te maken op basis van onderzoek in plaats van verouderde vooroordelen.

ABOUT THE AUTHOR

Natalie Nikolina studied law at Utrecht University (the Netherlands) and Warwick University (England). She graduated with honours (cum laude) in 2008. She continued her education at Utrecht University where she attained a Master's degree in Legal Research with the dual specialization in comparative family law and human rights. During her PhD research she conducted multidisciplinary research in the Netherlands, England and Belgium. Natalie currently works as a researcher in comparative sexual orientation law at Leiden University.

European Family Law Series

1. *Legal Recognition of Same-Sex Couples in Europe*, K. Boele-Woelki and A. Fuchs (eds.)
2. *European Family Law in Action Volume I: Grounds for divorce*, K. Boele-Woelki, B. Braat and I. Sumner (eds.)
3. *European Family Law in Action Volume II: Maintenance Between Former Spouses*, K. Boele-Woelki, B. Braat and I. Sumner (eds.)
4. *Perspectives for the Unification and Harmonisation of Family Law in Europe*, K. Boele-Woelki (ed.)
5. *Family Law Legislation of the Netherlands*, I. Sumner and H. Warendorf
6. *Indépendance et interdépendance patrimoniales des époux dans le régime matrimonial légal des droits néerlandais, français et suisse*, B. Braat
7. *Principles of European Family Law Regarding Divorce and Maintenance Between Former Spouses*, K. Boele-Woelki, F. Ferrand, C. González Beilfuss, M. Jänterä-Jareborg, N. Lowe, D. Martiny and W. Pintens
8. *Inheritance Law Legislation of the Netherlands*, I. Sumner and H. Warendorf
9. *European Family Law in Action Volume III : Parental Responsibilities*, K. Boele-Woelki, B. Braat and I. Curry-Sumner (eds.)
10. *Common Core and Better Law in European Family Law*, K. Boele-Woelki (ed.)
11. *All's well that ends registered?*, I. Curry-Sumner
12. *Model Family Code – From a global perspective*, I. Schwenzer and M. Dimsey
13. *Harmonisation of Family Law in Europe. A Historical Perspective*, M. Antokolskaia
14. *Brussels II bis: Its Impact and Application in the Member States*, K. Boele-Woelki and C. González Beilfuss (eds.)
15. *Tensions between Legal, Biological and Social Conceptions of Parentage*, I. Schwenzer (ed.)
16. *Principles of European Family Law Regarding Parental Responsibilities*, K. Boele-Woelki, F. Ferrand, C. González Beilfuss, M. Jänterä-Jareborg, N. Lowe, D. Martiny and W. Pintens
17. *Juxtaposing Legal Systems and the Principles of European Family Law on Divorce and Maintenance*, E. Örücü and J. Mair (eds.)
18. *Convergence and Divergence of Family Law in Europe*, M. Antokolskaia (ed.)
19. *European Challenges in Contemporary Family Law*, K. Boele-Woelki and T. Sverdrup (eds.)
20. *Children and their parents*, M. Vonk
21. *La capacité de l'enfant dans les droits français, anglais et écossais*, L. Francoz-Terminal
22. *Joint Parental Authority*, C.G. Jeppesen de Boer

23. *Debates in Family Law around the Globe at the Dawn of the 21st Century*, K. Boele-Woelki (ed.)
24. *European Family Law in Action Volume IV: Property Relations between Spouses*, K. Boele-Woelki, B. Braat and I. Curry-Sumner (eds.)
25. *Foundational Facts, Relative Truths. A Comparative Law Study on Children's Right to Know Their Genetic Origins*, R. Blauwhoff
26. *Imperative Inheritance Law in a Late-Modern Society. Five Perspectives*, Christoph Castelein, René Foqué and Alain Verbeke (eds.)
27. *Juxtaposing Legal Systems and the Principles of European Family Law on Parental Responsibilities*, Esin Örücü and Jane Mair (eds.)
28. *La justice des mineurs en Europe*, Yann Favier and Frédérique Ferrand (eds.)
29. *The Future of Family Property in Europe*, Katharina Boele-Woelki, Jo Miles and Jens M. Scherpe (eds.)
30. *The Place of Religion in Family Law: A Comparative Search*, Jane Mair and Esin Örücü (eds.)
31. *Reconstructing Marriage. The Legal Status of Relationships in a Changing Society*, Caroline Sörgjerd
32. *Legal Recognition of Same-Sex Relationships in Europe*, Katharina Boele-Woelki and Angelika Fuchs (eds.)
33. *Principles of European Family Law Regarding Property Relations Between Spouses*, Katharina Boele-Woelki, Frédérique Ferrand, Cristina González Beilfuss, Maarit Jänterä-Jareborg, Nigel Lowe, Dieter Martiny and Walter Pintens
34. *Der nacheheliche Unterhalt: Grundlagen und Ausgestaltung im deutschen Unterhaltsrecht und in den Prinzipien der Commission on European Family Law*, Philipp Beuermann
35. *Family Law and Culture in Europe: Developments, Challenges and Opportunities*, Katharina Boele-Woelki, Nina Dethloff and Werner Gephart
36. *Children's Rights in Intercountry Adoption. A European Perspective*, Claire Fenton-Glynn
37. *Nordic Cohabitation Law*, John Asland, Margareta Brattström, Göran Lind, Ingrid Lund-Andersen, Anna Singer, Tone Sverdrup
38. *European Family Law in Action Volume V: Informal Relationships*, Katharina Boele-Woelki, Charlotte Mol and Emma van Gelder (eds.)
39. *Divided Parents, Shared Children. Legal Aspects of Residential Co-Parenting in England, the Netherlands and Belgium*, Natalie Nikolina

www.ingramcontent.com/pod-product-compliance
Ingram Content Group UK Ltd.
Pitfield, Milton Keynes, MK11 3LW, UK
UKHW051927100926
8556IPUK00022B/1408

9 781780 683416